Libraries, Literacy, and African American Youth

LIBRARIES, LITERACY, AND AFRICAN AMERICAN YOUTH

Research and Practice

Sandra Hughes-Hassell, Pauletta Brown Bracy, and Casey H. Rawson, Editors

LIBRARIES
UNLIMITED™

An Imprint of ABC-CLIO, LLC

Santa Barbara, California • Denver, Colorado

Copyright © 2017 by ABC-CLIO, LLC

Library of Congress Cataloging-in-Publication Data

Names: Hughes-Hassell, Sandra, editor. | Bracy, Pauletta Brown, editor. | Rawson, Casey H., editor.
Title: Libraries, literacy, and African American youth : research and practice / Sandra Hughes-Hassell, Pauletta Brown Bracy, and Casey H. Rawson, editors.
Description: Santa Barbara, CA : Libraries Unlimited, [2017] | Includes bibliographical references and index. | Description based on print version record and CIP data provided by publisher; resource not viewed.
Identifiers: LCCN 2016044071 (print) | LCCN 2016026929 (ebook) | ISBN 9781440838736 (E-book) | ISBN 9781440838729 (paperback : acid-free paper)
Subjects: LCSH: African Americans and libraries. | Libraries and community—United States—Case studies. | Children's libraries—Services to minorities—United States—Case studies. | School libraries—Services to minorities—United States—Case studies. | African American children—Books and reading. | African American teenagers—Books and reading. | African American children—Education. | African American teenagers—Education. | African American students—Social conditions. | Literacy—Social aspects—United States.
Classification: LCC Z711.9 (print) | LCC Z711.9 .L43 2017 (ebook) | DDC 027.6/308996073—dc23
LC record available at https://lccn.loc.gov/2016044071

ISBN: 978-1-4408-3872-9
EISBN: 978-1-4408-3873-6

21 20 19 18 17   1 2 3 4 5

This book is also available as an eBook.

Libraries Unlimited
An Imprint of ABC-CLIO, LLC

ABC-CLIO, LLC
130 Cremona Drive, P.O. Box 1911
Santa Barbara, California 93116-1911
www.abc-clio.com

This book is printed on acid-free paper ∞

Manufactured in the United States of America

Contents

Preface

**. . . one of the fundamental tasks of educators is to make sure that
the future points the way to a more socially just world, a world in
which critique and possibility—in conjunction with the values of reason, freedom, and equality—function to alter the grounds upon which
life is lived.**

—Giroux (2010, para. 8)

Throughout our careers, each of us has explored how she can help improve
the quality of literacy and life outcomes for African American youth. Our motivations for engaging in this work vary. Sandra's involvement began early in
her teaching career, when as a novice teacher, she realized that she was failing the Black second graders in her rural Virginia classroom. Her commitment
intensified when, as the director of the Philadelphia Library Power project, she
saw the unequal distribution of resources, lack of opportunity, and other forms
of oppression and discrimination that negatively affected the lives of youth of
color in the "City of Brotherly Love." Pauletta began her professional career in
a middle-school library media center in Pittsburgh, Pennsylvania, where she
observed disparities in academic success among students enrolled in the ethnically balanced school. Motivated by these conditions, she has promoted the
role of libraries in fostering literacy through culturally responsive pedagogy.
Casey taught science in a high-poverty urban middle school that transitioned
to one of the nation's first single-gender public schools (a young women's academy) in her second year of teaching. In the course of that shift, her eyes were
opened to the intersections of race, socioeconomic status, and gender in her
students' lives, as well as the multiple ways in which their opportunities were
constrained by inequity.

Serendipitously, we found ourselves in the same area of North Carolina—Pauletta at North Carolina Central University, and Sandra and Casey at the University of North Carolina at Chapel Hill (UNC-CH). The three of us formed a partnership based on our commitment to social justice and our conviction that libraries do change lives.

In June 2012, with funding from the Institute for Museum and Library Services (IMLS), we convened a group of public and school librarians, researchers, library administrators, policymakers, authors, publishers, and educators who, over the course of three days, focused on the question of how libraries might participate in and become leaders of national efforts to improve the quality of literacy education for African American male youth. At this summit, titled "Building a Bridge to Literacy for African American Male Youth: A Call to Action for the Library Community," participants passionately explored three essential questions: (1) Why should libraries focus on the literacy needs of African American male youth? (2) What do we know about existing research, programs, and resources for these youth? and (3) What actions must the library community take? The summit resulted in a report (http://bridgetolit.web.unc.edu/?page_id=12) that presents the summit outcomes, the characteristics of effective library service for African American male youth, the fundamental knowledge needed by library and information science professionals, an expanded research agenda, and recommendations. A website (http://bridgetolit.web.unc.edu) was also created to support librarians in their efforts to meet the literacy needs of Black male youth. Since the summit, we have broadened the scope of our work to include African American female youth whose lives and life outcomes are also negatively affected by social inequities.

In this book, we explore how libraries can create more equitable and just services and programs for African American youth—services and programs that help to improve their literacy and life outcomes. Our goal is to introduce readers to key research concepts, such as Critical Race Theory (CRT), culturally relevant pedagogy, racial identity development, enabling texts, counterstories, and equity literacy; and to offer meaningful illustrations of how school and public librarians are using these concepts to effect real change in the lives of African American youth. We have selected powerful and inspiring concepts-in-practice examples to highlight in the second half of the book; however, the book is not intended to be a how-to-guide or a compilation of best practices. Instead, our intention is (1) to spur dialogue and reflection about how libraries must change to better meet the needs of African American youth, and (2) to motivate librarians to examine their beliefs, attitudes, and commitment to diversity, equity, and social justice. As Antero Garcia notes, best practices is a "buzzword-driven form of highlighting a superior approach and ignores the cultural contexts in which teacher practices are developed" (p. 9). We know that context drives practice.

Our definition of literacy is broad, encompassing traditional literacies, as well as information literacies, critical literacies, digital literacies, and media literacies. This expanded view of literacy is concurrent with the concept of literacy as described in *The Future of Library Services for and with Teens: A Call to Action* (Braun et al., 2014), which describes literacy as "more than a cognitive ability to read and write, but as a social act" (p. 6) that is part of cultural knowledge and behavior and that has purpose—to enable youth to act on their world in powerful ways.

We have used the terms *Black* and *African American* interchangeably in this book, but it is important to note that these terms do have distinctions. The use of the term *Black* rose to prominence in the 1960s as an alternative to *Negro* or *colored*; however, *African American* became a preferred term in the late 1980s because of its connection to the historical context and heritage of many Black Americans (Martin, 1991). The U.S. Census Bureau currently offers a single category for both of these options ("Black or African American") on census forms (U.S. Census Bureau, 2013), and a recent Gallup poll found that roughly two-thirds of Black Americans have no preference between them, with the remaining respondents evenly split (Jones, 2013). Nevertheless, some activists, researchers, and authors have recently begun arguing for use of the term *Black*, as it is more inclusive of the full range of diversity within the Black community which includes, for example people of Caribbean descent. In addition, the term not only respects the complexity inherent in the identity and experience of people who belong to the African diaspora, but it also does not distinguish between American-born and foreign born Blacks who live in the United States. Our decision to use the terms interchangeably is consistent with other writings on culturally relevant pedagogy, literacy, and school reform (c.f. Boykin, 2013; Delpit, 2002; Edwards, McMillon, & Turner, 2010; Lewis, Casserly, Simon, Uzzell, & Palacios, 2013).

The book is divided into two sections. Part One focuses on the research, with an emphasis on highlighting key theoretical frameworks and models that will help school and public librarians transform their services, programs, and collections to be more responsive to the strengths, experiences, and needs of Black youth. In Part Two, we turn from theory to practice, profiling several programs in public and school libraries and other agencies that serve Black youth.

An overarching theme of this book, and all our work, is *voice*. One of the main ways that the dominant culture marginalizes people of color is by silencing their voices. In this book, we focus on the scholarship of Black researchers. We include the work of African American librarians. We showcase the voices of African American youth by including their reflective writing, poetry, and artwork throughout the book. And we provide a space for African American parents to share their experiences as well.

We invite you to apply the research presented in this book; to adopt and adapt the practices described, molding them to fit the context of your community; and to share this book with your colleagues. We ask you to join us in creating the socially just world that Henry Giroux describes and African American youth deserve.

> Sandra Hughes-Hassell
> Pauletta Brown Bracy
> Casey H. Rawson

Acknowledgments

The editors express their appreciation to the contributors to this volume. Without their enthusiasm and dedication to the project, it would not have happened.

We also thank the graduate students who worked on the project with us:

- Constance Caddell, graduate assistant, North Carolina Central University
- Julie Stivers, graduate assistant, The University of North Carolina at Chapel Hill
- Trent McLees, graduate assistant, The University of North Carolina at Chapel Hill

Your assistance was invaluable.

Finally, we thank the Black youth who inspire our work. To you, we are indebted.

Part I

Focus on Research

1

Literacy Education for African American Youth: A Social Justice Issue for Librarians

Sandra Hughes-Hassell and Casey H. Rawson

A just library is one whose resources are put to active, deliberate use in support of social change and in the recognition of the special rights of oppressed groups.

—Furner (2007, p. 11)

We believe that high-quality literacy instruction for African American youth is more than simply a nice but abstract goal for librarians to keep in the back of their minds; instead, it is a critical social justice issue and a professional mandate that needs to be brought to the forefront of library practice. *Social justice* is a term that is often used in discourses of equity and equality but rarely defined explicitly, perhaps because it is frequently assumed that all participants in such discourses share a similar conception of the term (Darling-Hammond, French, & Garcia-Lopez, 2002). However, social justice is a complex, multifaceted concept, encompassing ideas and ideals of equity and fairness, morality and politics, power and privilege, and opportunities (or lack thereof) for social and economic growth and mobility among certain groups of individuals (Clark, 2006; Rawls, 1972, 2001). In this book, we use the conception of social justice as fairness, as described by political philosopher John Rawls (1972, 2001), who asserted that social justice is attained when equal access to liberties, rights, and opportunities is assured to all, including and especially the least-advantaged members of society. In Rawls's view, in order for social justice to occur, society must provide more opportunities for success—including educational success—for those who are or have been victims of institutional inequity. National statistics show that African American youth are one group in the United States that is negatively affected by institutional inequities.

In this chapter, we explore some of the institutional inequities encountered by African American youth on their literacy journeys. We then outline the basic tenets of critical race theory (CRT), a framework that can provide structure and purpose for librarians who are ready to answer the call for socially just collections, services, and programs for Black youth. Finally, we translate theory into practice by closing the chapter with a series of action steps that librarians can take immediately to improve the literacy, and therefore the lives, of African American youth in their communities. This chapter also will define many of the key terms used throughout the rest of the book, including *racism, counterstories, enabling texts, culturally relevant pedagogy,* and *equity literacy.*

In this chapter, we
- Explore institutional inequities.
- Define key terms.
- Introduce CRT.
- Identify immediate action steps that librarians can take.

INSTITUTIONAL INEQUITIES FACED BY AFRICAN AMERICAN YOUTH

To understand the magnitude of the inequities that African American youth face, we invite you to take this quiz (see Figure 1.1). Our intent is not to measure what you know, but to prompt you to reflect on your perceptions about the educational opportunities available to African American youth in the United States and to compare it to the reality.

So what do the data presented in this quiz tell us? First, the data released by the U.S. Department of Education's Office for Civil Rights (2012) show that Black students are more likely to attend schools that lack quality resources, including credentialed teachers, rigorous courses, qualified guidance counselors, and extracurricular activities. In addition, this data shows that African American youth frequently miss instructional time due to suspensions and expulsions. During the 2009–2010 school year, one in five Black males and one in nine Black females received an out-of-school suspension (U.S. Department of Education, Office for Civil Rights, 2012). This is particularly troubling, as research shows that Black students are not engaged in more frequent or serious misbehavior than their White peers are, but rather are disciplined more harshly for similar offenses (Rudd, 2014). While dropouts overall are at an historic low, the 2013–2014 national graduation rate was only 72.5 percent

FIGURE 1.1 Educational Opportunity Quiz

1. Teachers in elementary schools serving the highest percentages of African American and Latino youth are paid less than their colleagues working in the **same school district** at schools serving the lowest percentage of African American and Latino students. How much less? (U.S. Department of Education's Office for Civil Rights, 2012)
   A. $2,250
   B. $1,000
   C. $4,500

2. What proportion of high schools serving the most African American and Latino students offer calculus? (U.S. Department of Education's Office for Civil Rights, 2012)
   A. One-half
   B. Two-thirds
   C. One-third

3. African American students are more likely to be suspended or expelled than their White peers for the same or similar offenses. How much more likely? (U.S. Department of Education's Office for Civil Rights, 2012)
   A. 3½ times
   B. 2 times
   C. 4 times

4. Schools serving the most African American and Latino students are more likely to employ teachers who are newest to the profession, and therefore the least experienced. How much more likely? (U.S. Department of Education's Office for Civil Rights, 2012)
   A. 3 times more likely
   B. 1½ times more likely
   C. 2 times more likely

5. White students make up nearly 63 percent of students enrolled in gifted and talented education programs. What percent of African American students are enrolled in these programs? (U.S. Department of Education's Office for Civil Rights, 2012)
   A. 25 percent
   B. 19 percent
   C. 10 percent

6. Research shows that low teacher expectations negatively affect the ability of African American students to reach their full academic potential. After controlling for other factors, for what percent of the difference between predicted

performance and actual performance do teacher expectations account? (Wildhagen, 2012)

A. 20 percent

B. 5 percent

C. 42 percent

7. How many school librarians did the School District of Philadelphia employ in the 2013–2014 school year to work with their over 150,000 students? (Segal, 2013)

   A. 150

   B. 95

   C. 15

8. How many times more likely are children who do not reach proficiency in reading by third grade to leave school without a diploma than proficient readers? (Hernandez, 2011)

   A. Two times

   B. Four times

   C. Six times

9. What percentage of African American fourth graders and what percentage of African American eighth graders scored at or above proficiency in reading on national tests in 2013? (NAEP, 2013)

   A. 18 percent and 17 percent

   B. 25 percent and 21 percent

   C. 15 percent and 12 percent

10. What is the national graduation rate for African American males? (*Education Week*, 2013)

    A. 66 percent

    B. 52 percent

    C. 75 percent

Answer Key: 1. a   2. c   3. a   4. c   5. b   6. c   7. c   8. b   9. a   10. b

for Black students (a moderate improvement over 67 percent in 2010–2011, but significantly lower than the 87.2 percent graduation rate among White students in 2013–2014) (U.S. Department of Education, 2016).

The National Assessment of Educational Progress (NAEP, 2014) data demonstrate that the need for improved literacy education for African American youth is undeniable. Only 18 percent of African American fourth graders and 17 percent of African American eighth graders performed at or above proficiency in reading in 2013. This is not a new issue; 25 years ago, Janice Hale-Benson (1989) asked how it was that "schools reproduce failure for Black

children generation after generation" (p. 84). Of course,
schools are only one piece of a
literacy education puzzle;
however, because schools are
explicitly tasked with teaching
children reading, much of the
scrutiny falls on them when the
evidence shows so many students failing to attain literacy.

> For too many African American youth, the school rung of the literacy ladder is broken, which makes it critically important for both school and public libraries—traditionally important providers of literacy education and resources—to strengthen their services to this population.

Sara Mead (2010) described literacy education as climbing a ladder: "If any plank in the ladder is weak or missing, a child will be at risk for continued school failure. But if other rungs are strong, they can compensate for those shortcomings, enabling children to keep moving toward educational success" (para. 14). For too many African American youth, the school rung of the literacy ladder is broken, which makes it critical for both school and public libraries—traditionally important providers of literacy education and resources—to strengthen their services to this population.

Unfortunately, however, the data show that inequities extend to public and school library systems. Currently, many Black youth live in communities where school and public libraries are underfunded, provide minimal collections and limited access to computers, or employ few full-time youth services librarians (Kozol, 2012; Neuman & Celano, 2001). For example, during the 2013–2014 school year, the Public School District of Philadelphia, with a total student enrollment of more than 150,000, employed only 15 school librarians (Segal, 2013). In New York City, where the public library system is the single largest provider of free broadband access in the city, circulation rose 59 percent and program attendance rose 40 percent from 2002 to 2011 (Center for an Urban Future, 2013), with young adults accounting for much of this increase and teen attendance rising by 77 percent. However, over this same time period, city funding for public libraries fell by 8 percent.

The inequities described here combine with other factors to create life outcome gaps for many African Americans in the United States. Black males continue to comprise the largest portion of male inmates held in state or federal prisons, making up roughly 37 percent of the population (Bureau of Justice Statistics, 2014). The imprisonment rate for Black females (113 per 100,000) is more than twice the rate of White females (51 per 100,000) (Bureau of Justice Statistics, 2014). African American adolescents and young adults are more than eight times more likely to be the victim of homicide than Whites in the same age group (National Center for Health Statistics, 2009). The unemployment rate for African American males is more than double that of White males (U.S. Bureau of Labor, 2014). Many of these statistics have actually become more troubling in recent years. For example, income and wealth inequality are greatest when we look at them across race. The median wealth of White households was 13 times the median wealth of Black households in 2013, compared with 8 times the wealth in 2010 (Board of Governors of the Federal Reserve System, 2014).

While these and other sobering statistics about African Americans cannot and should not be used to paint a comprehensive picture of this community, these numbers do indicate life outcomes for many African Americans that are inequitable, and therefore incompatible with a just society. Some might argue that social institutions and systems are objective, color-blind, and race neutral, and that as a result, equal opportunity is available to all Americans. As Daniel Solórzano (1997) and William Tate (1997) explain, proponents of this narrative believe that if African Americans and other people of color are not successful, it is because of a deficiency in them—that is, their race is inferior, their cultural values are dysfunctional, or they just are not working hard enough. We, however, agree with scholars who reject this deficit model ideology and argue that the sources of inequality are not located within people of color, but instead are imposed on them by inequitable social practices (see, e.g., Gorski, 2014; Parker & Stovall, 2004; Solórzano, 1997; Tate, 1997). This perspective is grounded in research and guided by the tenets of CRT.

CRT is a multidisciplinary approach developed by legal scholars in the 1970s to address the effects of race and racism in the U.S. legal system (Bell, 1992; Delgado & Stefanic, 2001). Since then, it has been applied within the context of education to examine the role that race plays in a number of areas, including curriculum (Ladson-Billings, 1998), school funding (Alemán, 2007), and school discipline policies (Dixson, 2006). It also has been applied in library science to examine the cultural responsiveness of school library programs to the needs of urban youth (Kumasi, 2012) and the cultural relevance of texts used for literacy instruction (Hughes-Hassell, Barkley, & Koehler, 2009).

Solórzano (1997) has identified five defining elements of CRT, which he argues can be applied to contemporary social problems. We believe that these tenets must guide the efforts of librarians as they work to address the literacy and life outcomes of African American youth. For each tenet, we provide a brief overview and then present a passage from a piece of youth literature that exemplifies its core idea. We do this both to illustrate how the tenets might manifest themselves in the lives of Black youth and to demonstrate that literature can be used to engage youth in conversations about race, power, and privilege.

KEY TENETS OF CRT

The centrality of race and racism. CRT scholars assert that race and racism are defining characteristics of American society—that both are embedded in the structures, policies, and practices of most American institutions and that both work to the detriment of people and communities of color (Solórzano et al., 2005). CRT scholars argue that racism, whether intentional or not, has played and continues to play a dominant role in determining educational, judicial, employment, health care, and other inequities in the United States for communities of color. This focus on the systemic nature of racism—as opposed to thinking in terms of individual prejudices—may be new. When most people hear the word *racism,* they think of particular forms of prejudice or bigotry that are demonstrated by certain types of people. CRT defines racism more broadly as "individual, cultural, institutional, and systemic ways by which differential consequences are created for groups historically or currently defined as White being advantaged, and groups historically or currently defined as [people of color] as disadvantaged" (Racial Equity Tools, n.d.). Racism encompasses issues of prejudice and issues of power and privilege. According to Beverly Tatum (1997), "racial prejudice when combined with social power—access to social, cultural, and economic resources and decision-making—leads to the institutionalization of racist policies and practices" (pp. 7–8). That is, the perpetuation of the systems that advantage Whites.

Solórzano (1997) identifies four dimensions of racism that must be understood and examined: (1) micro- and macro-components, (2) institutional and individual forms, (3) conscious and unconscious elements, and (4) the cumulative impact on both the individual and the group (p. 6). It is important to note that while CRT scholars focus on the centrality of race and racism, they also recognize that racism intersects "with other forms of subordination and discrimination such as gender and class" (Solórzano, 1997, p. 6).

Definitions Important to Understanding Racism in the United States

Race: "A group that is *socially defined* . . . on the basis of *physical* characteristics, including skin color and facial features" (Van den Berghe, 1967, p. 11, emphasis added). "Race is a social construction. Despite myths to the contrary, biologists tell us that the only meaningful racial categorization is that of human" (Tatum, 1997, p. 16).

Racism: Systems of advantage based on race (Wellman, 1977).

Cultural racism: "Representations, messages, and stories conveying the idea that behaviors and values associated with White people or 'Whiteness' are automatically 'better' or more 'normal' than those associated with other racially defined groups" (Racial Equity Tools, 2013, p. 2); e.g., they can be seen in advertising, movies, books, the curriculum, policies, laws, etc.

Individual racism: "The beliefs, attitudes, and actions of individuals that support or perpetuate racism"; often manifested as microaggressions (Racial Equity Tools, 2013, p. 4).

Institutional racism: "Ways in which institutional policies and practices create different outcomes for different racial groups" (Racial Equity Tools, 2013, p. 4); e.g., overassignment of Black youth to special education classes.

Microaggressions: "Brief and commonplace daily verbal, behavioral, or environmental indignities, whether intentional or unintentional, that communicate hostile, derogatory, or negative racial slights and insults towards people of color" (Sue et al., 2007, p. 271).

Structural racism: "The normalization and legitimization of an array of dynamics—historical, cultural, institutional, and interpersonal—that routinely advantage Whites while producing cumulative and chronic adverse outcomes for people of color" (Villarosa, 2012, p. 52); e.g., include lower access to health care, higher rates of incarceration, inequitably funded public schools, etc.

> **White privilege:** "The unquestioned and unearned set of advantages, enti-
> tlements, benefits and choices bestowed on people solely because they are
> White. Generally White people who experience such privilege do so with-
> out being conscious of it" (Racial Equity Tools, 2013, p. 9).

Youth Literature in the Spotlight

An example of a young adult book that brings attention to the racism inherent in U.S. institutions is *We Beat the Street* (Davis et al., 2005). This nonfiction text chronicles the journey of
Sampson, George, and Rameck, three friends from a tough neighborhood in Newark, New
Jersey, to college and then medical school. Their journey is not trouble free. Along the way,
they make mistakes, face disappointments, and nearly fail. At one point, Rameck's dreams
are almost ended by a justice system that adheres to the single story of young Black men as
perpetrators of crime. As Rameck and his friend Dax, a law student, are driving home from a
professional prizefight, they are followed by the police.

> "Why they sweatin' us, man," Dax said. "We ain't done nothing wrong. Not one thing."
>
> "It's not about being wrong. It's about being black," Rameck said, anger and regret in
> his voice.
>
> "Why do they assume we're up to no good?" Dax asked bleakly.
>
> "Who knows?" Rameck answered as the three police cars followed their every turn
> and stop. "DWB—Driving While Black—is the newest crime, don't you know?" (Davis
> et al., 2005, p. 162)

The two young men are stopped and frisked, and their car is searched. When one of the
officers finds a small fishing knife in the glove compartment, Rameck is arrested and charged
with interfering with a police officer and possession of a deadly weapon. Rameck is cleared
of the charges only because the police lose the knife.

An historical context and multidisciplinary perspective. CRT scholars call for
issues related to race and racism to be examined within a historical context—
one that challenges the dominant narrative presented in schools that racism
no longer exists—using multidisciplinary methods (Solórzano, 1997). They
argue that understanding how race developed as a construct in this country,
as well as how the current biracial system formed and continues to be reproduced, are critical to dismantling institutional and structural racism and creating just and equitable opportunities for people of color.

Youth Literature in the Spotlight

An example of a young adult book that brings attention to the history of racism in this country and provides a lens through which to view current events is Sharon Draper's *Stella by Starlight* (2015). Set in the Jim Crow South in the 1930s, the book explores one community's experiences with segregation and discrimination. After Stella and her brother, Jojo, see members of the Ku Klux Klan (KKK) burning a cross near their home, the African American citizens of their neighborhood must become more vigilant than normal to protect themselves and their families. One of the key reasons for the Klan's increased activity was the decision by a number of the men to register to vote:

"I sure would like to cast my vote," Papa added.

Stella sat ramrod straight. What?

"Now, you know they don't want us to votin'. . . . Maybe that's why they all of sudden wearin' the bedsheets off their clotheslines again." . . .

"You know they've set up these poll taxes. . . . And a literacy test about the Constitution you gotta pass."

"Get ready for questions like 'How many bubbles in a bar of soap?' or 'How many wrinkles in an elephant's trunk?'" Spoon Man said.

Stella noticed that not one of the men even smiled. This was dead serious. (Draper, 2015, p. 150)

The passage of the Voting Rights Act in 1965 was intended to prevent the kind of discrimination that Stella's father faced; however, since the Supreme Court overturned key provisions of that act in 2013, many states have implemented strict voter identification rules—rules that many argue are intended to discourage, or even prevent, African Americans and other people of color from voting.

The challenge to the dominant ideology. CRT challenges the dominant deficit model ideology used to explain educational achievement differences. As Solórzano (1997) explains, the deficit model of thinking comes from two traditions: the inferiority paradigm and cultural deficit models. The inferiority model posits that people of color are inferior to Whites and that this deficiency causes the low educational attainment of students of color (Solórzano, 1997; Tate, 1997). From this perspective, little can be done to close the achievement gap—it is merely a natural consequence of the inferiority of students of color (Tate, 1997). Cultural deficit models contend that cultural values are to blame; that is, the cultural values transmitted from families of color to their children are dysfunctional and thus the cause of low academic achievement (Solórzano, 1997). These models characterize the cultural values held by many communities of color, such as cooperation rather than competition and the importance of present versus future orientation, as inferior. Deficit models argue that "since minority parents fail to assimilate and embrace the educational values of the dominant group, and continue to transmit or socialize their children with values that inhibit educational mobility, then they are to blame if the low educational attainment continues into succeeding generations" (Solórzano, 1997, p. 14).

CRT disrupts the deficit model ideology in two ways: (1) by recognizing that the sources of inequality are not located within students of color, but instead are caused by the historical dimensions, social construction, and political and social ramifications of racism (Parker & Stovall, 2004); and (2) by asserting that the experiential and cultural knowledge of people and communities of color is "legitimate, appropriate, and critical" (Solórzano et al., 2005, p. 275) to educating students of color. As librarians, we too must reject this deficit model, instead using the CRT framework to view and challenge inequities.

Youth Literature in the Spotlight

In *Ball Don't Lie* (2005), Matt de la Peña explores the concept of White privilege, challenging the idea that the United States is "a land of opportunity . . . where anyone . . . can succeed if they just pull up hard enough on their bootstraps" (olsson, 1997, p. 6). In this scene, Dante, a young African American male, explains the futility of believing in the idea of the American dream to Sticky, the novel's protagonist:

> Dante reaches down to grab a couple of stones off the ground. *See that wall in front of you?* he says. *In America, life's like a race to that wall. That's the way I see it.* He sets the first stone less than a foot from the wall, points and says: *If you born White and got money then you start the race way up here. Ahead of everybody . . .*
>
> *But say you ain't White and rich. Say you poor and black. Or you Mexican, Puerto Rican . . . You may not even have enough food to eat a balanced meal every night. . . . In this case you startin the race of life way back here.* He points to the second stone. *Only a fool would think someone who starts here has the same opportunities as cats startin at the first stone.* (de la Peña, 2005, pp. 229–230)

The centrality of experiential knowledge. CRT scholars view the experiential and cultural knowledge of people and communities of color as legitimate and critical to understanding the impact that race and racism are having on their lived experiences, including the educational opportunity gap that they experience, and embrace it through concepts such as counterstorytelling and culturally relevant pedagogy. Counterstorytelling is "a method of telling the stories of those people whose experiences are not often told including people of color, women, gays, and the poor" (Solórzano & Yosso, 2002, p. 26). CRT scholars believe that in addition to making sure that the voices of people of color are heard, counterstories validate their life circumstances and serve as powerful ways to challenge and subvert the versions of reality held by the privileged. Richard Delgado (1989), who introduced the concept, outlines a number of ways that counterstorytelling benefits groups that have traditionally been

marginalized and oppressed in the United States. By telling (and hearing) counterstories, members of marginalized groups:

1. Gain healing by understanding the historic oppression and persecu-
   tion their community has faced,
2. Realize that other members of their community have similar feelings
   and experiences, and that they are not alone,
3. No longer blame themselves or their community for being marginalized,
   and
4. Construct additional narratives to challenge the dominant narrative
   (Delgado, 1989, p. 2,437).

Members of the dominant culture also benefit from hearing counterstories.
Delgado (1989) argues that counterstories can help them overcome their "eth-
nocentrism and the unthinking conviction that [their] way of seeing the world
is the only one—that the way things are is inevitable, natural, just, and best"
(p. 2439).

Students' experiential and cultural knowledge are also embraced through
the practice of culturally relevant teaching, which we discuss further in Chapter 2. Gloria Ladson-Billings (2009) defines this practice "as a pedagogy that
empowers students intellectually, socially, emotionally, and politically by using
cultural referents to impart knowledge, skills, and attitudes" (p. 20). It recognizes the linguistic, literate, and cultural practices of communities of color as
resources to honor, explore, extend, and build on in formal educational settings.
In practice, culturally relevant pedagogy uses the "cultural knowledge, prior
experiences, frames of reference, and performance styles" of students of color
to make learning more relevant, meaningful, and validating (Gay, 2000, p. 29).
Key principles of culturally relevant pedagogy include:

1. "An authentic belief that students from culturally diverse and low-
   income backgrounds are capable learners" (Howard, 2003, p. 197)
   and can become intellectual leaders.
2. Legitimization of "students' real-life experiences as part of the 'official'
   curriculum" (Ladson-Billings, 2009, p. 127).
3. A commitment to enabling students to explore and make connections
   between their multiple identities.
4. The creation of a community of learners.
5. Engagement of students and teachers "in a collective struggle against
   the status quo" (Ladson-Billings, 2009, p. 128).
6. The recognition of the "political nature" of teaching (Ladson-Billings,
   2009, p. 128).

Youth Literature in the Spotlight

The short story "Confessions of a Black Geek" (Olugbemisola Rhuday-Perkovich, 2013) provides an example of a powerful counterstory. Even though the protagonist had all the

credentials to get into an Ivy League college—Advanced Placement (AP) classes, good grades, high Scholastic Aptitude Test (SAT) scores, a plethora of extracurricular experiences, etc.—when the acceptances rolled in, she began to hear racist remarks and complaints about affirmative action from her White classmates, their parents, and even some of her teachers. Instead of allowing these remarks to define her, she proudly affirmed her abilities:

> I'd gotten into the college of my choice because I'd worked every multidimensional bone in my body to get there.
> I didn't need to be in AP Bio to know how wrong it is to be reduced and flattened to a color (but I was). I wave my identity flag high and wide, marching-band style (yep, did that, too—polyester uniform and all).
> I'm Black. I'm a geek.
> And nobody can divide that beautiful partnership. (Olugbemisola Rhuday-Perkovich, 2013, p. 78)

A commitment to social justice and praxis. CRT contains an activist dimension. It challenges us not only to understand the social situation, but change it; it sets out not only to ascertain how society organizes itself along racial lines and hierarchies, but also transform it for the better (Delgado & Stefanic, 2001). A key goal of CRT is to bring about change that will lead to social justice (DeCuir & Dixson, 2004). CRT challenges researchers, practitioners, and policymakers to envision social justice as the struggle to eliminate racism, poverty, classism, and other forms of oppression while empowering groups that have been oppressed (Solórzano & Delgado Bernal, 2001). Social justice is a goal shared by the library community.

Youth Literature in the Spotlight

In the picture book *Sit-In: How Four Friends Stood up by Sitting Down*, Andrea Davis Pinkney (2010) tells the story of the four North Carolina college students who initiated the Greensboro lunch counter sit-ins to protest segregation. The book, told in pictures and words, provides all youth, but especially Black youth, with a powerful example of the role that young people can play in challenging systemic racism in the United States:

> So David, Joseph, Franklin,
> and Ezell sat quietly and still.
> With hearts full of hope.
> With Dr. King's words
> strong and close:
> "Be
> Loving
> Enough
> To absorb
> evil."

They sat straight and proud.
And waited. And wanted.
A doughnut and coffee,
with cream on the side. (Pinkney, 2010, unpaged)

Applying CRT to Library Practice

So at this point, you may be thinking, "Enough of the theory. What does all this discussion of theory mean to my work with African American youth? How is it going to help me close the literacy gap?" We believe that too often in education, we move from identifying a problem to immediately implementing solutions, without a thorough understanding of the bigger picture. The literacy and life outcome gaps confronting Black youth are situated in a larger historical, political, social, and legal context. There are no quick fixes. Short-term solutions do not address the enduring and fundamental problems that Black youth face. If we want the changes that we make to our library programs and services to have a lasting impact, they must be informed by a theoretical framework that enables libraries to identify, challenge, and address the larger systemic issues that lie at the heart of the problem.

In the final section of this chapter, we present six action steps, each informed by the tenets of CRT, which we believe that librarians must take today if we are to improve the quality of literacy education and life outcomes for African American youth. In the book *Change Is Come: Transforming Literacy Education for African American Students* (2010), Patricia Edwards and her colleagues repeat this refrain: "No more excuses, no more delays. Come on people" (p. 162). We agree. It is no longer sufficient simply to discuss what libraries "could" do or what libraries "should" do. It is time for us to act.

Action Step 1—Become culturally competent and equity literate.

To develop collections, programs, and services that reflect and support the literacy and life outcomes of African American youth, librarians must become culturally competent and equity literate. Cultural competence is "the ability to recognize the significance of culture in one's own life and in the lives of others; and come to know and respect diverse cultural backgrounds and characteristics through interaction with individuals from diverse linguistic, cultural, and socioeconomic groups; and to fully integrate the culture of diverse groups into services, work, and institutions in order to enhance the lives of both those being served by the library profession and those engaged in service" (Overall, 2009, pp. 189–190). More simply, "cultural competency goes beyond cultural awareness. It denotes an individual's ability to effectively interact with and among others whose values, behaviors, and environments are different from your own" (Michigan Education Association, n.d.). Cultural competency leads to improved educational outcomes for youth of color (Hanley & Noblit, 2009). For the library community, it also leads to culturally responsive practice, improved services, and an increase in library use (Overall, 2009).

The first step in becoming culturally competent is for librarians, particularly those who belong to the dominant White culture, to develop fully formed, personal racial and cultural identities. All of us need to have a strong sense of our individual cultural identity in order to support and serve African American youth. We must identify and deconstruct our personal biases, assumptions, and stances. Without this self-reflection, we cannot effectively and accurately understand, represent, and portray the multiple identities of the African American youth in our community. The journey to cultural competence is "a developmental process that evolves over an extended period" and involves intense work examining the issues of race, power, and privilege (Mestre, 2010, p. 8). You will read about one school librarian's racial equity journey in Chapter 12. In Chapter 13, you will hear from two librarians who are intentional in exploring their biases and privileges in their daily work with African American and Black teens.

Racial Equity Training Resources

- Racial Equity Institute: http://rei.racialequityinstitute.org/wpsite
- Courageous Conversations About Race, Pacific Educational Group: http://www.pacificeducationalgroup.com/public/pages/home
- Undoing Racism, People's Institute for Survival and Beyond: http://www.pisab.org
- National SEED (Seeking Educational Equity and Diversity) Project: http://www.nationalseedproject.org

Reflective self-knowledge is only the first step in the path toward becoming culturally competent. Librarians also must build authentic knowledge of "African American culture; a deeper understanding of the impact African American culture has on behavior, learning styles, and preferred teaching styles; and a genuine appreciation for the valuable repertoire of experiences African American students bring to school" (Edwards et al., 2010, p. 7). Too often, African American youth and their communities are painted with a broad brush and viewed as a monolithic group—one that is defined by the racial biases and stereotypes that pervade the media and popular culture. We must get to know African American youth as members of a cultural community, but also as individuals, each with "unique life experiences and influences" (Hughes-Hassell & Agosto, 2010, p. 9). As David Kirkland (2013) explains, teaching literacy to Black youth involves first understanding them deeply and knowing their ways with words. Only then can we "excite those potentials within [them] to release the energies of their literacies" (Kirkland, 2013, p. xv). Patricia Overall (2009) suggests a number of ways that cultural knowledge can be built, including researching "historical, demographic, linguistic, and social information" about diverse communities, interacting with people from diverse communities, and connecting with "confidants who are able to provide insights into cultural differences between community members and library professionals" (p. 193). In Chapters 2 and 3, we will discuss two cultural concepts that are central to supporting the literacy development of African American youth—Black cultural ethos and racial identity development.

Understanding our cultural identity and the culture of diverse communities is not enough, however. Librarians must become equity literate; that is, they must be able to "identify, analyze, and transform those structural and cultural aspects of society that maintain the subordination and marginalization" of African American youth (Solórzano, 1997, p. 6). Paul Gorsksi has identified four abilities that are key to developing equitable schools and libraries, including:

- *Recognize* even subtle forms of bias, discrimination, and inequity;
- *Respond* to bias, discrimination, and inequity in a thoughtful and equitable manner;
- *Redress* bias, discrimination, and inequity, not only by responding to interpersonal bias, but also by studying the ways in which bigger social change happens; and
- *Cultivate and sustain* bias-free and discrimination-free communities, which requires understanding that doing so is a basic responsibility for everyone in a civil society (Gorski, 2013, p. 21).

Action Step 2—Identify racial inequities and biases in school and library policies, interactions, and materials and respond to them in an equitable and proactive manner.

Many of the inequities present in schools have infiltrated school and public libraries; in fact, school and public libraries often reinforce these inequities. For this reason, we begin this section by elaborating on three of the inequities most frequently encountered by Black youth in schools.

Low teacher expectations are a prevalent disparity in many schools and have been found to negatively affect the academic performance of Black youth. In their book *Creating the Opportunity to Learn,* A. Wade Boykin and Pedro Noguera (2010) cite 25 years of systematic empirical data that reveal that teacher expectations fall along racial lines and document the fact that low teacher expectations have adverse academic effects on many Black and Latino children. They outline specific and concrete teacher behaviors that convey differences in expectations to youth of color, including giving White students more praise, affirmation, and positive feedback and providing White students with more product- and process-based questions. They also cite research that shows that lower teacher expectations for Black and Latino students are specifically linked to lower levels of reading achievement.

As librarians, we need to ask ourselves, "When I'm planning programs or instruction, what are my expectations for African American youth? Are my expectations lower because of media stereotypes or my implicit biases and assumptions about their literacy levels? Am I interacting differently with youth based on race?"

Biases are often found in the materials used to teach literacy. There is a large body of research demonstrating that both the reading achievement and reading motivation of African American youth are affected by the availability of diverse literature (e.g., Allington & Cunningham, 2007; Bell & Clark, 1998; DeLeón, 2002; Purves & Beach, 1972) or, as Bena Heflin and Mary Alice Barksdale-Ladd (2001) describe it, "literature that offers them personal stories, a view of their cultural surroundings, and insight on themselves" (p. 810). However, Jane Gangi (2008) has found that there is an *unbearable Whiteness* in literacy instruction in the United States. That is, most of the resources that teachers use for literacy instruction and guiding youth recreational reading choices advantage White children and marginalize children of color. Other research supports Gangi's conclusions (e.g., Astolfi, 2012; Hughes-Hassell, Barkley, & Koehler, 2009; McNair, 2008a, 2008b).

As librarians, we need to examine our behaviors to ensure that we are not reinforcing the "Whiteness" of literacy instruction during storytime and readers' advisories, when recommending books to parents, or when suggesting books for classroom teachers to use to embed in the language arts/reading curriculum. School librarians need to be particularly careful to ensure that book club order forms and book fair selections do not exclude the voices and viewpoints of people and communities of color.

Racial and ethnic biases extend to other areas of the curriculum. Despite repeated calls for multicultural education and curriculum revisions (e.g., Banks, 1993a, b, 1994, 1995), the social studies, history, and English curricula in most schools remain predominantly Eurocentric. The changes that we make are minimal and may include discussing the contributions of a few select African Americans in our social studies classes (often the same few), adding the writings of a few select African American writers to the English curriculum, and observing Black History Month. Few high schools offer courses in African American history or literature.

In her book *Why Are All the Black Kids Sitting Together in the Cafeteria?* Beverly Tatum (1997) discusses the frustration that Black students feel because they have learned little about their cultural history in elementary or secondary school. She argues that when African American youth do not see themselves in the curriculum, and when they do not learn about the contributions of the Black community in the arts, sciences, politics, and so forth, they are not only deprived of exposure to African American role models, but they are also denied an understanding of the long history of Black intellectual achievement. This not only negatively affects their identity development, but it reinforces the notion that "academic excellence is an exclusively White domain" (Tatum, 1997, p. 64). And, if students are already alienated from school, it further alienates them.

Librarians need to collaborate with the education community to transform the structure of the curriculum so that it enables youth to view concepts, issues, events, and themes from the perspectives of diverse racial, ethnic, and cultural groups (Banks, 2009). As James Banks (2009, p. 21) explains, "Only by looking at events from many different perspectives can we fully understand the complex dimensions of American culture and society." In Chapter 2, we provide additional details about how schools must be transformed.

Now we turn to libraries. As much as we would like to believe that libraries are objective and race neutral, there is evidence to the contrary. As Jonathan Furner (2007) argues, because race is unarguably embedded in other social systems, it is reasonable to assume that libraries as institutions are "infected with racism" (p. 4). He identifies several possible manifestations of racism in the library:

1. Denying that racism continues to exist in the U.S. or that it is still a problem.
2. Being indifferent to or even ignoring that racism impacts the library workplace and culture.
3. Hiring staff that do not represent the racial or ethnic backgrounds of the communities served.
4. Providing inadequate library resources that lead diverse communities to report high levels of dissatisfaction with the library.
5. Implementing policies and procedures that privilege the needs of the dominant group over the needs of diverse local communities. (Furner, 2007, p. 12)

In a special issue of *Children and Libraries* devoted to diversity, Allie Bruce (2015), a school librarian who identifies as White, provides a list of 10 privileges afforded to White children who visit her library simply because Bruce herself is White. Bruce's intent for this article is to challenge librarians who belong to the dominant White culture to examine the potential impact that their race has on the youth who visit libraries and their families. She explains, "Just as it is essential to name Whiteness to render privilege visible, it is equally important to specifically name the privileges afforded by Whiteness" (Bruce, 2015, p. 4). Each of the privileges that Bruce lists is compelling and worth considering. All of them not only highlight the advantages afforded to White youth in libraries but also demonstrate the prevalence of structural racism (often unconscious and unintentional) in libraries that serve youth of color. Here, we have selected three to highlight:

- If a White child is labeled a "reluctant" or "struggling" reader, she and her family need not worry that such a label will be attributed to poor parenting, poverty, or the lower intelligence of her race.
- White children can return books late without having that lateness reflect on their race.
- White children can enter my library knowing that decisions about which books to buy and what materials to teach have been determined by people who share their racial history and background, and that those books and materials testify to the existence of, and do not contain dehumanizing stereotypes of, their race. (Bruce, 2015, p. 4)

Bruce's observations also challenge librarians to ask, "What about youth of color? What do they think about the library?" Kafi Kumasi (2012) reports that many youth of color feel like outsiders in the library, noting that they infrequently

see their culture represented in pictures or books in the library, thus reinforcing "Whiteness as the normative and superior cultural influence in the school
library" (p. 37). The youth she interviewed wished that school librarians were
more open-minded and would sponsor programs that "celebrated their cultural history and literary tradition" (Kumasi, 2012, p. 35). Young Black men
that we have interviewed have described libraries as restrictive and intimidating environments. One explained it this way, "I got disciplined . . . for talking.
Also, moving around a lot. I couldn't sit still, always going somewhere and
looking at something or touching something" (Black Males Speak, 2011).
Kumasi (2012) urges librarians to examine the biases and assumptions that
they hold about youth of color, particularly urban youth, and to resist actively
the stereotypes perpetuated by the media about these young people. As she
notes, it is important that librarians "not allow outward conditions such as
dress, speech patterns, and other cultural signifiers" to shape their perceptions of these youth (Kumasi, 2012, p. 35).

Finally, as the youth that Kumasi interviewed noted, diverse books are missing from many school and public library collections. The reasons given are
varied, including the small number of books that feature diverse characters
published each year (cf. Horning et al., 2014) and the lack of diversity found
on many of the booklists that librarians use to guide their purchasing decisions (cf. Kurz, 2012; Rawson, 2014). Unfortunately, implicit biases and privilege also influence the selection practices of some school and public librarians.
As Amy Koester, better known as the "Show Me Librarian," points out, "This is
a problem because our decisions affect the capabilities of young readers to find
books in which they can find themselves and in which they can meet new
people" (Koester, 2015, para. 22). She goes on to explain that many librarians
say, "I don't need diverse titles because we don't really have many readers of
color in our community" (para. 22) or "Books about diverse characters just
don't circulate here" (para. 5) to justify their decision not to purchase diverse
literature. Koester argues that statements such as these imply that "we as
selectors view diverse books as inherently less-than . . . [and] . . . show a fundamental disrespect for the youth we are serving" (para. 13).

Librarians, whether as members of the school community or as taxpaying
citizens, need to be courageous—willing to point out the racial biases and inequities like the ones we have presented here that are implicit in many of our
schools and libraries. We need to push for achievement data to be disaggre-
gated and examined through a CRT lens—a lens that focuses on what the data
say about our instructional techniques, teacher expectations, curricula, and
the materials that we are using with African American youth. We need to push
for discipline policies to be examined. And, perhaps most important, we need
to examine our own practices to identify our role in perpetuating the inequitable systems that negatively affect African American youth.

Action Step 3—Challenge the dominant ideology.

It is imperative that librarians challenge the dominant ideology that places
lower expectations on African American youth and blames them or their

communities for their struggles while minimizing, or even ignoring, the structural forces that have led to the unequal distribution of resources, lack of opportunity, and other forms of oppression and discrimination faced by the African American community. The dominant ideology is a deficit model that ignores the important cultural strengths that youth of color and their communities possess which, when capitalized on, can lead to increased academic achievement, positive racial identity development, improved self-confidence and self-esteem, and increased resiliency (Hanley & Noblit, 2009). So what can librarians do to challenge the deficit model?

First, we can help shift the discussion in our schools and communities from focusing on the achievement gap to focusing on the opportunity gap, or as Ladson-Billings (2006) calls it, the educational debt. In her presidential address to the National Council of Teachers of English (NCTE), Ladson-Billings maintains that our emphasis on the achievement gap is misplaced and counterproductive, arguing that "the historical, economic, sociopolitical, and moral decisions and policies that characterize our society have created an educational debt" (Ladson-Billings, 2006, p. 5). She characterizes the achievement gap as the outcome of this debt, caused by exclusionary policies and practices that deny equitable and high-quality education to youth of color, funding disparities that place different values "on the education of different groups of students, and the disparity between what we know is right and what we actually do" (Ladson-Billings, 2006, p.8). As Kirkland (2012) notes, her "shift in metaphor from gap to debt suggests that those who occupy the low side of the gap are not at fault for failing to get an education. . . . We are only paying some and not others" (p. 2).

Second, as Edwards and her colleagues (2010) suggest, we can challenge the perception in many communities that Black families are "disadvantaged" or "at risk" when their literacy practices differ from those of White-middle class families. Literacy traditions within the Black community include storytelling; reading the Bible, church hymnals, and other religious texts; call and response; spoken-word poetry; hip hop and rap; and code switching (Delpit, 2002; Fisher, 2008; Hale, 2001; Morrell, 2004b). Many of these practices are collaborative in nature, and all of them are purposeful—that is, they hold social, personal, political, or spiritual significance. Edwards and her colleagues (2010) emphasize that the kinds of literacy practices enacted in African American families and communities can be used in schools and libraries to build bridges to literacy.

Research shows, however, that too often, educators ignore the strengths and rich literary experiences that their African American students possess, focusing instead on "the experiences and language their students are missing" (McManus, 2016, para. 15). When they do this, they "default to teaching practices such as vocabulary drills and rote repetition that emphasize obedience and quiet behavior"—experiences that "limit students' opportunities to develop language, but also negatively affect students' views of themselves as learners" (McManus, 2016, para. 16). In Chapters 7, 8, 10, 11, 13, and 14, we highlight some practical examples of culturally relevant curricular and programmatic interventions that have been successful with African American youth.

Third, we can challenge the stereotyping of African American youth, especially African American male youth, as disengaged or illiterate when in fact many of them are avid readers. As Kirkland (2012) explains, "We attach adjectives, like 'disengaged reader,' to these young men . . . I gave a Beowulf reading to an English class that a few young Black men were in. They weren't reading Beowulf. But when I followed up on them outside the classroom, they were reading magazines, comic books, newspaper articles—especially the sports section—events that were tied to their lives. So they weren't disengaged readers. They were very much engaged. The issue was disengaged classrooms and disengaged text" (p. 1). Alfred Tatum (2009) agrees, arguing that literacy instruction for African American adolescent males must include "(re)connecting them to texts that *are* useful and texts that *matter to them*" (p. xiv, emphasis in original). In Chapter 5, we introduce Dr. Tatum's idea of enabling texts.

To be clear, neither Kirkland or Tatum is saying that the use of engaging texts is enough to overcome a student's limited reading ability. What they are saying is that explicit instruction is more effective when we incorporate texts that are developmentally appropriate, texts that matter to students, texts that not only develop their literacy skills but also support their identity development, and texts that act as road maps for doing, thinking, and being. They are also saying that literacy instruction *must* begin from a place of respect—respect for the literacy practices already present in these young people's lives. As Kirkland (2013) explains, "Being Black and male myself, I never thought it would be my job to convince others that Black men practiced literacy. . . . I have found the current neglect of/disregard for the literacy of Black males to be a silence worth searching past" (p. 137).

Fourth, we can educate ourselves, and others, about why African American youth may be actively resisting learning literacy. The reasons are complex and varied, but they must be understood if we hope to educate Black youth in meaningful and effective ways. As Rebecca Powell (cited in Edwards et al., 2010) explains, for some African American students,

> a failure to learn *may be intentional.* That is, it is a resistance to literacy that is based upon a racist ideology of White privilege. It is resistance to a literacy that for them holds no meaning or promise, that historically has failed them in their quest to overcome the hegemonic focuses of power in our society. And it is a resistance to literacy that they find essentially irrelevant, that denigrates their cultural knowledge, that denies their voice. (Powell, 2009, p. 5, emphasis in original)

While we will return to this topic in Chapter 3, we also recognize that it is too multifaceted for us to unpack completely in this book. Therefore, we refer you to the following resources so that you can gain a thorough and deep understanding of this phenomenon:

- Coates, Ta-Nehisi (2015). *Between the World and Me.* New York: Spiegel & Grau.
- Edwards, Patricia A., McMillon, Gwendolyn Thompson, and Turner, Jennifer D. (2010). *Change Is Gonna Come: Transforming Literacy Education for African American Students.* New York: Teachers College Press.

- Emdin, Christopher (2016). *For White Folks Who Teach in the Hood . . . and the Rest of Y'all Too: Reality Pedagogy and Urban Education.* New York: Beacon Press.
- Kirkland, David (2013). *A Search Past Silence: The Literacy of Young Black Men.* New York: Teachers College Press.
- Tatum, Alfred W. (2009). *Reading for Their Life: (Re) Building the Textual Lineages of African American Adolescent Males.* Portsmouth, NH: Heinemann.
- Tatum, Alfred W. (2013). *Fearless Voices: Engaging a New Generation of African American Adolescent Male Writers.* New York: Scholastic.
- Tatum, Beverly Daniel (1997). *"Why Are All the Black Kids Sitting Together in the Cafeteria?"* New York: Basic Books.

Finally, we can challenge stereotypes of Black youth that are held by the dominant society—stereotypes that not only can negatively affect their academic achievement, but also cause them to place less trust in educators and to view schools as unsafe, uncaring institutions. As Claude Steele explains:

> Even though the stereotypes held by the larger society may be difficult to change, it is possible to create niches in which negative stereotypes are not felt to apply. In specific classrooms, within specific programs, even in the climate of entire schools, it is possible to weaken a group's sense of being threatened by negative stereotypes, to allow its members a trust what would be otherwise difficult to sustain. . . . For a great portion of Black students, the degree of racial trust they feel in their campus life, rather than in a few ticks on a standardized test, may be the key to their success. (Steele, 2003, p. 130)

The library can be one of those niches—a safe and welcoming space, free of discrimination and bias, where African American youth are viewed as individuals, where their strengths are recognized, and where they are held to high standards. For specific ideas for how to make the library a welcoming and equitable environment, see Chapter 6.

> The library can be one of those niches—a safe and welcoming space, free of discrimination and bias, where African American youth are viewed as individuals, where their strengths are recognized, and where they are held to high standards.

Challenging the Dominant Narrative— A Few Concrete Ideas

- Gather and present data that show the systemic inequities that lead to the educational debt for African American youth and other marginalized youth.

- Use asset-based and people-first language in all communications (e.g., educational debt versus achievement gap, cultural strengths versus cultural deficits, pushout rates versus dropout rates, and students living in poverty versus poor students).
- Stop using the term *at risk* to describe Black youth. Remind yourself and your colleagues that "Being labeled 'at risk' is like being voted least likely to succeed. For where there is no faith in your future success, there is no real effort to prepare you for it" (National Black Child Development Institute, 2014, p. 10).
- Challenge negative assumptions or comments made about African American youth and their families during meetings or informal interactions with colleagues.
- Lead professional development sessions related to building on African American cultural strengths, implementing culturally responsive literacy practices, honoring student voice, and engaging families and communities.
- Introduce staff to the history of literacy in the African American community.
- Highlight the work of African American authors, such as Philiss Wheatley, Frederick Douglass, Booker T. Washington, Paul Laurence Dunbar, Audre Lorde, W.E.B. Du Bois, Zora Neale Hurston, and James Baldwin, who are part of the rich textual lineage of the African American community.
- Engage Black youth in project-based learning, which has been shown to not only provide youth "the opportunity to engage with complex topics and construct their own knowledge, but also to develop vocabulary" (McManus, 2016, para. 13).
- Share "professional journals, books, or blogs related to anti-bias education" (Scharf, 2015, p. 19), racial equity, and African American literacy practices.
- Invite parents, guardians, and other members of the African American community to share information about literacy practices in the home.
- Conduct an audit of the library, "reading the messages conveyed by the images on the walls, the books on the shelves, and the arrangement of the furniture with an eye toward diversity, equity, and student empowerment" (Scharf, 2015, p. 9).
- Invite African American storytellers, spoken-word poets, and hip hop artists to lead library programs.
- Build alliances with colleagues within the library community or from outside networks who share your commitment to culturally responsive literacy education for African American youth and social justice.

Action Step 4—Incorporate counterstories into our practice and the collections.

Stories matter. Many stories matter. Stories have been used to dispossess and to malign, but stories also can be used to empower and to humanize. Stories can break a dignity of a people, but they also can repair that broken dignity.

—Adichie (2009)

Counterstories are key components of CRT in the following ways:

* They provide African American and Black youth with messages of racial and ethnic pride—messages that serve as "a protective factor that might buffer African American youth from the negative effects of perceived racial discrimination" (Harris-Britt et al., 2007, p. 669).
* They support racial identify development.
* They expose the impact of implicit bias, discrimination, and racism.
* They allow youth in the dominant culture to see how the world looks from someone else's perspective, thus "challenging their assumptions, jarring their complacency," and inviting them to action (Delgado 1989, p. 2440).

School and public libraries should be full of counterstories in the form of diverse literature that not only challenges the single story of African American youth, but also encourages and empowers them to take action in their own lives and in the world around them.

In creating diverse collections, we must look beyond award-winning titles, historical fiction, social issue books, and biographies. As author Jerry Craft (n.d.) points out, "Too many books for kids of color are biographies about slavery and the Civil Rights Movement. If the only books that White kids had were on Thomas Jefferson and Teddy Roosevelt, then maybe they wouldn't be so excited about reading either" (Publishers section, para. 3). Our collections need to be broad and deep, including all genres and formats. In creating diverse collections, we can utilize a wide-range of tools, including:

* We Need Diverse Books (http://weneeddiversebooks.org) and Diversity in YA (http://www.diversityinya.com), which highlight newly published titles, along with informational resources and reviews, across a broad definition of diversity;
* the We Need Diverse Book's Where to Find Diverse Books website (http://weneeddiversebooks.org/where-to-find-diverse-books) and the Cooperative Children's Book Center's searchable database of recommended titles (http://ccbc.education.wisc.edu/booksearch/advanced.asp);
* blogs such as Reading in Color (http://blackteensread2.blogspot.com/), Rich in Color (http://richincolor.com), and The Brown Bookshelf (http://thebrownbookshelf.com);
* lists like the African-American Reference Guide (http://tinyurl.com/lvdfkd5), which features recent titles by and about African Americans published between 2010 and 2015; and

- publishers focused on diversity, such as Lee and Low Books, Just Us Books, and Jump at the Sun.

As Julie Stivers and Sandra Hughes-Hassell (2015) point out, collecting diverse literature is only a starting point. It is not enough to promote diverse titles only in February, or only to diverse youth. Diverse books must be promoted year round, with all youth—just like the other books in our libraries. Every display—fantasy, graphic novel, adventure, whatever the topic—should include books with diverse characters. We must also be intentional in our efforts to incorporate these titles into our readers' advisory—and again, not just with African American youth, but with all youth. In addition to using diverse titles in individual readers' advisories, we must also incorporate them into book clubs, summer reading lists, classroom book talks, and library programming in meaningful ways. School librarians must collaborate with teachers to incorporate diverse literature across the curriculum. One resource that can help with this is Teaching Tolerance's *Perspectives for a Diverse America* (http:// perspectives.tolerance.org). This free, web-based curriculum "is a literacy-based, anti-bias, social justice curriculum that is aligned to the Common Core State Standards for Language Arts and Literacy—and to the Teaching Tolerance Anti-bias Framework." The curriculum contains a core "of central texts, including non-fiction essays and speeches, literature, songs, video clips, and maps that will help students consider and challenge multiple points of view."

Librarians also need to use diverse literature to engage youth in discussions about race and racism. This passage from Paul Gorski and Kathy Swalwell's article *Equity Literacy for All* (2015) illustrates how important these conversations are to African American youth:

"I'm invisible," Sean added, "but also hyper visible. Maybe twice a year there's a program about somebody's food or music, but that's about it. I don't see the purpose.

Then Cynthia, who had remained quiet through most of the hourlong discussion, slammed her fist on the table, exclaiming, "That multicultural initiative means nothing. There's racism at this school, and nobody's doing anything about it!" (p. 34)

Discussions about issues of race and racism often elicit anger, denial, guilt, and defensiveness. White people often feel vulnerable and attacked for being White and "prefer to believe that the problem is not that racism is present, but that it is being discussed" (Okun 2010, p. 2). People of color, too, may be uncomfortable, feeling as though they are being asked to speak for their entire racial, ethnic, or cultural group. Diverse literature can serve as a vehicle for overcoming the silence and discomfort that prevent open dialogue. As counterstory, it is nonconfrontational. It invites the reader to suspend judgment, listen for the point or the message, and determine the truth that the story contains (Delgado, 1989, p. 2,415). It acts as both a mirror—allowing teens of color to reflect on their own experiences—and as a window, providing the opportunity for White teens to view the experiences of others. The text becomes the tool for a conversation across racial and ethnic groups (Glazier & Seo, 2005).

Many authors of youth literature take a critical look at the impact of racism and poverty on the lived experiences of people and communities of color. Their characters are aware of the privileges that White youth share, and they recognize "how much less they themselves have been given by virtue of their birthright" (Buehler, 2010, p. 36). They are aware of the institutionalized racism present in the economic, educational, and judicial system. Diverse literature as counterstory can make the oppression and victimization of people and communities of color visible—visible to themselves and to the dominant culture. It can show that racism and inequality still exist in contemporary American society. It can help young people understand racism not only as personal prejudice and bigotry, but as a system of advantage—a system that is "perpetuated when we do not acknowledge its existence" (Tatum, 1997, p. 9). As Beverly Tatum (1997) argues, "talking about racism is an essential part of facing racism and changing it" (p. xix). Diverse literature provides a platform for these conversations.

In addition to providing counterstories in the form of diverse literature, librarians must make sure to connect youth with role models and mentors from the African American community—individuals who not only can assist with the development of literacy skills, but also offer counterstories and provide models of positive life outcome trajectories. Edwards and her colleagues (2009) note that there are many community organizations that can help African American children academically while ensuring that they remain connected to their Black cultural heritage, including (1) African American churches, (2) African American Greek-letter fraternities and sororities, (3) African American social organizations such as the National Association for the Advancement of Colored People (NAACP) and Jack and Jill of America, and (4) neighborhood organizations such as the Boys and Girls Clubs of America. Ernest Morrell, director of the Institute for Urban and Minority Education at Teachers College, Columbia University, encourages librarians to form partnerships with "teaching artists" who can lead programs on topics of interest to African American youth, such as video editing, sound recording, or writing and performing spoken-word poetry (Hughes-Hassell et al., 2011). In Chapters 9 and 10, you will read how the Free Library of Philadelphia and the Pearl Bailey Branch of the Newport News Public Library have leveraged the talents of their community members to support African American youth. Connecting youth with African American authors and illustrators is also important. In fact, Teresa Bunner (2014) describes it as "magic."

Finally, libraries can provide opportunities for African American youth to create their own counterstories. These can take the form of written pieces (as described in Chapter 8) or songs, social media entries (i.e., blog posts and Twitter messages), videos, formal presentations to policymakers, and so forth (as described in Chapter 4). The format of the counterstory is less important than its goals—to cultivate reading and writing "as tools or pathways for human development" (Hughes-Hassel et al., 2011, p. 6), and to "cast doubt on the validity of accepted premises or myths, especially ones held by the majority" (Delgado & Stefancic, 2001, p. 144). As Morrell explains, "Literacy is not just about decoding text. It's about becoming a superior human being that can act powerfully upon the world" (Hughes-Hassell et al., 2011, p. 6). Libraries must provide African American youth with opportunities to use literacy, and therefore their voices, to expose, critique, and challenge cultural, institutional, and structural phenomena that perpetuate racism and racial stereotypes.

Action Step 5—Integrate culturally relevant teaching practices in our instruction and programs.

As will be discussed in detail in Chapters 2 and 3, it is critical that librarians who work with African American youth integrate culturally responsive strategies into our instruction and programs. Edwards et al. (2010) explain: "One's *culture does influence learning style*, that is, the way we think about learning, including literacy learning" (p. 71; emphasis added). Hanley and Noblit (2009, p. 8), in their meta-analysis of 146 research studies focusing on the role of culture and identity development in promoting academic achievement and resilience among youth of color, identified five themes that we believe are important to designing culturally responsive library programs:

1. **Involve the community**—"Culture is constantly changing and varied." Libraries must reach out to community and family members as important sources of information "about the needs and resources of youth who they know in ways [librarians] cannot."
2. **Use culture to promote racial identity**—Library programs and instruction must involve "key aspects of [African American] youths' home culture and focus on developing strategies to use culture to construct positive racial identity."
3. **Use culture and racial identity as an asset**—Library programs must deploy an asset-based approach, recognizing African American youths' culture as a strength and reassuring them that racial stereotypes will not be used to define them, but instead they will be challenged and dismantled.
4. **Educate about racism**—Programs should provide accurate information about racial oppression and racism.
5. **Develop caring relationships**—Librarians must establish caring relationships with African American youth, but they must realize that what a caring relationship looks like will vary across cultures; that is, African American youth will interpret caring from the perspective of their culture, which may differ from the librarian's cultural definition.

Action Step 6—Embrace our role in social justice.

The literacy education and improved life outcomes for African American youth is a critical social justice and civil rights issue in American society, and we view it as one on which the library community can potentially have a tremendous impact. Historically, librarianship has adhered to a service- and empowerment-oriented value system (Lankes, 2011; Pateman, 2010). Addressing the literacy needs of Black youth requires that librarians actively embrace these values and focus on developing and providing services that are about social change—enabling, facilitating, and empowering African American youth and their communities, providing them with the information and resources they need and helping them level the economic, social, and political playing fields. Ernest Morrell reminds us:

> More Black males died in a decade in the United States from gunshots than all the casualties in Vietnam, Iraq, and Afghanistan combined. This is not inevitable. This is a choice. As long as we think of it as inevitability, we can absolve ourselves of the responsibility for not making the choice to do something to make it right. It is going to take all of us dedicating our lives to this. This is justice. This is fairness. Solidarity leads to action. (Hughes-Hassell et al., 2011, p. 19)

Often, librarians are hesitant to adopt a social justice position for fear of alienating the core user group or appearing to favor one user group over another (Pateman, 2010). It is important to remember that developing services for African American youth and other socially excluded people not only benefits the previously excluded, but the already included as well. Programs and services that are more closely tailored to meet the needs of the entire community are more likely to provide better services, resources, staff, and opening hours to all its users (Pateman, 2010).

That said, Alfred Tatum (2009) warns educators that "switching the focus to the literacy needs of *all* students prevents or obscures the literacy development of *certain* students. . . . The humanistic claim that we must focus on *all* is less humanistic in practice if the literacy needs of *certain* students are not fully addressed" (p. 61, emphasis in original). The library community must acknowledge that inequities exist for Black youth, and we must have the courage to address them.

CONCLUDING THOUGHTS

As this chapter has illustrated, African American youth are disproportionately affected by institutional and structural inequities, including underfunded school and public libraries, and that these inequities are perpetuated by a system that privileges Whites and marginalizes people and communities of color. Consequently, the life outcomes and opportunities for Black youth are "disproportionately constrained compared to their peers in the dominant white cultural group" (Hughes-Hassell et al., 2011, p. 26). We hope that this chapter has illustrated that these inequities and life outcomes are not inevitable—that change can happen. As Charlie Nelms, former chancellor of North Carolina Central University, said, "If we have the will . . . we can create the way" (Hughes-Hassell et al., 2011, p. 23). This chapter serves as the first step in helping libraries and librarians create the way.

NOTES

Portions of this chapter were previously published in the following sources:

Hughes-Hassell, S. (2013). Multicultural young adult literature as a form of counter-storytelling. *The Library Quarterly: Information, Community, Policy, 83*(3):

212–228; and Hughes-Hassell, S., Kumasi, K., Rawson, C. H., & Hitson, A. (2012). *Building a bridge to literacy for African American male youth: A call to action for the library community.* Unpublished manuscript, School of Information and Library Science, University of North Carolina at Chapel Hill, United States. Retrieved from https://bridgetolit.web.unc.edu/?page_id=12.

The Educational Opportunity Quiz was inspired by Gorski, P. C. (2013). *Teaching and reaching students in poverty: Strategies for erasing the opportunity gap.* New York: Teachers College Press.

2

Culturally Relevant Pedagogy and the Black Cultural Ethos

Pauletta Brown Bracy, Sandra Hughes-Hassell, and Casey H. Rawson

I was a curious boy, but the schools were not concerned with curiosity. They were concerned with compliance.

—Coates (2015, p. 26)

The achievement gap dilemma has given rise to prominent voices in the call to rehabilitate the educational system in the United States. At the center of the ongoing discussions about school reform is the education of African American youth. Many experts have offered suggestions about how to narrow the achievement gap, identifying measures and strategies to help African American students improve their test scores. According to Christine Sleeter (2012), at the time of desegregation during the 1970s, school districts began to experiment with various approaches to working with diverse student populations. A new entry into the discourse was the phenomenon of "culture." While some educators discussed the importance of creating school cultures to foster and support learning, others spoke of the imperative of cultivating the culture of the minority child to foster and support his or her learning. The new educational reform has carried different labels, including *culturally responsive pedagogy, culturally relevant pedagogy, culturally appropriate pedagogy, culturally compatible pedagogy,* and *culturally sensitive pedagogy.* However, all of these are characteristically anchored by the nexus of culture and schooling. Gloria Ladson-Billings (2009) describes culturally relevant teaching as "a pedagogy that empowers students intellectually, socially, emotionally, and politically by using cultural referents to impart knowledge, skills, and attitudes" (p. 20).

This chapter explores the construct of culturally relevant pedagogy through an examination of the works of seven scholars: Patrick Roz Camangian, Gloria Ladson-Billings, Geneva Gay, Tyrone Howard, Janice E. Hale, James Banks, and Christine C. Sleeter. Theorist A. Wade Boykin complements the collective body of scholarship with his seminal work on the *Black Cultural Ethos (BCE)* prototype, which is referenced by several of these scholars. Discussions highlight each scholar's perspectives on the subject. Throughout the chapter, we describe the characteristics of culturally responsive educators and offer research-based, culturally relevant strategies that school and public librarians can utilize in their work with African American youth.

In this chapter, we:
- Explore the constructs of culturally relevant pedagogy and the BCE
- Introduce the research of important scholars in the area of culturally relevant pedagogy
- Describe the characteristics of culturally responsive educators
- Offer research-based, culturally relevant strategies that librarians can use

BLACK CULTURAL ETHOS (BCE)

We begin with a discussion of A. Wade Boykin's influential work on the BCE. Boykin proposes that the key to developing talent in African American youth may lie in providing them with culturally sensitive and appropriate educational contexts that build on elements of African culture (Boykin, 1994). Other scholars concur (i.e., Delpit, 1988; Gay, 2000; Hale, 2001; Howard, 2010, Irvine, 2003; Ladson-Billings, 2009; Sleeter, 2012).

Boykin (1986) has identified what he calls the *triple quandary*—the African American experience as framed by the interplay of three realms of experiential negotiation—the mainstream, minority, and Black cultural realms. The *mainstream*, or Euro-American, realm is the most pervasive and affects *all* members of society. The *minority* experience is based on exposure to social, economic, and political oppression (often linked to race) and produces adaptive skills and strategies. Finally, the BCE is rooted in a traditional West African ethos and is "a culturally indigenous basis from which Afro-Americans interpret and negotiate social reality" (Boykin, 1986, p. 66). Boykin (1983) argues that the BCE is comprised of nine dimensions that characterize how African Americans perceive, interpret, and interact with the world, particularly those who live in low-income communities:

1. *Spirituality:* Permeating all sectors of one's life space is the conviction that greater powers than human ones are continually in play (Boykin, 1994, p. 249).

2. *Harmony:* Seeing oneself as, and in turn acting as though one were, inextricably linked to one's surroundings, rather than seeing oneself as distinct from one's surroundings (Boykin, 1994, p. 249).

3. *Movement:* Interweaving the mosaic of movement, music, dance, and percussiveness, represented by the musical beat (Boykin, 1994, p. 249).

4. *Verve:* Preferring the energetic, the intense, the stimulating, and the lively, and connoting a tendency to attend to several concerns at once and to shift focus among them, rather than to focus on a single concern in a rigidly sequential fashion (Boykin, 1994, p. 249).

5. *Affect:* Integrating feelings with thoughts and actions, such that it would be difficult to engage in an activity if one's feelings run counter to the engagement, and implying emotional expressiveness and sensitivity to emotional cues from others (Boykin, 1994, p. 249).

6. *Communalism:* Denoting the "awareness of the interdependence of people and acting in accordance with the notion that duty to one's group is more important than individual privilege and rights" (Hanley & Noblit, 2009, p. 26).

7. *Expressive individualism:* Cultivating a distinct personality and "putting one's own personal brand on an activity," with concern for style more than efficiency or accuracy (Boykin, 1983, p. 344).

8. *Orality:* Emphasizing attaching the knowledge gained and passed on through word of mouth, with reliance on the call-and-response mode of communication (Boykin, 1994, p. 249).

9. *Social time perspective:* Construing time in terms of significant events, rather than the clock and calendar, and behavior that is bound to social traditions and customs of the past that serve as guideposts for the future (Boykin, 1994, p. 249).

Boykin believes that the conflict created by the triple quandary affects many aspects of the African American experience, including schooling. According to Boykin (1986), African Americans are "incompletely socialized to the Euro-American cultural system; they are victimized by racial and economic oppression; and they participate in a culture that is at odds with mainstream ideology" (p. 66). He argues that the approaches to classroom teaching and learning are typically built on mainstream, or Euro-American, experiences and ways of learning. Rather than being seen as a strength, diversity of lived experience is viewed as a deficit that needs to be overcome. Table 2.1 summarizes the distinctions that Boykin draws between the BCE and the Euro-American cultural ethos.

Boykin and his colleagues have conducted extensive research on the elements of the BCE in search of instructional approaches and other methods to counter this deficit viewpoint, as well as to support the teaching and learning of African American children. The following selected studies compellingly speak to the vital role of Black culture in the educational process and offer concrete suggestions for how the BCE can be used to improve the educational experiences of African American and Black youth.

Exploring the dichotomy of learning preferences and instructional practices, Boykin and other researchers conducted a qualitative study to determine the types of cultural themes present in classrooms serving African American

TABLE 2.1 Traditional BCE and Euro-American Cultural Ethos

BCE	Euro-American Cultural Ethos
Emphasis on spirituality in the universe	Emphasis on materialism in the universe
Harmonic unity with nature and other people	Mastery over nature and individualism as a prized entity
Values feelings, expressiveness, and spontaneity	Values control of impulses, self-discipline, and dispassionate reason
An individual's duty is to the group, and possessions belong to the group	Individual rights are paramount, and the notion of private property is sacred

students (Boykin, Tyler, & Miller, 2005). Using the taxonomy of classroom life functions and cultural behaviors cited in the BCE to describe classroom dynamics, they found that themes associated with mainstream cultural ethos were more prevalent than those associated with a Black ethos. Moreover, the Anglo-cultural themes were more likely to be manifested in both verbal and behavioral, teacher-initiated expressions than in student-initiated expressions. Students themselves were more likely to initiate cultural expressions consistent with Black cultural ethos than those judged consistent with mainstream Anglo-cultural worldviews. In other words, there was a disconnect between the verbal and behavioral expressions of Black youth and their teachers, which negatively affected the schooling experience of the youth.

Communal behavior was the focus of four studies, two of which were discipline specific. In all four of these studies, the performance of African American students improved when teachers structured their classrooms as supportive, culturally respectful, and communal settings.

The first study examined the effects of communal and individual learning contexts on the long-term retention of a geography curriculum (Boykin, Lilja, & Tyler, 2004). Students were assigned to either a communal or an individual learning context over a three-week span. Overall, African American students in the communal learning context significantly outperformed students in the individual learning context on the culminating unit examination.

Mathematics was the topic of the second study, which sought to incorporate cultural themes into learning contexts (Hurley, Boykin, & Allen, 2005). Students were assessed after participation in one of two learning contexts, which differed in the degree to which they afforded the expression of a communal orientation. The conditions differed by learning structure (group work versus individual work); physical context (sitting together using shared materials versus sitting in individual desks with individual materials); reward structure (no reward versus criterion reward); and motivational prompt (communal versus individualistic). Black students who studied in a high-communal learning context outperformed their counterparts in a low-communal learning context, supporting the notion that the environment in which learning takes place is critical to determining how well and how much Black children learn.

Another discipline-specific study addressed three dimensions of BCE: social perspective of time (referred to as *sociality*), verve, and rhythmic expression (referred to as *movement*). Elaine Parsons (2008) noted that instructional environments that utilize BCE resemble the learning context advocated by science education reform, with instruction consisting of a variety of teaching strategies, including problem- and project-based learning and guided or open inquiry. Her research sought to answer three questions: "(1) With respect to BCE, what characterizes the natural instructional contexts of two middle school science teachers? (2) What characterizes the achievement of African American students in contexts that incorporate BCE and contexts that do not? (3) What achievement patterns, if any, exist in BCE and non-BCE instructional contexts?" (p. 665). The natural contexts of the teachers did not incorporate sociality, verve, or movement. Although natural opportunities to incorporate BCE were available to both teachers, neither took advantage of these opportunities. In contexts that did not incorporate BCE, Black students' achievement at pretesting and posttesting declined. One teacher moderated her setting to include the three dimensions as part of her instructional context; student achievement improved from pretesting to posttesting.

Another study investigated the capability of African American students to learn for transfer (i.e., to use skills, behaviors, and attitudes developed in one setting in another one) using an experimental design of culturally structured communal contexts (Serpell, Boykin, Serge, & Nasim, 2006). Communal learning contexts facilitated learning for both African American and White students; however, African American students scored better on the transfer tasks than White students and showed greater gains compared to the control group.

Pursing the communal dimension of the BCE in distinct strategies, Ebony Dill and A. Wade Boykin (2000) conducted a comparative study of the efficacy of communal, peer tutoring, and individual learning contexts, framed by three hypotheses: "(a) students will give greater endorsement to communal values as compared to individual values; (b) Communal Learning (CL) contexts will facilitate more text recall than individual criterion context and at least as much as the traditionally structured peer learning contexts; and (c) communal orientation will be positively related with performance and experiences under the communal learning context" (p. 69). Their findings supported the first hypothesis; students preferred communal themes over individualistic ones. As to the second hypothesis, communal learning was superior to both peer and individual criterion learning in facilitating text recall. Concerning the third hypothesis, no significant correlations were found; however, students indicated that they cared about their peers and especially liked the learning phase of the project because they were able to work collaboratively. The researchers concluded that Communal Learning contexts are more congruent with African American students' preferred learning modes, provide them with the opportunity to cultivate their own strategies and behaviors to facilitate learning, and foster a sense of interdependence and duty (pp. 74–75).

Verve was the topic of research that explored the relationship of "psychological verve" to the school performance and motivation of African American children. Noting the home environments of African American students to be high-energy, fast paced, socially oriented, and affording high physical stimulation (Boykin, 1982), Caryn Bailey and A. Wade Boykin (2001) used school-relevant problem-solving tasks in math, vocabulary, spelling, and picture sequencing and presented them to children in low- and high-variability contexts. In each type of academic task, considered separately, performance was significantly better in the high-variability context. The researchers concluded that variability manipulation seemed to have a pronounced and pervasive effect on Black students' academic task performance, intimating that presenting tasks in a high-variability (i.e., random-sequence) format may be more effective in classroom settings for facilitating the academic achievement of certain Black school children than the more traditional low-variability (i.e., blocked-sequence) format.

Movement expression in its varied "interconnectedness of music-linked movement, rhythm, percussive dance, kinesthetic movement, and gestures" was the subject of a study that involved story recall performance, as researchers sought to explore the impact of infused cultural components in both content and context (Cole & Boykin, 2008, p. 334). Children were placed in environments of high movement and syncopated music, low movement and syncopated music, high movement and no syncopated music, and low movement and no syncopated music. The Black children's highest performance of optimized story recall was in the condition of syncopated music and high movement. The lowest performance was in the environment that was devoid of any music or movement.

In a similar study, A. Wade Boykin and Rodney Cunningham (2001) examined the effects of incorporating cultural factors related to movement expression into the presentation and content of instructional materials. One context in this study allowed for high-movement expression such as dancing, running, and jumping, whereas another provided little movement expression, only walking and standing. The results were consistent with previous findings, confirming the prediction that African American children's overall performance was significantly better in the high-movement expression than the low movement–learning context.

An especially critical aspect of the classroom climate is the attitudes and perceptions held by teachers. Motivation and behavior were the focus of one study, which sought to discern if White elementary school teachers of African American students perceive behaviors linked to certain cultural forms as more advantageous to their classrooms than those linked to other cultural forms. In this research, Kenneth Tyler and colleagues (2006) investigated the themes of communalism and verve, along with competition and individualism. Using scenarios of hypothetical students behaving in ways consistent with the cultural themes, their analysis revealed that White teachers viewed competitive and individualistic students as significantly more motivated and achievement oriented than those who displayed communal and vervistic behaviors. Thus, the teachers' perceptions of optimal motivation and achievement were linked to mainstream values.

In a second study, based on the premise that students must demonstrate mastery of tasks across varied content disciplines that reflect mainstream cultural values, in contrast to values brought to school from home, Boykin and his colleagues (2006) investigated the presence of culture in learning activities and instructional practices of African American and American European elementary school teachers serving low-income, African American students. The themes explored in this study were individualism and competition (mainstream) and communalism and verve (BCE). The most common cultural practice endorsed by the teachers studied here was individualism, followed by competitive, communal, and vervistic practices. The researchers concluded that although research has shown African American student preference to the contrary, many teachers reinforce mainstream cultural values via their activities and behavior in the classroom.

Topics in another group of studies concerned cultural values in the home. Research findings have confirmed that practices associated with BCE facilitate academic success when incorporated into school-based learning. However, the practices are not always enacted in public schools serving African American students (Tyler, Boykin, Miller, & Hurley, 2007). Within this context, investigators sought to determine if African American students from low-income backgrounds prefer culture-based learning, and if such practices are fostered by parental socialization. In addition, they were interested in the extent to which students believe that their teachers accommodate their culture-based learning preferences. Their findings revealed that both at home and in school, students had the greatest learning and working preference for communal and vervistic behaviors. They also reported that their parents would prefer communal behaviors to individualistic and competitive behaviors. However, the students believed that their teachers had emphasized individualistic and competitive learning behaviors in class.

In the second study, researchers examined the role of culture in socialization patterns within low-income, African American households (Tyler, Boykin, Boelter, & Dillihunt, 2005). Parent participants in this study reported socialization practices present in their children's home activities and encounters with an emphasis on four cultural themes: communalism, verve, competition, and individualism. The parents reported that communal-based household socialization activities were significantly more common than individualistic, vervistic, or competitive activities. However, these parents also marginally endorsed individualistic socialization practices, which was consistent with other research showing evidence of individualistic tendencies among African American adults. The investigators concluded that although communalism is emphasized and is a relatively stable cultural socialization theme in African American households, both BCE themes and mainstream cultural themes are present in these contexts.

The research that Boykin and his colleagues have conducted offers clear and precise directions for the best ways to employ the BCE to educate African American youth. The findings are not only easily translatable into best practices for the classroom and library, but they also are compatible with educational philosophies such as constructivism, inquiry, and connected learning, which have been adopted by the library community. A number of research-based literacy strategies are found in the box "Examples of Literacy Strategies That Build on the BCE."

Examples of Literacy Strategies That Build on the BCE

Oral Tradition

- Incorporate storytelling, spoken word, call and response, poetry, reader's theater, and song into literacy instruction (Hale, 2001).
- Utilize literature circles, book discussion formats, and thinking protocols that allow students to respond orally to texts (Lazar et al., 2012).
- Engage students in retelling stories and reciting or performing poetry (Lazar et al., 2012).
- Have students participate in buddy and partner reading (Lazar et al., 2012).

Affect

- Use texts and other resources, such as TED talks and popular culture artifacts, that are stimulating and relevant to African American youth (Hale, 2001; Tatum 2009).
- Ask students to make text-to-self and text-to-text connections (Lazar et al., 2012).
- Allow students to write about what they know, including their personal lived experiences (Tatum, 2011).
- Utilize critical literacy techniques to analyze literary selections, as well as popular culture artifacts and other media (Christensen, 2002; Morrell, 2012).
- Incorporate the creative arts into literacy programs (Hale, 2001).
- Pay attention to and incorporate current events into literacy instruction (Tatum, 2006).

Verve, Movement, and Expressive Individualism

- Provide quiet spaces and spaces where activity and noise is allowed.
- Include hands-on activities, projects, and trips into the community.
- Make music, rhythm, movement, and variability part of literacy instruction when appropriate.

Communalism

- Utilize small cooperative groups that emphasize cooperation over competition (Hale, 2001; Tatum, 2006, 2009).
- Support student success by connecting youth with mentors and providing apprenticeship opportunities (Tatum, 2006, 2009).
- Utilize peer mentors and coaches (Boykin & Noguera, 2011).

Harmony

- Place literacy instruction/events in a meaningful context (Tatum, 2006, 2009).

- Find ways to help African American and Black youth see the implications that literacy has for their lives, their futures, and their communities (Tatum, 2006, 2009).
- Build on the historical legacy of literacy in the Black community (Tatum, 2006, 2009).

HUMANIZING PEDAGOGY

Patrick Camangian (2015) offers another related perspective for closing the achievement gap, which he labels "humanizing pedagogy." Humanizing pedagogy "draws on traditions of culturally relevant and critical pedagogies to develop critical literacies that foster the type of learning that leads to revolutionary transformation in lives," with the aim of "[teaching] students to love themselves, love people, and see humanizing education as part of a long history of struggle for radical social justice" (Camangian, 2015, p. 448). He contends that the implementation of humanizing pedagogy allows youth of color to critically examine the historical oppression and discrimination that their communities have experienced, with a focus on recognizing and deconstructing the psychological damage that this oppression has caused to their communities as a whole, as well as to themselves as individuals. By doing so, Camangian (2015) argues that youth of color will "cultivate a deeper knowledge of and compassion for the self" and begin to feel a greater "sense of control over their collective lives" (pp. 426–427). They will also be prepared to engage in social justice work and transform the oppressive suffering that communities of color (especially low-income urban communities) experience. Humanizing pedagogy is grounded in Paulo Freire's ideas of critical pedagogy and reflects several of the CRT tenets described in Chapter 1, specifically the centrality of experiential knowledge, the importance of counterstories, and a commitment to social justice and praxis. It also builds on many of the elements of the BCE.

Camangian explored humanizing pedagogy in a participatory action research project designed to enable the youth in his 12th-grade English course, most of whom were Black and Latino, to examine the causes of their academic and social struggles with the goal of transforming their lives. His findings suggest three culturally relevant practices that educators can use to enable youth of color to become academically successful, motivated, and compassionate leaders capable of disrupting oppressive and dehumanizing social and political conditions.

The first of these practices is *agitation,* which involves providing opportunities (and support) for "students to learn about and understand social [and political] issues in ways that resonate with the deeply intimate and often hostile ways they experience such issues" (Camangian, 2015, p. 432). The goal of agitation is to push "students to become unsettled about social conditions, ideology, and social practices that shape their experience" (Camangian, 2015, p. 436). In Camangian's study, his students explored the economic struggles faced by their community, including the exploitation and underdevelopment of the Black community. They approached this topic not only from an historical and political perspective, but also from a deeply personal viewpoint, sharing stories of how economic inequities affect their daily lives.

Agitation leads to *arousal*, the second practice, which involves youth of color in critiquing the White-dominated society and questioning the idea that social institutions such as schools are race neutral, objective, and fair, as the dominant narrative suggests. It requires students to engage in sophisticated analyses of society and of themselves. For example, arousal often leads youth of color to explore the systemic nature of racism and how it permeates social institutions. It may challenge youth of color to consider internalized racism, the acceptance and adoption by people of color of the dominant society's racist views, stereotypes, and biases of their own racial or ethnic group. And it may push youth to consider the intersection of identities such as race, ethnicity, gender, socioeconomic status, and sexual orientation.

The final practice, *inspiration*, challenges students to act and to inspire others—in other words, to engage in social justice work. For students to be motivated to "awaken the collective consciousness of others" (Camangian, 2015, p. 443), Camangian argues that educators must support students in the creation of authentic culminating learning products and help them develop leadership skills that will enable them to inspire others. In his study, Camangian's students shared their class-related work, their "narratives, poetry, and research projects to inspire critical thinking [and] transformative behaviors, and to open up space for participating classes to voice their social and political perspectives" (Camangian, 2015, p. 444).

Camangian (2015) argues that these three "practices have potential to engage students in meaningful academic learning, recognizing dehumanization to disrupt it, and cultivating humanizing behaviors" (p. 431). They move education from a focus on developing academic skills in order to raise test scores to preparing students to transform oppressive social and political systems. Additional examples of participatory action research that are grounded in humanizing pedagogy are described in Chapter 4.

CULTURALLY RELEVANT PEDAGOGY AND PRACTICE

Gloria Ladson-Billings (1995) began the development of a grounded theory of culturally relevant pedagogy in an ethnographic study about teaching practices during the 1988–1989 and 1989–1990 school years. Eight teachers of African American children were involved in the research. Data were collected through observing behaviors, conducting interviews, and performing analysis of videotaped sessions.

Three broad suppositions emerged, which she considered to be the theoretical underpinnings of culturally relevant pedagogy:

1. **Conceptions of self and others held by culturally relevant teachers.**
   The teachers:
   • believed that all students could achieve academic success;
   • saw their pedagogy as art—that is, "unpredictable, always in the process of becoming" (Ladson-Billings, 1995, p. 478);

- viewed themselves as members of the wider school community; and
- saw teaching as a way to give back to that community.

2. **How culturally relevant teachers structure social relations**. The teachers:
   - consciously created social interactions to help students attain cultural competence and critical consciousness;
   - maintained fluid, equitable, and reciprocal relationships with students;
   - demonstrated connectedness with students;
   - developed a community of learners; and
   - encouraged collaborative learning and responsibility toward peers.

3. **The conception of knowledge held by culturally relevant teachers.** The teachers believed that:
   - knowledge is dynamic and active,
   - knowledge must be approached from a critical stance,
   - teachers must be passionate about knowledge and learning,
   - scaffolding is critical to facilitate learning, and
   - teachers must use complex and multifaceted assessment strategies.

Summarily, Ladson-Billings (2009) characterizes teachers with culturally relevant practices as:

- having high self-esteem;
- seeing themselves as part of the community, seeing teaching as giving back to the community, and encouraging their students to do the same;
- seeing teaching as an art and themselves as artists;
- believing that all students can succeed;
- helping students make connections between their multiple identities; and
- seeing teaching as "pulling knowledge out"—like "mining" (p. 38).

Like Ladson-Billings, Geneva Gay emphasizes the importance of culturally relevant pedagogy and practice. She posits that the fundamental aim of culturally responsive pedagogy is "to empower ethnically diverse students through academic success, cultural affiliation, and personal efficacy" (Gay, 2000, p. 111). She describes it as making learning encounters more effective and relevant for diverse students by using elements of students' cultural knowledge, prior experiences, frames of reference, and performance styles. It is anchored on four "pillars of practice: teacher attitudes and expectations, cultural communication in the classroom, culturally diverse content in the curriculum, and culturally congruent instructional strategies" (Gay, 2000, p. 44).

Descriptively, culturally relevant pedagogy is:

- **Validating:** It not only recognizes that culture varies across ethnic and racial groups, but it acknowledges that *all* cultural heritages are legitimate and should be included in the curriculum. Doing so affirms students' cultural histories, connects their home and school experiences in meaningful ways, and positions academic excellence as the legacy and domain of all cultural groups, not just Whites. It also acknowledges that culture affects learning preferences and styles and thus incorporates a variety of instructional strategies. Finally, it recognizes the value of counterstories and integrates them across all areas of the curriculum.

- **Comprehensive:** It not only focuses on academic achievement, but it supports the development of positive racial and ethnic identity development. As discussed in Chapter 3, this is essential to academic success for youth of color, but it also helps students build relationships with their racial and ethnic communities—relationships that are important to the development of resilience. This sense of camaraderie prepares youth to engage in the collective struggle against racism and oppression. Finally, culturally relevant pedagogy focuses on teachers developing caring classroom environments and getting to know students as individuals.
- **Multidimensional:** It focuses on all aspects of the schooling experience, including student-teacher relationships, the learning environment, the classroom climate, the content of the curriculum, and instructional and assessment practices. It takes an asset-based approach, tapping into students' cultural knowledge, strengths, and prior experiences.
- **Empowering and transformative:** It focuses on the whole student, supporting personal and academic growth and raising cultural consciousness, thus empowering youth of color to transform themselves and the world around them. It positions academic success as an expectation for all youth and provides role models of people of color who are leaders in their fields.
- **Emancipatory:** It liberates youth of color by presenting a curriculum that includes references to the intellectual and political legacies of communities of color in this country. It helps them understand what it means to be Black, Latino, Asian, or Native American in the United States and instills in them a sense of pride in their culture and intellectual history.

Tyrone Howard builds on the work of Ladson-Billings and Gay (as well as other scholars who study culturally relevant pedagogy). As a result of his research, he has identified five principles of culturally responsive pedagogy:

- The adoption of an asset-based approach to educating culturally diverse students—one that challenges the dominant deficit-based system.
- The dismantling of normative beliefs about discourse, knowledge, language, culture, and history that privilege Eurocentric and middle-class standards and values.
- The adoption of a social justice stance that involves not only being aware of injustice and oppression, but also working to disrupt inequities, discrimination, and repression actively.
- The development of a deep, authentic, and culturally informed understanding of how to create a caring school environment that supports the academic, social, emotional, psychological, and cultural well-being of culturally diverse youth.

- The recognition of the complexity and dynamic nature of culture and the implementation of teaching strategies that allow students to use their personal culture and lived experiences to enhance their educational success (Howard, 2010).

PRINCIPLES OF PRACTICE FOR EFFECTIVE SCHOOLING

Janice Hale (2001) offers a culturally appropriate pedagogy of school reform, in which she identifies three principles or practices for effective schooling for Black youth:

Instruction
- Is grounded in a theoretical framework such as Boykin's BCE.
- Includes culturally relevant teaching strategies such as cooperative group work, kinesthetic learning experiences, hands-on activities, authentic real-world projects, and interrelated learning experiences that include field trips, speakers, and classroom visitors that have been found to benefit Black youth.
- Utilizes a comprehensive and culturally responsive curriculum and sets specific, clearly articulated, and shared goals for Black youth in each content area.
- Articulates the specific understandings, knowledge, and skills that students are expected to master for each unit, as well as how learning will be assessed (formatively and summatively).
- Infuses African, African American, and Afro-Caribbean culture across the curriculum and into each instructional unit.
- Creates an aesthetically pleasing learning environment that incorporates beauty and harmony.
- Emphasizes cultural legitimacy in teaching, curricular materials, and assignments.
- Implements academic rigor throughout elementary and middle school so that Black students can master honors or Advanced Placement (AP) English and history classes and advanced math and science courses such as calculus and physics in high school.

Instructional accountability infrastructure
- Includes a building-level instructional coordinator or curriculum leader that supports academic success for all youth. This includes providing professional development, planning with teachers, observing in classrooms, and providing meaningful feedback to teachers. It also entails monitoring student progress and providing the academic, social, and emotional support that each child needs to perform at the appropriate grade level.
- Understands the dynamics of African American family life, especially in inner-city communities, and seeks ways to help parents and families meet the expectations of involvement.

- Involves parents in ways that are culturally relevant, strengths-based, and meaningful.

Cultural enrichment
- Offers enrichment programs in the school and the community that build on and supplement classroom instruction.
- Provides programs that strengthen the connection between the school and the community in ways that motivate school engagement, build social skills, and teach nonviolent conflict resolution. This includes male mentoring programs, teen pregnancy intervention, and cultural enrichment activities. These programs ideally are organized and led by parents and communities.

MULTICULTURAL EDUCATION

No discussion of culturally relevant pedagogy would be complete without mentioning the work of James Banks, who calls for transformation of the *total* school experience to better meet the needs of youth of color. This includes critically examining and reforming the curriculum, the teaching strategies and instructional materials that we use, the attitudes and behaviors of teachers and administrators, and the culture of the school (Banks, 1993). Banks argues that anything less than comprehensive multicultural education reform is insufficient to change substantially the schooling experience and achievement levels of youth of color. In other words, it is not enough to tinker; to simply add content that celebrates the lives of influential African Americans (or members of other racial or ethnic communities) and their contributions to American society; or to include one book written by an African American or Black author to the required reading list for each grade level. He explains it this way:

> Because the assumption that only what is Anglo-American is American is so deeply ingrained in curriculum materials and in the hearts and minds of many students and teachers . . . we need to examine seriously the conception of American that is perpetuated in the curriculum and the basic cannon, assumptions, and purposes that underlie the curriculum. (Banks, 2009, p. 18)

Based on his research and that of other scholars, Banks developed a model of multicultural education that focuses on substantial transformation of the current educational experience and reflects many of the elements of BCE, humanizing education, and culturally responsive pedagogy discussed previously. It also addresses issues of cultural power. His conceptualization consists of five dimensions: (1) content integration, (2) knowledge construction, (3) prejudice reduction, (4) an equity pedagogy, and (5) an empowering school culture and social structure (Banks, 1993). A full discussion of each dimension is beyond the scope of this chapter, but here, we provide a brief overview of each one.

Content integration requires teachers across all subject areas to "use examples, data, and information from a variety of cultures and groups to illustrate key concepts, principles, generalizations, and theories in their subject area and discipline" (Banks, 1993, p. 5). This is the easiest dimension for schools to implement, and while it is necessary, Banks argues that it is not enough to bring about the changes needed to close the achievement gap or to enable African American youth to reach their full potential.

Knowledge construction calls for recognition that positionality influences how knowledge within each subject area and discipline is constructed. In other words, the biases, experiences, and perceptions of researchers and scholars affect their interpretation of historical events, their understanding of social and political movements, the scientific questions they ask and investigate, and so forth. The role of teachers is to help students become "active participants in knowledge building rather than passive consumers of the knowledge that is constructed by others" (Banks, 1999, p. 69).

Prejudice reduction focuses not only on supporting youth of color in the development of positive racial and ethnic identities, but also on helping all youth develop more positive feelings toward other racial groups. Strategies such as including counterstories across the curriculum in consistent, natural, and integrated ways; involving youth in discussions of race, racism, power, and privilege; and engaging youth in participatory action research can be used to help students develop more positive racial attitudes and values.

An *equity pedagogy* "exists when teachers use the techniques and methods that facilitate the academic achievement of students from diverse racial, ethnic, and social-class groups" (Banks, 1993, p. 6). The items included in the box "Examples of Literacy Strategies that Build on the BCE" (pages 38–39) are some of the techniques that Banks suggests.

The concept of an *empowering school culture and social structure* calls on educators to address systemic factors such as test bias, low teacher expectations, unequal discipline policies, lack of access to advanced coursework, failure of teachers to address microaggressions, and other inequities that prevent youth of color from having quality educational experiences. It also focuses attention on creating a school culture that empowers youth to work for a more just and humane society.

As Banks (1993) argues, each of these concepts must be implemented to bring about meaningful changes in schools. A school is a system, and as such, changes need to be made to all of its parts—the curriculum, the educators' attitudes and behaviors, the instructional materials and teaching strategies used, the relationships among students, and the school climate—if we are to improve the educational experience of African American youth.

What Do Culturally Responsive Librarians Do?

- Validate and affirm Black youth.
- Set high expectations, scaffold instruction, and provide frequent and substantial feedback.
- Provide Black youth with the skills and tools that they need to empower themselves.

- Exhibit caring, commitment, and respect for African American youth and their culture.
- Establish a caring environment and warm, personal, positive relationships with Black youth.
- Identify ways that the school or library culture (e.g., values, norms, and practices) may differ from Black youths' home culture, and develop strategies for bridging those differences.
- Build on Black youths' cultural backgrounds to develop engaging and effective programs, services, and collections, and to teach challenging academic knowledge and skills.
- Give Black youth a voice in what they learn and how they demonstrate understanding, as well as in program development.
- Create learning experiences that are culturally relevant and meaningful.
- Engage Black youth in identifying, examining, and discussing the value assumptions inherent in the construction of knowledge.
- Include students' interests and lived experiences in program development.
- Recognize that culture is not a fixed characteristic of individuals and instead bring an awareness of cultural possibilities to their work and get to know each student as an individual.
- Employ culturally responsive instructional strategies, processes, and assessments.
- Explicitly build on the cultural capital and funds of knowledge of the African American community.
- Advocate with Black youth and their families/communities.
- Serve in leadership roles within the school to help develop the infrastructure needed for all teachers to implement culturally responsible pedagogy (CRP).
- Involve parents in library programs and services.
- Create programming that bridges the gap between the school and the community.

CONCLUDING THOUGHTS

School librarians and public youth services librarians are bound by an ethic to serve youth in the most effective and culturally responsive ways. By its nature, pedagogy is most applicable in school settings, as it speaks directly to the manner in which teaching and learning occurs in tandem. Youth services librarians too engage in a teaching-learning dynamic through such activities as booktalking or book discussion groups or makerspaces. In working with African American youth, regardless of location (at school or in public), knowledge of culturally relevant pedagogy is a necessary requisite to ensure optimal service and personally rewarding library experiences. From this overview of culturally relevant pedagogy and Boykin's BCE construct (summarized in Table 2.2), implications for our profession clearly exist. The most essential element is culture. In our best efforts, it is our professional responsibility to cultivate

> In our best efforts, it is our professional responsibility to cultivate *cultural capital* among Black youth and among ourselves. We serve them best when we fundamentally embrace their culture.

cultural capital among Black youth and among ourselves. We serve them best when we fundamentally embrace their culture.

TABLE 2.2 Summary of Scholar Perspectives on Culturally Relevant Pedagogy

Scholar(s)	Concepts Discussed in This Chapter

A. Wade Boykin	• The triple quandary
	• BCE:
	  ◦ Spirituality
	  ◦ Harmony
	  ◦ Movement
	  ◦ Verve
	  ◦ Affect
	  ◦ Communalism
	  ◦ Expressive individualism
	  ◦ Orality
	  ◦ Social time perspective

Patrick Roz Camangian	• Humanizing pedagogy:
	  ◦ Agitation
	  ◦ Arousal
	  ◦ Inspiration

Gloria Ladson-Billings, Tyrone Howard, and Geneva Gay	• CRP:
	  ◦ Theoretical underpinnings (Ladson-Billings)
	  ◦ Characteristics of teachers employing CRP (Ladson-Billings)
	  ◦ Key descriptors (Gay) and principles (Howard) of CRP

Janice Hale	• School reform practices for effective schooling of Black youth

James Banks	• Comprehensive multicultural education reform:
	  ◦ Content integration
	  ◦ Knowledge construction process
	  ◦ Prejudice reduction
	  ◦ Equity pedagogy
	  ◦ Empowering school culture and social structure

Christine Sleeter	• Misconceptions about and oversimplifications of CRP

That said, as teacher educator Christine Sleeter (2001) observes, culturally relevant pedagogy is often oversimplified and misunderstood. It is viewed by some as merely a cultural celebration, and by others as a set of steps that teachers may use to get know their students better, as opposed to a paradigm shift. Culture is also considered by some educators as fairly fixed and homogenous, which results in a one-dimensional approach to working with students of color. Finally, many educators focus on culture alone as a way to bring about equity, consequently avoiding discussions of racism and other forms of oppression that underlie achievement gaps and alienation from school.

Thus, as librarians embrace the culture of African American students to better improve their schooling experiences, we need to remember our commitment to social justice and continue to challenge the dominant deficit model ideology used to explain educational achievement differences. We need to embrace culturally relevant pedagogy in all its complexity and fight to eliminate racism, poverty, and other forms of oppression that deny Black students access to high-quality instruction in our nation's schools. As Gary Howard (2006) writes, "We, through our consciousness and our commitment to social justice, can choose to direct our power, our personhood, and our profession toward the erosion and eventual extinction of White dominance" (p. 118).

3

Ethnic and Racial Development in African American Youth

Pauletta Brown Bracy, Sandra Hughes-Hassell, and Casey H. Rawson

> **We know at a very deep level that African American children do not come into this world at a deficit. There is no "achievement gap" at birth.**
>
> **—Delpit (2012, p. 5)**

As illustrated in Chapter 1, educators, social scientists, policymakers, and the public agree that African American youth face daunting challenges in everyday life. Beyond risk factors of health and general well-being, the approach to addressing the problems has focused on academic success. The achievement gap, which has garnered considerable attention the past few decades, has become *the* predicament in urban education reform. The most vulnerable people in this dilemma are African American males, who are known to be more disengaged with schooling than their female peers. Pedro Noguera (2008) assesses the nexus of the issue this way:

> The trouble with Black boys is that too often they are assumed to be at risk because they are too aggressive, too loud, too violent, too dumb, too hard to control, too streetwise, and too focused on sports. Such assumptions and projections have the effect of fostering the very behaviors and attitudes we find problematic and objectionable. The trouble with Black boys is that most never have a chance to be thought of as potentially smart and talented, or to demonstrate talents in the sciences, music, or literature. The trouble with Black boys is that too often they are placed in schools where their needs for nurturing, support, and loving discipline are not met. Instead, they are labeled, shunned, and treated in ways that create and reinforce an inevitable cycle of failure. (p. xxi)

The cycle of failure that Noguera describes is not the exclusive domain of African American males; however, they are the most visible victims of *a system of education that has failed to support the schooling needs of diverse youth in the United States.* We have purposely emphasized the phrase "a system of education that has failed to support the schooling needs of diverse youth in the United States" because we believe that it is the schools that have failed, *not* the youth. In her book *"Multiplication Is for White People,* Lisa Delpit (2012) writes, "We know at a very deep level that African American children do not come into this world at a deficit. There is no 'achievement gap' at birth. When we educators look out at a classroom of black faces, we must understand that we are looking at children at least as brilliant as those from any well-to-do-white community" (p. 5).

Delpit identifies a number of reasons that Black youth are not excelling in today's schools. One of the most troubling is the "deeply ingrained bias of equating blackness with inferiority" (Delpit, 2012, p. 9). Delpit argues that this perception affects not only how teachers view Black youth, but also how Black youth view themselves. She contends that educators who embrace this view tend to focus on remediation and low-level skills; they do not challenge Black youth to engage with complex concepts or to participate in discussions that require deep thinking because they believe that they are incapable of intellectually demanding work. Black youth often internalize these negative stereotypes and accept these low expectations, doubting their own competence, and as Delpit describes, they typically exhibit one of two behaviors: becoming invisible or acting out. Thus, according to Delpit, the real problem is not the achievement gap, but the expectation gap—a gap that causes a large number of educators not to teach and a large number of Black youth not to learn. She concludes:

> African American students are gifted and brilliant. They do not have a culture of poverty but a culture of richness that can be brought into classrooms to facilitate learning. *African American students learn when they are taught.* They must be helped to overcome the negative stereotypes about themselves and their communities that permeate our culture. (Delpit, 2012, p. 25; emphasis added)

Culturally relevant pedagogy, as described in Chapter 2, is one approach to supporting Black youth. We believe that paying attention to the psychology of African American youth, specifically consideration of who they are and how they navigate their maturation in and out of school settings, can also provide invaluable information to those who are committed to ensuring the prosperity and academic success of these young people. In this chapter, we pursue this topic through an exploration of racial and ethnic identity development theories. As Jean Phinney (1990) stated, "attitudes toward one's ethnicity are central to the psychological functioning of those who live in societies where their group and its culture are at best poorly represented (politically, economically, and in the media) and are at worst discriminated against or even attacked verbally and physically" (p. 499).

Before proceeding, it is important to distinguish racial identity from ethnic identity. According to André Branch (2012), although these terms are closely related, there are still distinctions to be drawn between them. *Ethnic identity* is "a sense of belonging to a particular ethnic group, in which one shares values, beliefs, traditions, language, and, in some cases, behaviors with others in the group" (p. 825). This sense of belonging can be influenced by interactions with those inside as well as outside the group. *Racial identity*, in contrast, relates to the ways in which one defines oneself based on parentage and is affected by physical traits such as skin color and hair texture.

> We believe that paying attention to the psychology of African American youth, specifically consideration of who they are and how they navigate their maturation in and out of school settings, can also provide invaluable information to those who are committed to ensuring the prosperity and academic success of these young people.

This chapter is divided into three sections. First, we look at various models of identity development, beginning with well-known standard models and then moving to models that specifically focus on racial and ethnic identity. Second, we discuss a sample of research that explores the relationship between racial and ethnic identity and the school success of African American youth. Finally, we suggest strategies that libraries can adopt to support both the racial and ethnic identity of African American youth and their literacy development.

In this chapter, we:
- Explore the constructs of racial and ethnic identity development
- Introduce the research of important scholars in the area of racial and ethnic identity development
- Explore the connection between positive racial identity development and academic achievement
- Offer strategies that librarians can use to support both the racial and ethnic identity of Black youth

MODELS OF IDENTITY DEVELOPMENT: THEORETICAL UNDERPINNINGS

Although *identity* is now a commonly used term, it is a relatively new concept, arising from the work of psychologist Erik Erikson in the 1950s and 1960s (Fearon, 1999). An individual's identity can be both *social* (defined by membership in a particular group with characteristic attributes and expected behaviors) and *personal* (focused on distinguishing features viewed as unchangeable or in which the individual takes pride), according to Fearon (1999). Many scholars have proposed models of identity development, and in many cases, these models highlight the period of adolescence as particularly critical and formative.

General Models of Identity Development

The earliest model of identity development was Erikson's (1950, 1963) model of psychosocial stages. He proposed that individuals progress through eight stages of identity development, and during each one, they face a crisis brought about by conflicting individual and societal needs. Successful navigation of each crisis results in the development of healthy personality traits and character strengths, while failure to do so may lead to stagnation and unhealthy personality traits. Erikson viewed adolescence as a critically important period in identity development, elaborating on this stage in his landmark book *Identity, Youth, and Crisis* in 1968.

Erikson (1968) described "the psychosocial aspect of adolescing" as the stage in which the individual develops "the prerequisites in physiological growth, mental maturation, and social responsibility to experience and pass through the crisis of identity" (p. 91). Although Erikson's model was not focused on racial identity, in a chapter entitled "Race and the Wider Identity," he used the term "Negro revolution" (p. 295) to describe the psychological journey that people of color must undertake to achieve psychological freedom from colonial thought patterns.

Psychologist James E. Marcia (1966, 1980) extended Erikson's work in his theory focusing on adolescent identity development. He defined identity as a self-structure—"an internal, self-constructed, dynamic organization of drives, abilities, beliefs, and individual history" (p. 159). As this structure becomes better developed, individuals can more easily express their own identities, acknowledge their own strengths and weaknesses, and make changes in their lives.

Marcia asserted that an identity crisis involving a period of search and exploration may lead to a clear commitment and an achieved, stable identity. He described four statuses, nonlinear in nature, which are undergirded by issues or tasks that are characteristic of late adolescence and are characterized by the presence or absence of crisis (a decision-making period) and the degree of commitment that one has toward occupation and ideology. These include:

Identity achievement. This stage involves an individual who has navigated a decision-making period and is pursuing occupational and ideological goals of his or her own choosing.

Foreclosure. This stage involves an individual who has committed to parentally chosen occupational and ideological goals. Individuals in foreclosure show little or no evidence of crisis.

Identity diffusion. This stage involves an individual without occupational or ideological direction; this status may manifest itself with or without a preceding decision-making period.

Moratorium. This stage involves an individual in an identity crisis, struggling with occupational and/or ideological issues.

Both Erikson and Marcia's models highlight the role of crisis or conflict in identity development and depict the process of identity development as occurring in phases throughout an individual's life. Other scholars have extended and adapted these and other models of identity development to address the question of how individuals develop racial and ethnic identities. Their work will be discussed in the following section.

Models of Racial and Ethnic Identity Development

In her groundbreaking book *Why Are All the Black Kids Sitting Together in the Cafeteria?* Beverly Tatum (1997) noted that "in adolescence, as race becomes personally salient for Black youth, finding the answer to questions such as, 'What does it mean to be a young Black person? How should I act? What should I do?' is particularly important" (p. 60) In other words, adolescence is a crucial period for the development of racial and ethnic identity. Several scholars have noted this and have developed models of racial or ethnic identity development that can help librarians and others understand some of what is going on behind the scenes in the lives of African American youth. The models discussed here are not the only models of racial or ethnic identity development, but are among the most influential of such models.

One of the earliest racial identity development models was developed by psychologist William E. Cross Jr. in 1971. Cross introduced the concept of *nigrescence* to describe the process through which individuals become Black or Afrocentrically

> Tatum (1997) notes that "in adolescence, as race becomes personally salient for Black youth, finding the answer to questions such as, 'What does it mean to be a young Black person? How should I act? What should I do?' is particularly important" (p. 60).

aligned. The Nigrescence model consists of five stages, the first two of which (*preencounter* and *encounter*) are especially relevant to adolescence.

In the preencounter stage, the racial identity of a young Black individual is shaped by early developmental experiences, including interactions with family members and the broader community. Surrounded by the dominant Eurocentric culture, Black youth in this stage have either neutral or negative attitudes toward Blackness. Those with neutral attitudes acknowledge their race but see society as essentially colorblind and do not recognize the implications of being a Black American; in other words, as Beverly Tatum (1997) states, "the personal and social significance of one's racial group membership has not yet been realized" (p. 55). Others in the preencounter stage may hold anti-Black views as a result of having absorbed negative, racist messages from the dominant culture. Often, these individuals also hold positive racial stereotypes of White people and White culture. These youth, according to Tatum (1997), "have absorbed many of the beliefs and values of the dominant White culture, including the idea that it is better to be White" (p. 55).

Cross (1995) argued that formal education plays a large role in the attitudes of Black youth toward their own race. The educational system in the United States, he contended, privileges a Western cultural and historical perspective and downplays the significance of the Black experience in the United States and the world. For example, Black youth may be miseducated about Africa's role in the development of global culture and the role of Blacks in the development of culture and history in the United States. In addition, Eurocentric notions of beauty and art are emphasized in educational settings (and, for many Black youth, at home as well), with the result that many Black youth enjoy so-called Black arts such as jazz and African dance, but place higher priority

Cross (1995) argues that formal education plays a large role in the attitudes of Black youth toward their own race. The educational system in the United States, he contends, privileges a Western cultural and historical perspective and downplays the significance of the Black experience in the United States and the world.

and status on White/Eurocentric art forms (e.g., ballet, classical music). As a result of this miseducation, these youth may hold a distorted view of the cultural, historical, political, and economic potential of Black people.

At some point, typically in adolescence, Black youth begin to grapple with "what it means to be a member of a group targeted by racism" (Tatum, 1997, p. 55). This grappling marks the transition into the *encounter* stage. Often, the encounter stage is initiated by an incident that forces an individual to acknowledge the personal impact of racism and challenges them to examine their own attitudes toward race. For example, a Black child may notice for the first time that that Black men are often depicted as dangerous criminals in the media, or that there are no Black students in their school's honors classes (Tatum, 1997). These encounters can shatter an individual's current worldview and sense of self, pushing him or her toward nigrescence—the process of accepting and affirming a Black identity (Cross, 1995). Cross noted that for many youth, the encounter stage involves feelings of guilt, anger, and anxiety as they discover that they have been erroneously minimizing or denying the significance of race in their daily lives.

Another psychologist, Janet E. Helms, developed a model of racial identity development based on Cross's Nigrescence model. Helms's (1993, 1995) model, known as the *People of Color Racial Identity Ego Statuses and Information-Processing Strategies*, is comprised of five stages and focuses on the idea that a major goal of racial identity development is overcoming psychological manifestations of societal racial stereotypes and negative self- and own-group conceptions. In other words, to develop a healthy racial identity, people of color must recognize and overcome internalized racism. Helms's model contains the following stages:

Conformity (preencounter): As in the Nigrescence model, individuals in this stage devalue characteristics of their own race and instead give allegiance to White standards of merit.

Dissonance (encounter): In this stage, individuals are ambivalent, confused, or both about their own racial group and self-definition.

Immersion/emersion: Individuals in this stage idealize their own socioracial group and denigrate that which is perceived to be White. Individuals in the immersion/emersion stage value own-group commitment and loyalty and use own-group standards to define themselves.

Internalization: Individuals in this stage are positively committed to their own socioracial group, define racial attributes within themselves, and have the capacity to assess and respond objectively to members of the dominant group.

Integrative awareness: In this stage, an individual has the ability to value his or her own identities, as well as to empathize and collaborate with members of other marginalized or oppressed groups.

Jean S. Phinney (1989, 1993) proposed a model of racial identity development specifically focused on adolescents, based on existing models of ego and identity development (including those of Cross and Marcia). Phinney's three-stage model depicts a progression from a stage in which adolescents accept the values and attitudes of the dominant culture without meaningful exploration of their own ethnicity (the *unexamined ethnic identity* stage), through a stage in which they initiate an ethnic identity search and attempts to learn more about their ethnicity and its meanings (*ethnic identity search/moratorium*), and finally to a stage in which they have achieved a confident sense and acceptance of their own identities (*ethnic identity achievement*).

Phinney (1995) suggested that studies about ethnic identity development among adolescents can provide insight into the adjustment problems of minority youth. Early adolescents typically have not explored their ethnicity, but they may have some preconceived ideas gleaned from parents or society in general. At this stage, they may have internalized the negative stereotypes and rejected their group membership as a result. During adolescence, they begin exploration, learning about their culture, and accepting it and themselves, as well as embracing their group. Those in stage 3, who have achieved ego identity, are likely to have a positive psychological adjustment because they have developed a way of dealing with negative stereotypes and prejudice. They do not internalize negative self-perceptions and are clear about the meaning of ethnicity for them.

One final model of ethnic identity development is the typology of cultural identity developed by James A. Banks (2009). The Banks typology acknowledges that ethnic groups are not monolithic, but rather highly complex, and that ethnic identity development may be a nonlinear process. Banks argued that a person's attachment to and identity with a particular ethnic group varies with "the times in one's life, and the situation and settings in which one finds oneself. Depending on experiences, social class, and many other variables, ethnicity may be important to an individual or not" (p. 62). Thus, although the six stages in Banks's model are labeled numerically, this model allows transfer between stages in any direction over the course of an individual's life. These six stages include:

Stage 1: Cultural psychological captivity. Individuals exhibit self-rejection and low self-esteem as a result of internalizing beliefs about their ethnic or cultural group perpetuated by the dominant culture.

Stage 2: Cultural encapsulation. Individuals believe that their cultural group is superior to others and associate primarily with members of their own ethnic group.

Stage 3: Cultural identity clarification. Individuals develop positive attitudes toward their own cultural group, are able to articulate their own cultural identity, and exhibit self-acceptance. As a result, they are able to accept and respond more positively to other cultural groups.

Stage 4: Biculturalism. Individuals function in two cultural or ethnic communities. They have a healthy sense of cultural/ethnic identity and the skills necessary to participate in their own culture, as well as a second culture.

Stage 5: Multiculturalism and reflective nationalism. Individuals can function (at least at a minimal level) in multiple cultural or ethnic communities and are capable of understanding, appreciating, and sharing the values, symbols, and institutions of multiple cultures.

Stage 6: Globalization and global competency. Individuals have clear and positive cultural, national, and global identities and can function effectively in a variety of national and international cultural communities.

Table 3.1 summarizes the stages in each of the reviewed models of racial or ethnic identity development. While not all these models describe a linear progression, each of them does include an early stage, in which young people of color either lack knowledge about their own racial identity or have absorbed negative stereotypes about their own race; and a later stage, in which individuals have come to accept and articulate their own racial identity and are able to place that identity in a broader sociocultural context. Between these two stages, there is often a turbulent period of uncertainty, anger, doubt, and anxiety. For adolescents, whether they successfully navigate this period and achieve a positive, consistent, and healthy racial identity depends in part on

TABLE 3.1   Comparisons of Racial Identity Development Models

Cross (1971, 1995)—Nigrescence Model	Helms (1993, 1995)—People of Color Racial Identity Ego Statuses and Information-Processing Strategies (IPS)	Phinney (1989, 1993)—Stages of Ethnic Identity Development	Banks (2009)—Banks Typology of Ethnic Identity
Preencounter	Conformity (Preencounter)	Unexamined identity	Cultural Psychological Captivity
Encounter	Dissonance (encounter)	Ethnic identity search	Cultural Encapsulation
Immersion/emersion	Immersion/emersion	Achieved ethnic identity	Cultural identity Clarification
Internalization	Internalization		Biculturalism
Internalization/commitment	Integrative awareness		Multiculturalism/reflective nationalism
			Globalization/global competency

the extent to which the process of racial identity development is supported in educational settings.

THE RELATIONSHIP BETWEEN RACIAL IDENTITY AND SCHOOL SUCCESS: WHAT DOES THE RESEARCH SAY?

In this section, we present a number of research studies that explore the relationship between racial identity and school success. Each of the studies suggests concrete, research-based considerations for how schools can support the racial and academic identities of Black youth.

Racialized Identities

Na'ilah Nasir (2012) conducted an ethnographic study exploring the relationship between identity and learning in African American adolescents. Among the assumptions of this study were that both learning and identity are cultural and contextual and that considering the racial identities of students is critical in a stratified society such as that of the United States, with its long history of racism and inequality.

Based on the data that she collected from extensive observation of several African American youth, Nasir described three types of resources that can support Black youth in both their racial identity development and their academic achievement. These include *material resources* that can help students connect to the classroom environment and view themselves as successful learners, such as the physical organization of the classroom, items on display in the room, and backpacks. *Relational resources,* positive interpersonal connections with peers and teachers, can help students feel more connected to education as a practice. Finally, students' racial identity development and academic achievement can be supported by *ideational resources*, which Nasir defined as "ideas about oneself and one's relationship to and place in a practice and the world, as well as ideas about what is valued and what is good" (p. 110).

Nasir (2012) identified five principles of teaching for identity building to inform a theoretical model of how schools might better support racialized and academic identities for African American youth. They are:

- Establish "caring relationships among members of the school community," where all students are "viewed as competent, intellectually strong, and inherently worthy."
- Create spaces where students are authentically cared about as people.
- Provide access to material resources for all students.
- Adopt culturally relevant practices.
- Hold explicit conversations about race and handling discrimination. (p. 163)

Critical Race Achievement Ideology

Dorinda Carter (2008) conducted a qualitative study of nine high-achieving Black students attending a predominately White suburban high school. The research was guided by the following questions:

1. How do high-achieving African American students describe and understand the behaviors they employ in classroom, social, and extracurricular domains in a predominately White high school?
2. How do these students' perceptions of values, behavioral norms, and expectations in these domains inform the behaviors they employ in those different domains within the school context?
3. How, if at all, do these students view these domains as fundamentally different along racial lines? (Carter, 2008, p. 472)

Carter discovered that these high-achieving students in many cases viewed their own academic success as an act of resistance against the idea that school success is reserved for White students. These students were very much aware of the race-based obstacles to academic achievement, but they also had a strong sense of individual agency. She proposed the phrase *Critical Race Achievement Ideology (CRAI)* to describe the framework in which these students operate academically, socially, and culturally. Presented in terms of six dimensions, the CRAI ideology proposed that high-achieving Black students:

- see themselves as achievers and believe that hard work and individual effort are key to academic success;
- view academic achievement as a raceless concept that can be attained by anyone, yet view their personal academic success as fundamentally embedded in their racial identities;
- maintain a "critical consciousness about racism" (p. 484) and are aware of how race affects their own and others' current and future opportunities;
- are pragmatic about the value of education to their future success;
- are committed to multicultural competence and are able to move within and between school subcultures, including the dominant (White) culture; and
- maintain a strong racial/ethnic identity and high academic achievement by developing strategies for overcoming racism in the academic context.

Racial Discrimination

Racial and ethnic discrimination is the unfair and prejudicial treatment of individuals on the grounds of race or ethnicity. A number of researchers have posited that addressing barriers to success for Black youth requires an understanding of the impact that discrimination can have on their psychosocial functioning. Table 3.2 summarizes several studies suggesting that discriminatory experiences, both in and out of school, negatively affect the academic

TABLE 3.2   Studies Exploring Linkages Between Discrimination and Psychological Functioning of Black Youth

	Purpose	Findings
Wong, Eccles, and Sameroff (2003)	Examined the relationship between discrimination and the academic, social, and behavioral development of African American adolescents	Discrimination by teachers and peers has a negative impact on the psychological development and academic achievement of Black youth. Strong ties with their racial community and an understanding of their cultural heritage not only serve to protect Black youth from the negative impact of discrimination, but also promote positive social, behavioral, and academic growth.
Smalls, White, Chavous, and Sellers (2007)	Examined the relationships among racial identity, racial discrimination, and academic engagement among African American adolescents	Experiencing racial discrimination is a risk factor for lower academic engagement. Positive racial identity is an important resilience factor. Embracing racial identity may enhance school engagement.
Roberts and Taylor (2012)	Examined the linkages between discrimination, racial identity and academic performance among African American adolescents	Ethnic identity was positively related to academic achievement for all students. The relationship was strongest for Black males.

engagement of Black youth, as well as their growth in other domains. Importantly, the studies indicate that the achievement of strong racial identities can buffer Black youth from the negative impact of implicit and overt acts of racism and discrimination and is correlated with high academic motivational attitudes and behaviors.

Cool Pose

In *Cool Pose: The Dilemma of Black Manhood in America*, Richard Majors and Janet Billson (1992) write about the dilemmas of Black masculinity and explore a coping strategy called "cool pose," or "the presentation of self many Black males use to establish their male identity" (p. 4). Citing the influence of West African culture on African American culture, Majors and Billson assert that each of the nine dimensions defined in Boykin's *Black Ethos*—spirituality, harmony, movement, verve, affect, communalism, expressive individualism, oral tradition, and social time perspective—are manifest in a single expression: being cool.

Majors and Billson (1992) describe cool pose as "a ritualized form of masculinity that entails behaviors, scripts, physical posturing, impression management, and carefully crafted performances that deliver a single, critical message: pride, strength, and control" (p. 4). They argue that cool pose provides Black males with a sense of confidence and security that allows them to cope with the widespread negative perceptions of Black men that are communicated by the dominant White society. It also allows Black males to express their distrust of the dominant society, as well as their anger about the discriminatory and oppressive policies and practices that negatively affect their lives, especially if they live in inner cities.

In K–12 schools, Majors and Billson argue, cool pose frequently places Black males in conflict with school personnel whose values and attitudes typically reflect middle class, White norms and expectations. As a result, the expression of culture-specific behaviors such as strutting, rapping, speaking in an aggressive or ostentatious manner ("woofing"), participating in trash-talk competitions ("playing the dozens"), using slang, wearing hats or expressive clothes, or wearing pants with loosened belts ("sagging") often results in disciplinary action, including suspension or even expulsion from school. In other words, what young Black men consider stylish or cool, school personnel often interpret as disruptive and threatening.

> Majors and Billson (1992) argue that cool pose is crucial for preservation of pride, dignity, and respect, furnishing the Black male with a sense of control, inner strength, balance, stability, confidence, and security.

Brian Wright (2009) argues that while schools often establish rules to prevent Black males from adopting a cool pose, it should be viewed instead as a unique strength that some African American males possess. He sees cool pose as a catalyst—a direct link to academic success—but only if teachers and school personnel rethink their understanding of this form of Black masculinity. He calls on educators to embrace "the adaptive behaviors that [young Black men] associate with cool pose which reflect social competence, pride, dignity, self-esteem and respect" (p. 126).

Oppositional Culture: Acting White

One of the most well known, but often disputed, explanations for the achievement gap is the theory of oppositional culture that was proposed by Signithia Fordham and John Ogbu. Fordham and Ogbu (1986) contend that the low academic performance exhibited by youth of color is an adaptive response to the requirements of White cultural imperatives. We will first discuss Fordham and Ogbu's ideas and then provide a look at research that questions its explanatory value.

Fordham and Ogbu (1986) argue that in response to biases and discrimination (including inferior schooling and a job ceiling that denies them access to employment opportunities that take full advantage of their education, their credentials, and their qualifications), Black Americans have developed a survival strategy and coping mechanism that they call *collective identity*. This term refers to "a people's sense of who they are, their 'we feeling' or 'belonging.' People express their collective identity with emblems or cultural symbols which reflect their attitudes, beliefs, feelings, behaviors, and language or dialect" (Ogbu, 2004, p. 3). This collective identity allows Blacks to define themselves in opposition to how the dominant group views them.

Along with collective identity, Fordham and Ogbu (1986) assert that Black Americans have also developed an oppositional *cultural frame of reference* that serves to protect their Black identity and maintain boundaries between them and Whites. Beverly Tatum (1997) explains it this way: "Certain styles of speech, dress, and music, for example, may be embraced as 'authentically Black' and become highly valued, while attitudes and behaviors associated with Whites are viewed with disdain" (p. 61).

Fordham and Ogbu (1986) argue that understanding the oppositional identity and cultural frame of reference are important in improving the schooling experience of Black youth, many of whom have learned that if they assume the White cultural frame of reference, their own cultural identity will be adversely affected. In other words, they believe that if they adopt the standard academic practices that school requires, they will be "acting White" and, as a result, giving up their Black identity. Fordham and Ogbu assert that some members of racial and ethnic groups thus underachieve academically, not because they are incapable but because they view school and the educational system as extensions of the White dominant culture that threatens their group's cultural identity and survival. Tatum (1997) notes that while this frame of reference is not adopted by all Black youth, there are Black youth who describe feeling alienated or rejected by their Black peers because of their academic success.

Fordham and Ogbu's theory has been challenged repeatedly since its development. Garvey Lundy (2003) is particularly vocal in his criticism, stating that adoption of this stance has two negative consequences. First, it shifts the focus away from the systemic nature of racism in our schools, and conveniently allows educators to assume erroneously that Black students as a whole reject academic success; that is, Black youth are at fault, not the schools. Second, it denies the possibility that Black students who are asserting a collective Black identity are not rejecting academic success, but instead are rejecting White cultural hegemony—the continued domination by the White culture. Their failure to learn, then, may be an intentional act of protest.

Stereotype Threat

Stereotype threat theory focuses on "how societal stereotypes about groups can influence the intellectual functioning and identity development of individual group members" (Steele, 1997, p. 613). Introduced by Claude Steele, this theory assumes that to maintain high levels of academic achievement, students must see such achievement as part of their identity and hold themselves accountable to high academic standards. When those standards are met, students think positively of themselves and can sustain academic motivation.

Unfortunately, negative stereotypes about African Americans are too often prevalent in American schools, and this factor can bear negatively on academic success. Steele (2003) argues, "The success of Black students may depend less on expectations and motivations—things that are thought to drive academic performance—than on trust that stereotypes about their group will not have a limiting effect in their school world" (p. 122). For Black youth who identify with the domains in which the negative stereotypes apply, the threat of the stereotypes can be felt sharply, thus hampering their achievement.

> Steele (2003) argues, "The success of Black students may depend less on expectations and motivations—things that are thought to drive academic performance—than on trust that stereotypes about their group will not have a limiting effect in their school world" (p. 122).

Steele (2003) concludes that while the stereotypes held by the broader society are difficult to change, schools must be places where negative stereotypes do not apply. In other words, within schools, "it is possible to weaken a group's sense of being threatened by negative stereotypes, to allow its members a trust that would otherwise be difficult to sustain" (p. 130).

Resiliency

Acknowledging that environmental disadvantage and stress can lead to behavioral and psychological problems among children, David Miller and Randell McIntosh (1999) suggest that these conditions can be overcome and lead to a favorably adjusted adulthood. This positive adaptation despite negative environmental circumstances is called *resiliency*. In research on resilience and protective factors with 131 urban African American adolescents, Miller and McIntosh (1999) investigated the influence that racial socialization and racial identity have on resilience and how these factors promote academic engagement and achievement in African American adolescents. *Racial socialization* refers to the values, norms, morals, and beliefs that African American parents and caregivers communicate to their children to prepare them to adapt to and live in a racist world. As discussed in the previous sections of this chapter, *racial identity* refers to a sense of group belonging based on cultural commonalities. The findings of the study suggest that a positive racial identity can "protect African American adolescents against the discrimination and daily hassles that they experience as they to seek to perform well in school" (p. 166). Similarly, African American youth can use the strategies that they learn through racial socialization to deal with the racial stressors and other distractions that they experience at school in more productive ways—ways that do not interfere with their academic success.

Additional Research on Racial and Ethnic Identity Among African American Youth

Belgrave, Faye Z., & Joshua K. Brevard (2015). *African American boys: Identity, culture, and development.* New York: Springer.

Burt, Janeula M., & Glennelle Halpin (1998). "African American identity development: A review of the literature." Presentation at the Mid-South Educational Research Association, New Orleans, November 4–6.

Decuir Gunby, Jessica T. (2009). "A review of the racial identity development of African American adolescents: The role of education." *Review of Educational Research* 79(1): 103–124.

Harper, Brian E. (2007). "The relationship between Black racial identity and academic achievement in urban settings." *Theory into Practice,* 46(3), 230–238.

Phinney, Jean S. (1990). "Ethnic identity in adolescents and adults: Review of research." *Psychological Bulletin,* 108(3): 499–514.

Wright, Brian L. (2009). "Racial-ethnic identity, academic achievement, and African American males: A review of literature." *Journal of Negro Education,* 78(2): 123–134.

TRANSLATING RESEARCH INTO PRACTICE

The studies outlined in this chapter demonstrate that positive racial identity and culturally relevant pedagogy (see Chapter 2) can play major roles in promoting academic success and resilience in African American youth. As Hanley and Noblit (2009) argue, "In-school and out-of-school programs can be designed to develop these linkages and to more generally promote the wider project of racial uplift" in African American communities (p. 11). In this final section, we draw on the theories and research discussed earlier in this chapter to present a number of concrete ways that the library community can recognize and build positive racial identity development in African American youth.

First, we must be intentional in providing resources and programs that support positive racial identity development in Black youth. The earlier we begin this support, the better. Research shows that infants as young as four weeks enjoy looking at human faces in picture books (Hasson, 1991). As early as six months, infants begin to notice skin differences (Katz, 1993). By the age of two, children begin to ask questions about differences in skin color (Derman-Sparks, 1993). And by the age of three, children notice physical differences, including facial feature shapes and hair texture, which leads them to categorize people and begin to form attitudes about people of different races and ethnic groups (Phinney & Rotherman, 1987; Tatum, 1997; Van Ausdale & Feagen, 2001). Exposure to diverse children's literature, beginning with board books, has been shown to bolster the self-esteem and cultural identity of children of color (Hansen-Krening, 1991; Jalongo, 1988). According to Tatum (1997), by providing children of color with counterstories that offer positive cultural images and messages about their race, adults not only encourage positive racial identity development, but also mitigate the impact of stereotypes. In Chapter 7, you will read about Black Storytime, a program developed by librarian Kirby McCurtis that incorporates stories, music and movement, rhymes, and activities to help families build their children's early literacy skills, as well as promote positive cultural images in order to affirm children's self-esteem and support growth of their Black identity.

In the K–12 environment, it is important for school librarians to take the lead in examining the school curriculum and the wider school culture to ensure that it does not reinforce the view that academic excellence is reserved exclusively for White students or the belief that if you are African American and want to be smart, you must "act White" or deny your cultural and community heritage. As Tatum (1997) points out, "if young people [both Black and White] are exposed to images of African American achievement in their early years, they won't have to define school achievement as something for Whites only. They will know that there is a long history of Black intellectual achievement" (p. 65). School librarians can help teachers infuse contributions of the African American community into the curriculum in meaningful ways that counter the miseducation of Black youth that Cross describes. They can also ensure that the curriculum provides youth with the opportunity to view issues, topics, and events from multiple perspectives (Banks, 2009).

Beverly Tatum (1997) provides an example of another way that librarians can reinforce Black youth's positive racial identity—make sure that when we are discussing issues related to race relations such as slavery, Jim Crow, the Civil Rights movement, and today's Black Lives Matter movement, that we do so honestly and in ways that "empower children (and adults) with the vision that things can change" (p. 42). She argues that too often, when issues or events like this are discussed, the Black community is portrayed as helpless victims and not enough attention is given to the resistance and activism of the Black community, or for that matter, to "what White people have done to oppose injustice" (p. 42). Again, one of the simplest ways to do this is to make sure to provide resources, such as books, primary documents, videos, and so forth, that allow youth to experience the harsh reality but also see the power of the Black community's opposition. Another way that this can be done is by engaging Black youth in Youth Participatory Action Research (YPAR), a technique grounded in experience and social history that allows youth of color to understand and change the world (see Chapter 4).

We must also ensure that libraries are spaces free of discrimination and stereotypes. The research is clear—discrimination and negative stereotypes adversely affect the academic achievement of African American youth, particularly males. While the vast majority of educators say that their schools are free of racial and ethnic tension, this is not actually the case, as shown by the growing number of complaints about this that the Office for Civil Rights (2015) has received. As discussed in Chapter 1, the systemic nature of racism in this country suggests that discrimination and bias, and even racial tension, extend to libraries. Teaching Tolerance offers an array of tools that educators and librarians can use to examine the school and library climate (see http://www.tolerance.org/map-it-out). Throughout this book, we provide strategies that librarians can employ to address both institutional and individual sources of prejudice and discrimination and to make libraries safe spaces for all youth. Most importantly, as discussed in Chapters 1 and 4, librarians must be willing to address issues of race and racism when they arise.

In addition, we must continue to educate ourselves and all library staff about the importance of racial identity development for African American youth. Willis Hawley (n.d.) notes that too often, diversity-related topics such as this are relegated to episodic workshops or one-off learning modules. He contends that there is little evidence supporting the idea that this is an adequate strategy for developing understanding or implementing change. In fact, often this approach can reinforce negative perceptions. Instead, ongoing, reflective opportunities to discuss the kind of research presented in this chapter and its implications for practice must be provided.

Finally, in order for librarians to support the racial identity development of Black youth, we must do our own racial identity work. This is especially true for White librarians. Most Whites do not see themselves as racial beings, tending to see race "as something other people have, not something that is salient to them" (Tatum, 1997, p. 94). However, as Gary Howard explains, we live in a highly racialized society; thus, it is important for "each of us to understand our own position and level of awareness vis-à-vis the categories of race" (p. 88). For Whites, this means developing "a positive White identity based on reality, not on assumed superiority" (Tatum, 1997, p. 94)—an identity that recognizes and examines the negative historical implications of Whiteness in the United States, but moves beyond guilt toward action. Howard (2006) proposes a model of White racial identity that involves three developmental tasks:

1. Acknowledging the reality of White racism in its individual, institutional, and cultural manifestations.
2. Abandoning racism and engaging in active resistance to its many forms.
3. Developing a positive, nonracist, and authentic connection to White racial and cultural identity. (p. 92)

His model identifies three White identity orientations—fundamentalist, integrationist, and transformationist—that reflect where Whites are in the developmental process of completing the developmental tasks and, thus, forming a positive racial identity. Howard's goal is to show White educators that there are different ways to be White, to provide them with a positive direction for growth, and to communicate that they have "a *choice* as White people to be champions of justice and social healing" (p. 116; emphasis in original). A full exploration of White identity development is beyond the scope of this book, but Beverly Tatum's (1997) *Why Are All the Black Kids Sitting Together in the Cafeteria?* and Gary Howard's (2006) *We Can't Teach What We Don't* Know are excellent resources for White educators who would like more guidance on this critical work.

CONCLUDING THOUGHTS

Patricia Edwards and her colleagues (2010) contend that African American youth must "constantly strive toward reclamation of their academic careers and literacy lives" (p. 54). They do this by using four strategies: (1) building resilience through double consciousness (i.e., creating an identity that allows them to express their Blackness in a way that is authentic to them); (2) developing a cool, smart, and Black pose; (3) connecting to the school through community; and (4) engaging with caring teachers (p. 54). We believe that librarians can assist Black youth in "reclaiming school success" by being the trusted, caring adults that Black youth describe, who have positively affected their lives and thus, their academic success. We can serve as mentors, allies, and advocates who recognize the connection between Black identity development and school success, and we can help Black youth develop the commitment and motivation needed to overcome the stereotypes and discrimination that they face. We can also actively challenge the culture of low expectations that surround many Black youth in the United States. Edwards and her colleagues note that "one teacher can make the difference in the life of an African American student" (p. 62). We argue that one *librarian* can make the difference in the life of Black youth.

Key Points About Racial Identity Development

- In addition to the identity exploration that all teens engage in, Black teens explore their racial identity, focusing on questions such as "What does it mean to be a young Black person? How should I act? What should I do?" (Tatum, 1997, p. 60).
- Positive racial identity development is central to academic success and resilience for Black youth.
- Racial stereotypes and discrimination negatively affect the positive racial identity of Black youth.
- Stereotype threat, or the fear that negative stereotypes about Black youth will affect our treatment of them and our expectations for them, must be challenged.
- The identity of Black youth is often in conflict with the expectations of the dominant culture, which can lead to disengagement of, and even active resistance by, Black youth.
- The behaviors of some Black youth that adults often object to, such as those captured by the term *cool pose,* are a part of their identity and need to be viewed as a strength to be built upon.
- Racial identity in adolescence lays the groundwork for actualized adult racial identities.

4

Cultivating Voice and Agency

Sandra Hughes-Hassell

When students are allowed to speak and to write their truth, they begin the process of introspection, inquiry, and critical thinking.
—Bathina (2015, para. 1)

All young people have a political identity, a yearning sense of injustice that they want to do something about. What we need to do is map their political intensity onto an intellectual trajectory. To ask them, what are you going to do about it? And then, give them tools to take action.
—Hughes-Hassell et al. (2012, p. 8)

Much of the discourse about literacy and Black youth focuses on raising test scores and closing the achievement gap; however, literacy plays a much larger role in the lives of Black youth. It is connected to intellectual growth, identity, resiliency, resolve, and a positive life trajectory. It is also a powerful tool of voice and agency.

The concept of voice is a key tenet of Critical Race Theory (CRT) and is tied to the centrality of experiential knowledge and the concept of counterstories. As Richard Delgado and Jean Stefancic (2001) note, the life experiences and opinions of people of color are legitimate and appropriate for countering the dominant, often deficit-oriented narrative about people of color, examining and challenging oppression, and informing decisions about institutional policies and practices. Personal narratives "not only shift the lens through which many in the dominant culture view people of color" (Hughes-Hassell et al., 2010, p. 17), but also empower people of color to express their lived experiences, including their insights into how society is structured to marginalize and oppress them, how racism affects their daily lives, and how they believe that society needs to be reformed to create a just society. Christopher Knaus (2009) argues that it is imperative that we create avenues through which the voices of youth of color can "develop, thrive, and express in culturally affirming and relevant ways" (p. 142).

However, as Pamela Quiroz (2001) notes, "Language is merely the tool through which voice is expressed. For voice to be empowering, it must be *heard*, not simply spoken" (p. 328, emphasis added). Simply put, "if [youth] speak, then adults must listen" (Cook-Sather, 2006, p. 367). Dana Mitra (2004) argues that the development of student voice instills agency in youth, which can be defined as the "belief that they could transform themselves and the institutions that affect them" (p. 681). Mitra also proposes that in the process of developing and sharing their voices, youth can acquire the skills and competencies to work toward personal and social change and establish meaningful relationships with adults and their peers (p. 681). Louie Rodríguez and Tara Brown (2009) agree, arguing that when adults work with youth to develop their agency, they are helping "young people develop the knowledge, leadership skills, and sociopolitical power needed to redress mounting educational and social injustices" (p. 32).

In this chapter, we focus on how cultivating voice and agency is connected to the literacy development of Black youth. First, we begin with a discussion of what we mean by voice and agency, and why both are important to the literacy development of Black youth. Then we present concrete ideas for how librarians can not only create diverse, welcoming, and transformative environments where African American youth can develop their voices to "speak and write their truths," but also provide youth with opportunities to use their voices in meaningful ways to effect change.

In this chapter, we:
- Define voice and agency
- Explore the connection between voice, agency, and academic achievement
- Present concrete ideas for how librarians can create environments where African American youth can develop their voices to effect change

DEFINING VOICE

The McDougald Terrace Branch of the Durham public library system in North Carolina closed in 2012. Prior to its closing, the library provided programming focused on literacy and youth development targeted to the African American youth who lived in the neighborhood where the branch was located. When librarian Heather Cunningham learned that the library was to be closed, she and Craig Varley, a graduate student at the University of North Carolina at Chapel Hill (UNC-CH), invited local youth to use digital cameras to document the final summer that the library was open. Their photos were collected, organized, and published through Lulu.com in a book entitled *McDougald Terrace Library*. Interspersed among the photos were poems created by the youth as part of Youth Ink Writing Workshops taught by the Sacrificial Poets, a local spoken-word poetry group. This poem, written by an 11-year-old male student, shows the power of writing to define self:

"I Am From"
I am from a place where people don't care about you.
But it's goin' change cause I'm goin' take my family another way.
And it's a easy way out getting an education.
I'm taking my dream, like Martin Luther King.
See I'm making it, chillin' with my fam
Dream chasin' it
People ain't tryin' to give us a chance
We had to take it
But wit my fam, wit me
I promise
I'm goin' make it. (McDougald Terrace Library, 2013)

This is voice.

In Portland, Oregon, Linda Christensen's urban high school students, who are predominantly African American, write personal essays to "analyze how their lives have been shaped by the 'single stories' told about them—stories that are informed by stereotypes, discrimination, injustice, and racism" (Christensen, 2012, p. 19). Their essays contain vignettes that include dialogue and setting to "evoke what it means to be young and black" (p. 24). She notices that each time she gives this assignment, at some point students stop writing the essay only because it is an assignment, instead becoming truly passionate about their writing. When she asks them why, they say, "We got to write about issues that were real in our lives, and someone listened and cared" (p. 24). One young man wrote:

> As a black male in America, I never let my guard down to racism. Because if I do, it will smack me right in the face. We are easily stereotyped and people automatically think we are up to no good . . . When encountering racism, I just move on with my life, so I will stop being affected by other people's portrayals of me. (Christensen, 2012, p. 25)

This is voice.

Ernest Morrell (2002, 2006) coordinated a series of research seminars that allowed youth living in East Los Angeles to attend the University of California, Los Angeles (UCLA) for several weeks during the summer to work with UCLA faculty and graduate students. One year, they focused on inequitable access to educational opportunities for youth of color in Los Angeles (LA), particularly those living in lower-socioeconomic communities. They developed a research question, designed their study, and read literature related to the sociology of education. They collected data by surveying other youth about their experiences; analyzing curricula; interviewing teachers, parents, and civil rights lawyers; using geographic information systems (GISs) to map educational attainment by race, ethnicity, and socioeconomic status across LA; and using digital photography to document the differences in facilities. After analyzing their data, these young people who attended the lowest-performing schools in LA produced videos and made presentations calling for change, "orally with accompanying PowerPoint slides to an audience of academic faculty members, community members, parents, and elected officials" (Morrell, 2002, p. 76). As the excerpt given here from their presentation shows, "motivated and empowered by the prospect of addressing a real problem in their communities, the students learned the tools of research, read difficult texts, and produced their own text of high academic merit" (Morrell, 2002, p. 76):

> The differences are exposed. The demands are voiced. Like the Chicano, Black, and Women's civil rights movements before us, we are engulfed in social and educational reform. We demand equity and the preservation of our civil rights. We demand that all our schools in urban and suburban communities be taught equally and be provided with the same quality educational resources. (Morrell, 2006, p. 123)

This is voice.

As these examples demonstrate, voice has multiple dimensions. One dimension recognizes that Black youth have stories to tell, that their stories are important, and that by telling their stories, they can shape a "richer narrative about what it means to be young [and] African American . . . in the United States" (Tatum, 2013, p. 10). This dimension validates their existence; helps them "wrestle with issues and circumstances related to their academic, personal, and social identities, and to the identities of others" (Tatum, 2013, p. 8); and gives them tools and counterstories that can be used to "dismantle the mistaken assumptions" made about them (Christensen, 2012, p. 19). This dimension encourages African American youth to use their voices for real purposes and real audiences and demonstrates the value of doing so for personal, civic, and political reasons. This dimension corresponds most closely with how the term *voice* is used in the teaching of writing and demonstrates a desire for student engagement, communication, and knowledge creation (Cook-Sather, 2006).

Another dimension includes a social action component. It recognizes that African American youth not only possess expert knowledge about issues facing their school and communities, but that they can also provide unique insight into how these issues should be investigated and addressed (Rodríguez & Brown, 2009). This aspect focuses on "shifting the role of [African American] youth from simply giving voice to one of becoming change agents" (Rodríguez & Brown, 2009, p. 19). This aligns with the definition of voice as participation that critical theorists advocate (Cook-Sather, 2006). This dimension of voice is a central component of Youth Participatory Action Research (YPAR), a research method "in which people directly affected by a problem under investigation engage as co-researchers in the research process, which includes action, or intervention, into the problem" (Rodríguez & Brown, 2009, p. 23). YPAR not only "supports inquiry, discovery, problem solving, and knowledge construction" (Rodríguez & Brown, 2009, p. 23), but it also challenges the dominant, deficit-oriented view of people of color and other marginalized groups. In addition, it allows youth to confront issues such as racism, classism, sexism, and cultural bias explicitly.

DEFINING AGENCY

Agency can be defined as the power to act. In educational settings, the most basic form of agency is the ability of Black youth to influence class topics, activities, and final products, as well as the individual decisions that they make as writers and readers. In school and public libraries, this would also include the ability to influence collection development and programming decisions, as well as the freedom, support, and tools and resources to pursue their personal interests and passions. Agency can also entail African American youth "sharing their opinions of problems and potential solutions" (Mitra, 2004, p. 652) in their schools, libraries, or communities by participating in focus groups, completing surveys, or doing other activities that are developed, administered, and acted on by adults. Demetria Tucker and Sonya Scott, librarians at the Pearl Bailey Branch Library in Newport News, Virginia, share an example of this type of agency in Chapter 10. Perhaps the most empowering form of agency involves African American youth participating in YPAR; that is, collaborating with adults to (1) identify an issue affecting their own education, school, library, or community; (2) determine how best to study the issue; (3) conduct the research study; and (4) develop and enact solutions that effect change.

THE IMPORTANCE OF CULTIVATING VOICE AND AGENCY

Research suggests that efforts to increase youth voice and agency make a difference in the attitudes, behaviors, and engagement of all youth (Mitra, 2004). At the classroom level, studies have found that youth improved academically when teachers constructed their classrooms in ways that valued youth voices; this was particularly true when youth were given the power to work with their teachers to improve curricula and instruction (Mitra, 2004; Oldfather, 1995; Rudduck & Flutter, 2000). Penny Oldfather (1995) showed that increasing student voices in schools helped to reengage alienated youth, provide them with a stronger sense of their own abilities, and build their awareness that they can make changes in their schools. Students reported valuing their schools, and thus their education more when their teachers heard their voices and "honored" them (Mitra, 2004; Oldfather, 1995). Increasing student voices in classrooms has the added benefit of improving students' understanding of how they learn, thus enabling the teacher to build on their learning strengths in designing instruction (Johnston & Nicholls, 1995; Mitra, 2004).

Youth voice initiatives have also been found to affect youth development positively. Research with elementary-aged youth (Mitra & Serriere, 2012) and adolescents (Mitra, 2004) found that when youth engage in student voice

> Youth voice initiatives also give African American youth a platform to assert their identities as intelligent young people who have much to offer the world.

efforts, they show growth in three important areas—agency, belonging, and competence. Agency can act as a source of social capital for youth, leading to further educational, employment, and enrichment opportunities. Belonging, or the development of supportive interaction with adults and peers, positively relates to academic success and motivation. In addition, *competence,* which is defined as the ability of youth to develop new skills and abilities, actively solve problems, and be appreciated for their talents, increases feelings of self-efficacy and builds leadership skills (Mitra, 2004; Mitra & Serriere, 2012).

For African American youth, the cultivation of voice and agency is critical. Building a culture of literacy means "helping African American students take ownership of literacy and see it as personally meaningful to their lives" (Edwards et al., 2009, p. 146). Linda Christensen explains:

> Students, no matter what their reading and writing ability, are capable of amazing intellectual work. They act up and get surly when the curriculum feels insulting. Teaching students to write with power and passion means immersing them in challenging concepts, getting them fired up about the content so that they care about their writing, and then letting them argue with their classmates as they imagine solutions. Great writing doesn't take place in isolation from the world. Global warming? Getting pulled over by the police because you're black and young and running down the street? Plant closures? Domestic abuse? Forest, river, and salmon loss? Toxic dump in your back yard? Students will rise to the "challenge" of a rigorous curriculum about important issues if that rigor reflects the real challenges in their lives. Too often the rigor offered students is a "rigor" of memorization and piling up of facts in order to earn high scores on end-of-course tests. (Christensen, 2009, para. 25)

As Jyothi Bathina (2015) notes, when African American youth are "allowed to speak and to write their truth, they begin the process of introspection, inquiry, and critical thinking" (para. 1). They develop literacy skills within a context that not only reflects and respects their life experiences, but also recognizes and builds on the linguistic capital and knowledge base of the African American community.

Youth voice initiatives also give African American youth a platform to assert their identities as intelligent young people who have much to offer the world—identities that are often suppressed in schools by (1) a curriculum that relies on rote-and-drill educational approaches and rewards students for being quiet and not critically questioning lessons or (2) low expectations held of them by teachers—or, tragically, both (Knaus, 2009). Knaus (2009) explains:

> Listening and validating voice shows students that they too can create knowledge, but also that they already have a solid foundation from which to build. Educators have to begin to hear student experiences as knowledge, to begin to frame personal and cultural knowledge as relevant to already entrenched curriculum. (p. 145)

Providing opportunities for African American youth to take part in YPAR has multiple outcomes. First, it engages students because through YPAR, they are empowered to investigate issues that are important and meaningful to them and their communities—the kinds of issues that Christensen has mentioned. Second, the research project itself becomes a context for literacy learning. Participating in the research allows African American youth to develop and utilize multiple literacies (i.e., traditional literacies, as well as information literacies, critical literacies, digital literacies, and media literacies) to learn, to demonstrate understanding, and to advocate for change. It also helps them learn academic literacy—the language and tools necessary to be successful in colleges and universities (Morrell, 2004a). Third, it builds leadership skills and confidence and instills a sense of social responsibility. For example, Ernest Morrell (2006) reports that several of the youth involved in the research seminar at UCLA described earlier in this chapter continue to advocate for social justice. One has founded an organization dedicated to the struggle for educational justice; another has created a support group for entering students of color at her college campus; and still another has worked with kids in inner-city Boston (Morrell, 2006, p. 125). Other researchers report similar findings (e.g., see Irizarry, 2011). Finally, by participating in YPAR initiatives, African American youth develop relationships with adults who serve as mentors—helping them develop their literacy skills, offering counterstories, and providing models of positive life outcome trajectories.

A Word of Caution

Researchers who study youth voice and agency initiatives warn that adults who want to engage these elements must be genuine in their efforts; that is, we must "be open to change and willing to change" (Cook-Sather, 2006, p. 382). We must be committed to respecting and responding to "a diverse set of perspectives and not just tolerat[e] or tokeniz[e] them" (Cook-Sather, 2006, p. 382). Many Black youth have felt silenced and rendered invisible much of their lives by the structures of racism. In his classic novel *Invisible Man,* Ralph Ellison described his invisibility in American life: "I am a man of substance, of flesh and bone, fiber and liquids—and I might even be said to possess a mind. I am invisible, understand, simply because people refuse to see me" (quoted in Colesante & Biggs, 2015, p. 459). Including the voices of African American youth in schools or libraries is not engaging or empowering in and of itself—"we must listen and act on [youths'] words not once but again and again" (Cook-Sather, 2006, p. 382). The purpose of developing voice and agency is to help African American youth develop confidence in their lives, in their abilities, and in the idea that although they may not "be able to change society overnight" (Cook-Sather, 2006, p. 382), literacy gives them tools to act upon the world in powerful ways.

Adults who encourage African American youth to "write and speak their truths" must also be prepared for those truths. The lives of African American youth, regardless of socioeconomic status, are affected by race and racism. Many feel disrespected, discriminated against, and even dismissed because of their identity. Some may have experienced prejudice firsthand, as they have been "pulled from police cars, followed in stores, [and] suspended for refusing to obey ridiculous orders" (Christensen, 2012, p. 19). Some may live in neighborhoods that are plagued with poverty, violence, and drugs. We must be ready for their realities—their experiences are too important to be silenced—and we must be prepared to discuss their realities with them. As Knaus (2009) argues, for some of these young people, "without space to voice their conflicting experiences and feelings, academic engagement seems a distant hope" (p. 136).

Finally, some youth may not embrace the idea of voice, or they may be slow to participate in voice initiatives. For some African American youth, silence is their form of resistance (Kirkland, 2013). Alison Cook-Sather (2006) explains, "Silence can be powerful—a withholding of assent, a political act" (p. 369). For others, silence represents resignation. They have no reason to trust that their voices are valued because for so long, their voices have gone unheard, or worse, have been silenced. And for others, silence indicates fear. Past experiences have taught them that it is not safe to speak (Cook-Sather, 2006). As Cook-Sather (2006) notes, whatever the causes of the silence, it must be considered in any initiatives aimed at cultivating voice and agency.

Ways That Libraries Can Cultivate Voice and Agency

In a world where the experiences of African American youth are often disregarded, "to be able to connect beyond the façade, to be able to tell a story that's deeply personal, challenges . . . the dehumanizing that's happening in classrooms" and in society (Pettaway, 2015).

In the final section of this chapter, we provide ideas and strategies that librarians can use to cultivate voice and agency, increase the authenticity and relevance of library programs, give programs greater purpose, and consequently increase the engagement and learning of African American youth.

Host Writing Workshops

Building literacy and cultivating voices by hosting writing workshops is programming that many libraries already participate in, but it is especially important that libraries serving African American youth invest in the staff and resources necessary to make these workshops a core part of their strategic plan. As librarians Autumn Winters and Elizabeth Gregg (2010) explain, "Libraries are one of the best places to teach [youth] that their writing matters" (p. 162). A key component of writing workshops must be the opportunity for African American youth to share their stories with their friends, families, and communities. This can be done by building open-mic nights into writing programs or by using print-on-demand publishing tools, cloud-based tools like Storybird, or apps like Bitstrips to publish youths' work. Using traditional web tools like websites, blogs, and wikis is another way that youth can share their work with an authentic audience. The manner in which the stories are made available to a wider audience is not important. As teachers Mariela Nuñez-Janes and Tim Sanchez explain, "it's the publishing of the stories themselves that's important" (quoted in Pettaway, 2015, para. 15). In a world where the experiences of African American youth are often disregarded, "to be able to connect beyond the façade, to be able to tell a story that's deeply personal, challenges . . . the dehumanizing that's happening in classrooms" and in society (Pettaway, 2015, para. 14).

Next, we provide overviews of five examples of writing workshops that help cultivate youth voices and build literacy skills. Each contains a citation to the article, book chapter, book, or website where you can learn more about the project in question.

In their article "Cuentos del Corazón/Stories from the Heart," Jessica Singer Early and Tracey Flores (2015) describe a writing workshop that they implemented for bilingual second graders and their families. The workshop goals included making the families feel "honored for their language abilities and [enabling them] to use their native languages in the writing and reading process" (p. 14). The focus of the workshop was giving families time to write together. The workshop facilitators used multiple strategies to create "a safe space and sense of community to empower families to share their stories and cultivate their voices" (p. 19). Libraries could easily adapt this workshop for African American youth and their families. As discussed in Chapter 1, the literacy practices of the African American community are often underutilized or disregarded by educators. A family-focused writing workshop would allow libraries to build on literacy traditions within the African American community such as storytelling, call-and-response, and spoken-word poetry. It also supports communalism, one of the nine dimensions of Black Cultural Ethos (BCE) discussed in Chapter 2.

In "Before It's Reading, It's Writing: Urban Teens as Authors in the Public Library," Autumn Winters and Elizabeth Gregg (2010) describe Write On!—a writing workshop for urban teens developed by the Durham County library in partnership with the UNC-CH Writing Center. The goal of Write On! was to teach "young people to redefine their relationship with the written word by turning them into writers as well as readers" (Winters & Gregg, 2010, p. 153). As Winters and Gregg (2010) explain, Write On! was developed to counter the way that urban teens experience writing in schools, where their audience is usually the teacher and their only purpose is to demonstrate that they have developed a core set of literacy skills. Instead, they wanted the teens that they worked with to see that what they write does matter. UNC-CH students served as coaches and created a supportive, trusting, and collaborative atmosphere, much like that in a college-level writing class, for the teens. At the end of each session, which ran 14–15 weeks, the youths' writings were published, which Winters and Greggs (2010) argue, "subvert[ed] the typical relationship among librarians, books, and kids" (p. 162). Winters and Gregg describe the specifics of the program in their book chapter, making it easily replicable by other libraries.

In his book, *Fearless Voices: Engaging a New Generation of African American Adolescent Male Writers*, Alfred Tatum (2013) provides a detailed description of the summer writing institute that he has led since 2008 with African American adolescent males at the University of Illinois at Chicago. His goal: for the young men to "use their pens to change course . . . to seek power and promise in their own words" (Tatum, 2013, p. 13). Each writing session begins with the following preamble:

> "We, the Brother Authors, will seek to use language to define who we are, become resilient beings, write for the benefit of others and ourselves, and use language prudently and unapologetically to mark our times and mark our lives. This, we agree to, with a steadfast commitment to the ideals of justice, compassion, and a better humanity for all. To this end, we write!" (Tatum, 2013, p. 14)

The book contains examples of the young men's poems and short stories, which Tatum publishes on a website where they are accessible to the youth, their families, and the broader community. He also shares them through his own academic writings and presentations. Tatum's institute is replicable by libraries either on their own or in collaboration with other community organizations, as you will read in Chapter 8, where Teresa Bunner describes the Blue Ribbon Mentor Advocate summer writing institute.

Author Matt de la Peña conducted a weeklong artist-in residency program with 14 seventh and eighth graders, primarily African American and Latino, at Mount Vernon Middle School in Raleigh, North Carolina, in March 2016. The students selected to work with de la Peña were identified as struggling but motivated students. Beginning in January, the students participated in literature circles where they discussed a number of de la Peña's books, including *Mexican White Boy* (2010) and *The Living* (2013). Once de la Peña arrived at the school, the students participated as a group in a two-and-a-half-hour writing workshop with him each morning and then met one on one with him in the afternoons. Each teen produced at least one polished piece of writing, which they shared with their families in a culminating celebration on Friday. Librarian Julie Stivers described the power of the residency this way:

> The **14** students—two groups of **7**—who engaged with Matt in a series of writer workshops displayed their powerful, creative, and brave voices over the course of an exciting and intense week. Our students have been given many labels at other schools: *low-performing, at-risk, failing*. They've shed those untruths and become writers—a powerful label to wear while moving through school. And the world. (personal communication, April 26, 2016; bold in original)

To learn more about this program, go to www.libequity.web.unc.edu.

Adopt the Connected Learning Framework

Connected Learning is an educational framework that seeks to make learning not only relevant, but also available to all youth in their personal, academic, and work lives. It focuses on the "potential of digital media" to support learning that is "socially embedded, interest driven and oriented toward educational, economic, and civic opportunity" (Roc, 2014, p. 3). Developed by Mimi Ito and her colleagues at the Digital Media and Learning Research Hub, the framework "centers on an equity agenda of deploying new media to reach and enable youth who otherwise lack access to opportunity" (Ito et al., 2013, p. 8). Connected Learning environments, whether in classrooms, libraries, museums, maker-spaces, or digital media labs, "embody the values of equity, social belonging, and participation" (p. 8), with the following goals:

- Developing lifelong learners who possess both basic literacy skills and higher-order thinking skills.
- Connecting academics to a youth's interests and linking him or her to inspiring peers and mentors.
- Utilizing digital and networked technologies to link learning in the school, home, and community.
- Enabling youth to make, create, and produce—all powerful pathways to deeper learning and understanding.
- Building communities and collective capabilities for learning and oppor-tunity (Ito et al., 2013).

The Future of Library Services for and with Teens: A Call to Action, published by the Young Adult Library Services Association (YALSA), describes Connected Learning as "the core of library services for and with teens," arguing that "con-nected learning provides a foundation for what teens need and want from libraries" (Braun et al., 2014, p. 10). We believe that Connected Learning also provides a platform for librarians to support the literacy development of Afri-can American youth.

The cultivation of voice and agency is at the heart of Connected Learning. Connected Learning only "happens when a young person is pursuing knowl-edge and expertise around a subject *they care deeply about*—something that is relevant to them and to their communities—and when they are supported in this pursuit by mentors, friends, peers, institutions, and caring adults" (Ito, 2013, p. 6, emphasis added). When librarians align their programming and ser-vices with the core principles and values of the Connected Learning frame-work, Black youth are able to express themselves authentically in ways that represent their lived experiences, explore their personal passions, connect with a network of peers and experts, and solve problems in their communities. They not only gain academic literacy skills and content knowledge, but they also realize the power of their voices and what it means to be a member of a com-munity of creators.

A study of the YOUMedia Labs learning space at the Chicago Public Library found that the youth who participated, the majority of whom were African American, reported improvement in their academic skills, including school-work, writing skills, and communication with adults, as well as a better understanding of the types of opportunities available to them after high school (Sebring et al., 2013, p. 38). They also increased their digital skills, feeling more confident in their abilities to record music, make videos, use multiple types of media to create something, and post something on the Internet. In addition, as this quote from one of the study participants illustrates, the youth devel-oped identities as talented, intelligent, and capable individuals: "I have access to things that I couldn't have used before to get what I need to get done. And now I feel like what was already within me has been exposed to me or revealed to me, and now I'm using it" (Sebring et al., 2013, p. 31).

A more detailed discussion of Connected Learning and how it is being implemented in public and school libraries across the nation is beyond the scope of this book. Our intent was to introduce this framework, show the connection between it and the literacy development of African American youth, and identify resources where you can learn more about how to use the framework to guide your practice (see the "Connected Learning Resources" box). Chapter 9 contains information about the Free Library of Philadelphia's Maker Jawn initiative, which illustrates the power of Connected Learning to support the literacy needs of African American youth, as well as other youth who have been marginalized.

Connected Learning Resources

- Connected Learning: An Agenda for Research and Design: http://dmlhub.net/wp-content/uploads/files/Connected_Learning_report.pdf
- Teaching in the Connected Learning Classroom: http://kpeppler.com/Docs/2014_Peppler_Teaching-in-the-CL-classroom.pdf
- Connected Learning TV: http://connectedlearning.tv
- Digital Media and Learning Research Hub: http://dmlhub.net

Utilize Protocols and "Written Conversations" as Part of Your Programs and Instruction

Protocols, according to the National School Reform Faculty (Mattoon, 2015), are "structured processes and guidelines that promote meaningful and efficient communication, problem solving, and learning" (p. 1). They are often used by teachers working in professional learning communities to improve projects, plans, or materials and "to look at student work with specific objectives and needs in mind" (Mattoon, 2015, p. 1). They can also be used with youth to build trust and promote participation in classrooms and other learning environments. Perhaps most important, protocols can be used to ensure equity and the inclusion of all viewpoints. As Joseph McDonald and his colleagues explain, protocols help make room for differences in "life experiences—derived, for example, from race, ethnicity, class background, sexual orientation, ability/disability, age, and so on" (McDonald et al., 2013, p. 13).

Written conversations are a concept introduced by Harvey and Elaine Daniels (2013) in their book *The Best Kept Teaching Secret: How Written Conversations Engage Kids, Activate Learning, Grow Fluent Writers . . . K–12*. The Danielses argue that written conversations such as dialogue journals, write-arounds, silent literature circles, threaded discussions, and blogs are a proven way to structure powerful interactions among youth of all ages. They outline a number of benefits of written conversations, including:

- enabling active, engaged learning;
- providing effective differentiation for diverse groups of youth;
- building fluency, confidence, and a positive attitude toward writing;
- offering models of various writing styles and purposes;
- creating a climate of collaboration and community; and
- inspiring students to advocate and take action (Daniels and Daniels, 2013, p. 2).

Both protocols and written conversations are effective strategies to utilize with African American youth. They not only allow youth to develop literacy skills in purposeful ways, but they also show respect for knowledge and culture, thus allowing Black youth to turn their knowledge into a strength. Another benefit is that when we incorporate protocols into our work, we are engaging African American youth in active learning—a key principle of culturally relevant pedagogy. Finally, the use of protocols counters an experience that some African American youth report—raising their hands to participate in discussions, only to repeatedly watch the adult leading the discussion call on the White youth in the group instead. While this type of silencing may be unintentional and unconscious, it is an implicit bias that protocols help address. Next, we discuss three protocols that we have successfully used with African American youth in library programs. We also point you to resources where you can find additional examples to incorporate into your work (see the box "Protocol Resources").

Protocol Resources

Daniels, Harvey, & Daniels, Elaine. (2013). *The best kept teaching secret: How written conversations engage kids, activate learning, grow fluent writers . . . K–12*. Thousand Oaks, CA: Corwin Literacy.

McDonald, Joseph P., Mahr, Nancy, Dicter, Alan, & McDonald, Elizabeth, C. (2013). *The power of protocols: An educator's guide to better practice*. 3rd ed. New York: Teacher's College Press.

National School Reform Faculty Protocols and Activities: http://www.nsrfh armony.org/free-resources/protocols.

Visible Thinking: http://www.visiblethinkingpz.org/VisibleThinking_html _files/VisibleThinking1.html.

Text Graffiti is a protocol promoted by Teaching Tolerance in its *Perspectives for a Diverse American* curriculum (n.d). Similar to the Danielses' concept of written narratives, this technique provides youth with an opportunity to think, reflect, and respond silently before engaging in group discussion. We have used it to engage teens in discussions of race and racism, but it can be used to initiate conversations on any topic. Text graffiti exposes youth to an excerpt from a text (e.g., a short story, novel, poem, or nonfiction work) prior to having them read the full piece. Students read selected passages out of context, silently comment on the passages, in either writing or drawing, and then respond to their peers' comments. After reading and responding to a number of their peers' comments, the youth engage in a small-group discussion, and then a large-group discussion, about the text's theme or claims, all while keeping the discussion anchored to the text. This strategy can be used across all content areas and with multiple kinds of texts. Figure 4.1 shows a handout that we created to text graffiti a passage from Nikki Grimes's *Bronx Masquerade*.

Another protocol that allows African American youth to formulate and share their ideas, first in writing and then through performance, is the Circle of Viewpoints thinking routine from Harvard's Visible Thinking Project (Harvard Project Zero, n.d.). The purpose of this protocol is to help young people "consider different and diverse perspectives involved in and around a topic" (Harvard Project Zero, n.d., para. 1). It can be used "to open discussions about dilemmas and other controversial issues" (Harvard Project Zero, n.d., para. 2) or to initiate and guide literature discussions. The protocol involves brainstorming

FIGURE 4.1 Sample Text Graffiti

GRAFFITI THIS TEXT

Passage from *Bronx Masquerade* (Grimes, 1998)

White folks! Who they think they kidding? They might as well go blow smoke up somebody else's you-know-what, 'cause a Black man's got no chance in this country. I be lucky if I make it to twenty-one with all these fools running around with AK-47s . . . Life is cold. Future? What I got is right now, right here, spending time with my homeys. Wish there was some future to talk about. I could use me some future. (p. 8)

Directions

1. Read the text silently.
2. Respond to the text in writing:
   - Write what you think the text might mean and why you think so.
   - Draw a representation of what you think the text might be talking about.
   - Explain what the text makes you wonder.
   - Write what the text tells you about people.
   - Write about the kind of conflict the text is describing.
   - Tell how this text reminds you of something in your own life or in the world. What? How?
   - Tell how this text reminds you of something else you have read. What? How?
3. Pass your response to the person to your right.
4. Write a response to another person's graffiti thoughts.
5. Repeat steps 2–4 until everyone in the small group has written on each sheet.
6. Return the sheet to its original "owner."
7. Read all the comments.
8. Engage in a small-group discussion, using your writings to help guide the discussion.

FIGURE 4.2   Circle of Viewpoints Routine (Harvard Project Zero, n.d.)

I AM THINKING OF ____ FROM THE POINT OF VIEW OF _____.

I THINK . . . *describe the topic from your viewpoint. Be an actor—take on the character of your viewpoint.*

A QUESTION I HAVE FROM THIS VIEWPOINT IS . . .

a list of different perspectives and then using the script skeleton shown in Figure 4.2 to explore each one. Youth select a specific perspective and then complete the script from that point of view. After all the participants have written their scripts, the youth gather in a circle and perform their points of view. A facilitator records their ideas and questions. Once everyone in the circle has spoken, the facilitator leads the discussion by asking: "What new ideas do you have about the topic that you didn't have before?" and "What new questions do you have?" (Harvard Project Zero, n.d., para. 6). We have used this protocol in library programs to examine the concept of cultural appropriation in *Shadowshaper,* by Daniel José Older (2015), and to discuss bullying with a group of middle school students.

We have also found Write-Arounds, advocated by Daniels and Daniels (2013), to be an effective strategy to increase engagement and encourage deeper thinking among African American youth. In write-arounds, three to five youth sit side by side, "writing notes to each other, serially exchanging these notes, commenting and building upon each other's ideas" (Daniels & Daniels, 2013, p. 156) for about 10–15 minutes. Youth can respond by posing questions, making connections to ideas from readings or class discussions, reacting to each other's statements, connecting to their personal experiences, and drawing. Variations on this activity include having youth write on large pieces of butcher block paper, whiteboards, or chart paper, or to use a digital collaborative tool such as Google Apps. The goals are to acknowledge everyone's ideas and to encourage youth to dig more deeply into a topic. Buffy Hamilton, a school librarian in Georgia, utilizes this strategy frequently with high school students across content areas. You can read about her experiences with write-arounds on her blog *The Unquiet Librarian* (https://theunquietlibrarian.wordpress.com). In Chapter 13, you will read how teen librarian Faith Burns used write-arounds as a tool for empowering teens at the Main Branch of the Durham Public Library to design and evaluate an after-school program for elementary school students.

Develop Programs That Allow Youth to Use Their Voices to Engage with the World

The power of YPAR to cultivate voice and agency is undeniable. The YPAR projects that Ernest Morrell and his colleagues have engaged in with urban youth, as well as those that Jason Irizarry has taken part in with Latin@ youth, demonstrate this. As one young woman explains, "We are smart . . . I learned [through participating in this research project] that by myself, it is hard to change things, but if teachers work together with students, we can do anything" (Irizarry, 2011, p. 205). Another agreed, noting, "I'm in my senior year of high school and for the first time I am beginning to enjoy learning. I attribute my passion for education to having an opportunity to learn about things that are important to me" (Irizarry, 2011, p. 49).

We believe that as librarians, we must embrace our social justice roots and develop library programs that provide African American youth with opportunities to use their voices to engage with the world, to educate other African American youth, and to critique and challenge the systems of oppression and inequity that affect communities of color and continue to be reproduced in American society. Research, inquiry—these are the purview of librarians. We need to incorporate this aspect of our professional knowledge into our work with African American youth as readily as we do our love of literature or our excitement about new technologies. We can develop programs that allow youth to investigate and report on matters that are important to them and to their community. If we live in a city or town with a university (or multiple universities), we can seek out faculty, graduate students, and even undergraduate students to partner with us to develop long-term YPAR initiatives. If we do not have access to those kinds of resources, we can work alone or with other librarians or teachers to develop less complex, short-term projects.

> "We are smart . . . I learned [through participating in this research project] that by myself, it is hard to change things, but if teachers work together with students, we can do anything" (Irizarry, 2011, p. 205).

Linda Christensen, the teacher in Portland whose work with students we discussed earlier in this chapter, has had students "travel to local colleges to teach graduate education students about the history of the SATs, the politics of language, and the power of praise poetry in the Harlem Renaissance. They have walked to elementary and middle schools to read books they have written about abolitionists and Ebonics. They have distributed report cards grading cartoon videos on their representation of people of color to video stores and local newspapers. They have created table-tents for elementary schools about women we should honor, and they have testified about changes that need to happen in their schools" (Christensen, 2009, para. 26). Even young children can engage in initiatives like these. Lenny Sánchez (2014) describes an interdisciplinary project in which teams of third graders examined challenges in their inner-city neighborhood such as having "insufficient and unsafe equipment for students to play on during recess" (p. 185). Each of these examples could have been the result of a public library program or collaboration between a school librarian and teacher.

Teen librarian Wick Thomas is one librarian who is working to foster teen activism. His work with teens in Kansas City, Missouri, is described in a special November 2015 issue of *School Library Journal* that focuses on teens and libraries. In March 2015, Thomas and over 100 teens, many from families that are suffering from economic difficulties, rallied at the state capital "to talk to legislators about how the proposed budget cuts to libraries would adversely affect *their lives*" (Thomas, 2015, para. 2, emphasis added). In addition, the teens in his Library Advisory group planned and implemented the Kansas City Public Library Youth Empowerment Summit. Here, the teens held workshops "on how to access power in their communities and effect change. Sessions covered topics such as the Black Lives Matter movement, LGBTQ [lesbian, gay, bisexual, transgender, and queer] issues in high school, mental illness, and how to be a better activist" (Thomas, 2015, para. 7). As Thomas (2015) explains, "Young adults care about these issues, and having a space to discuss them helped them better understand the power that they currently hold—and solidifies our role as a radical, necessary institution" (para. 8). These are the kinds of programs that librarians, both public and school, must be developing if we want to improve the literacy and life outcomes of African American youth.

Make Space to Talk About Race, Power, and Privilege in the Library

Regardless of where they live, whether in the suburbs of Washington, D.C., a college town like Chapel Hill, or the Englewood neighborhood of Chicago, Black youth know the names Trayvon Martin, Michael Brown, Eric Garner, Tamir Rice, Freddie Gray, and Sandra Bland. The tragic deaths of these young Blacks have affected Black youth deeply, personally, and as a community. As Christensen (2013–2014) argues, there must be spaces where Black youth can, if they wish, give voice to their feelings about these awful events—spaces where they have the opportunity to become part of the national conversation on racial profiling, excessive police force, and flaws in the justice system in authentic, real ways. Libraries can be these spaces.

In her article "Trayvon Martin and My Students: Writing Toward Justice," Christensen (2013–2014) quotes Marc Lamont Hill, a professor at Morehouse College, who describes the message sent to Black youth by these recent events: "You're less valuable and less worthy of protection, love, and investment than other folks. And when that message is received, it wears on your spirit. It's tough to live in a world where you're seen as less than" (Christensen, 2013–2014, p. 22). Lamont Hill goes on to say, "There needs to be conversations about what if feels like to be followed in the store, chased out of the mall, or to not be welcomed on the other side of town. Give [Black youth] the space to ask questions, vent and cry and be vulnerable in a world that almost demands them to be hard at all times" (Christensen, 2013–2014, p. 23). By providing that space, librarians demonstrate to Black youth that their experiences matter—that we stand with them in naming and addressing the prejudice, bias, discrimination, and inequities that they face, and that we will help them "develop the skills and language they need to explore these complex and controversial issues" (Gorski & Swalwell, 2015, p. 38). We are not saying that librarians have to have the answers. What we do need to do is give Black youth the chance to see that their anger, fears, and hopes are being recognized by the wider community.

Like Gorski & Swalwell (2015), we recognize that "this is a daunting task" (p. 37), and not one that everyone will feel comfortable embracing. It can be accomplished, however, with the kind of racial equity training that we discussed in Chapter 1 and will cover later in this book in Chapter 12, and by joining professional and community-based networks, such as We Need Diverse Books (http://weneeddiversebooks.org), Reading While White (http://reading whilewhite.blogspot.com), and Black Lives Matter (http://blacklivesmatter .com) where these issues are being discussed. The American Association of School Librarians (AASL), the Association for Library Service to Children (ALSC), and YALSA are also committed to helping librarians understand their personal and cultural values, beliefs, and identities; to understand the effects of racism and discrimination on youth; and to develop strategies for addressing and dismantling racism in libraries.

CONCLUDING THOUGHTS

The soul of a people lives in that people's voice and is streamed in the continuous sounds that run deep like rivers through their lineage.
—Kirkland (2013, p. 40)

This quote from David Kirkland captures why we believe that it is so critical for librarians to focus on cultivating the voice and agency of African American youth. Voice matters! As librarians, we should be addressing the literacy development of Black youth, not simply to help close the achievement gap, but because literacy is a powerful tool of voice and agency. Libraries must be spaces where Black youth are encouraged to develop their voices, to tell their stories, and to share their unique perspectives on how we can work together to create the just society they deserve.

5

Stories Matter

Sandra Hughes-Hassell, Casey H. Rawson, and Julie Stivers

Out of all the texts in the world, why do we put these texts in front of African American adolescent males living in economically deprived communities?
—Tatum (2009, p. 42)

It's a beautiful thing when I have to tell my Black male students to stop reading in class so that they can pay attention . . . and that has happened several times since we started [the Black male book club].
—Butts (2011, para. 3)

Much has been written about how to improve literacy rates among children and teens of color, and a good deal of this research focuses on the choice of texts. Research has stressed the importance of providing children and adolescent readers with texts that reflect their personal experiences and accurately portray characters like themselves and their families, friends, and peers (Allington & Cunningham, 2007; Bell & Clark, 1998; DeLeón, 2002; Gangi, 2008; Purves & Beach, 1972). The availability of such texts affects both reading achievement and reading motivation in students (Allington & Cunningham, 2007; Bell & Clark, 1998; Gangi, 2008; Heflin & Barksdale-Ladd, 2001). Research shows that "when readers interact with literature that relates to their culture-specific experiences, their reading comprehension performance will improve" (McCullough, 2008, p. 7). It also suggests that youth of color who typically display antipathy toward reading may react differently when provided with texts that are culturally relevant, as author Sharon Flake describes:

Black boys will read. But to get them off to a flying start, we've got to give them books that remind them of home—who they are. When this happens, they fly through books—even the most challenged readers. They hunger for the work like a homeless man finally getting a meal that's weeks overdue. (Flake, 2007b, p. 14)

In a recent book, Alfred Tatum (2009) takes the idea of culturally relevant texts a step further, arguing that African American adolescent males need exposure to texts that not only contain characters who look, act, and think as they do, but also encourage and empower these young people to take action in their own lives and in the lives of others around them. Tatum (2009) maintains that one reason that African American male youth suffer academically, emotionally, and culturally is a lack of exposure to "texts that they find meaningful and that will help them critique, understand, and move beyond some of the turmoil-related experiences they encounter outside school" (p. xii). Tatum calls such writing *enabling texts.*

Tatum's argument for using enabling young adult and adult texts with Black adolescent males applies to male and female Black youth of all ages. Today, there are numerous picture books and middle-grade novels that allow Black youth to explore and view concepts, issues, themes, and issues from multiple perspectives and in relation to their multiple identities. Examples include picture books such as *One Million Men and Me* (2007) and *Tea Cakes for Tosh* (2012), both by Kelly Starlings Lyons, and middle-grade novels like *The Cruisers* series by Walter Dean Myers (2010a, 2011, 2012, 2013) and *Unstoppable Octobia May* (2014) by Sharon Flake. If teachers and librarians wait until middle school or high school to connect Black youth with meaningful and engaging texts, they may be missing opportunities that are difficult to recapture. The love of reading and writing needs to be cultivated early, and youth, even in the elementary grades, need to begin to understand the role that literacy plays in shaping their life outcomes.

In this chapter, we first define the characteristics of enabling texts. We then discuss how librarians might use enabling texts in their work with Black youth. Finally, we include a sample list of enabling texts that feature African American protagonists.

In this chapter, we:
- Define the concept of the enabling text.
- Identify the characteristics of enabling texts.
- Explore the connection between culturally relevant and enabling texts and academic achievement.
- Discuss how librarians might use enabling texts in their work with Black youth.
- Provide a sample of enabling texts that feature African American protagonists.

DEFINING AND IDENTIFYING ENABLING TEXTS THAT FEATURE AFRICAN AMERICANS

How can educators, librarians, and parents identify texts that are culturally relevant, powerful, and able to make a positive difference in the lives of
their readers? This is a difficult task, particularly given the small number of
books featuring African American characters published each year (Horning
et al., 2014). While any given book with an African American protagonist may
hold the interest of Black readers, many of these texts fall short of the benchmarks set for enabling texts, which promote a healthy psyche and serve as a
road map for being, doing, thinking, and acting, according to Tatum (2009). In
fact, as Tatum (2009) argues, some books with Black characters actually "reinforce a student's perception of being a struggling reader incapable of handling
cognitively challenging texts" (p. 65). He calls such texts *disabling texts.*
Included in his definition of disabling texts are books that are developmentally
inappropriate—that is, books that may be on the students' reading level but
"ignore their need for human development" (p. 67). As an example of this type
of disabling text, Tatum describes a case in which a *Berenstain Bears* book,
written for primary students, was selected for instructional use with a
16-year-old Black male (p. 67).

Also included in his definition of disabling texts are books that serve mainly
to reinforce the stereotypes of Black communities, especially Black urban areas.
Some titles in the street fiction genre in particular may meet this criterion; as
Brooks and Savage (2009) discuss, many of these books "embod[y] the potential to valorize infidelity, criminal activity, and a wide range of unprincipled and
even stereotypic behaviors" (p. 50). However, as these researchers also note,
street fiction novels are scattered along a "nuanced and varied" continuum, so
dismissing all street fiction as disabling shortchanges the genre (p. 51). It also
denies the ability of Black teens to take a critical stance as readers and judge
for themselves the authenticity of the text or the author's intent in writing the
book.

To help teachers, librarians, and parents identify texts that have the potential to motivate Black youth to become better readers and to help them define
themselves, we have used Tatum's definition of enabling texts to create the
rubric shown in Figure 5.1 (Tatum, 2009, p. 77). Unless otherwise noted, each
characteristic was derived from Tatum's work. In the next section, we use sample enabling texts to illustrate each element of the rubric.

Characteristics of Enabling Texts

Provide a Healthy Psyche

Tatum (2009) argues that enabling texts portray characters who practice
self-reflection, leading readers to look within and to define themselves. The process of self-definition is often an explicit part of an enabling text's narrative.
Take, for example, David, the protagonist in the novel *Pull* (Binns, 2010). After
a tragedy strikes David's family, he must decide whether to risk splitting apart

FIGURE 5.1 Enabling Text Rubric

Characteristic	Definition
Provides a healthy psyche (Tatum, 2009)	• Leads Black youth to look within • Shows Black youth defining themselves
Provides a modern awareness of the real world (Tatum, 2009)	• Connects to issues/questions that students find essential today • Takes place within the context of their life experiences • Deals with issues that are important to Black youth • Presents real environments/conditions Black youth face inside and outside school
Focuses on the collective struggles of African Americans (Tatum, 2009)	• Provides insight into issues related to social justice • Allows youth to take a critical look at their oppression and oppressors and to examine the academic & social ills they face • Contains content that will cause youth to take action in their own lives • Challenges youth to think about their existence
Serves as a road map for being, doing, thinking, and acting (Tatum, 2009)	• Reflects an improved human condition • Suggests steps/strategies/supports for improving life • Speaks to the power of the individual and of the collective
Recognizes, honors, and nurtures multiple identities (Tatum, 2009)	• Academic • Social • Cultural • Sexual • Economic • Communal • Gendered • National • Personal • International
Demonstrates resiliency (Tatum, 2009)	• Focuses on self-reliance • Focuses on self-determination • Shows Black youth, adults, or both as problem solvers • Challenges victim mentality
Interesting and provocative (Tatum, 2009)	• Thematically engaging • Complex—multilayered • Developmentally appropriate • Fast-moving and provocative • Taps into feelings, imagination, and intellectual curiosity
Avoids caricatures (Tatum, 2009)	• Reflects the diversity within racial and ethnic groups • Avoids common tropes associated with Black youth (e.g., the teen mother, the hoopster, or the gang recruit) • Avoids stereotypical portrayals of other youth of color (e.g., the nerdy Asian) • Portrays youth of color as complex and multidimensional
Includes a mentor or role model	• Provides guidance or offers wisdom to the protagonist • Often an adult or elderly member of the African American community • Not didactic or preachy

his younger siblings in order to pursue a college education and basketball career (his mother's dream for him) or to keep his family together by foregoing college in favor of an apprenticeship with a construction foreman. David eventually chooses the latter path, explaining his decision to his high school basketball coach this way:

> You asked me what I want for my future. I want the wind. And mortar and bricks too . . . I want to look over the plans for something that never existed before. I want to dream up those plans and make them real . . . And I'll be taught by a master. And in the meantime, I'll be keeping my family together. Not because I feel guilty, and not because I have to. I'm doing it because I want to. (Binns, 2010, p. 302)

David comes to this decision after a good deal of introspection, and his thought processes are clearly documented throughout the novel. At the end of the novel, David summarizes what he has discovered through his deliberate decision making: "People can learn if they're willing. Learn to live their own lives, and overcome their own faults. They can decide not to crash and burn, and not to be ruled by other people's dreams" (Binns, 2010, p. 307). Novels like this one provide teens with a healthy model for their own decision making.

Provide a Modern Awareness of the Real World

As Tatum (2009) notes, enabling texts connect readers with the world around them by honestly portraying characters, issues, problems, and environments that African American youth might encounter in the real world. Two important facts related to this characteristic of an enabling text should be considered. First, *real* is a relative term—that is, what each reader finds realistic will vary depending on that person's experience.

One reader might relate to Coe Booth's *Tyrell* (2007), whereas another reader might identify more with the twins in Kwame Alexander's *The Crossover* (2014). This is one reason

> Not all Black teens will identify with a protagonist who must check his clothing for gang colors before leaving his home each morning.

that it is critical to offer a spectrum of novels that reflect the lives of Black youth in our libraries and classrooms, so no one single story is being presented. Just as we should not assume that a White child or teenager comes from a middle-class, dual-parent, suburban home, we should also take care not to assume that all African American youth come from urban, poverty-stricken, violent communities (Hughes-Hassell et al., 2010). Not all Black teens will identify with a protagonist who must check his clothing for gang colors before leaving his home each morning, as the characters in *Chameleon* (Smith, 2008) must do. This does not mean that gritty urban fiction cannot be enabling or is not realistic—undeniably, many people do live in situations like these and both persevere and grow despite the challenges they face. However, educators, parents, and librarians must recognize that some African American readers may find it difficult to connect with the characters in such novels. As one Black teen noted in a discussion of *Autobiography of My Dead Brother* (Myers, 2005)—a book that meets the criteria of an enabling text—"I mean it was a good book, but since I'm not in a gang, it wasn't anything I could relate to" (personal communication, March 15, 2011).

The second important factor to keep in mind when considering which texts offer a modern awareness of the real world is that books other than contemporary, realistic fiction can meet the criteria for this category. Tatum (2009) recommends that teachers also use historical works, such as *Narrative of the Life of Frederick Douglass* (Douglass, 1845/1997). These texts, while seemingly not at all modern, still offer truths that resonate with Black youth today. While the world has changed in the decades since such historical texts were written, adolescents can still draw parallels between the people, events, and issues in these texts and their modern-day lives. According to author Sharon Draper, studying the past allows us to "understand some of the social, economic, and political realities of the present. The past is a teacher from which we can learn much" (as quoted in Hinton-Johnson, 2009, p. 92). Similarly, genre fiction (such as fantasy and science fiction) should not be automatically discarded for failing to represent the "real world." Like historical texts, genre novels often present modern, real-world problems and issues indirectly; they require only a small leap from the reader to bridge seemingly fantastical narratives with the realities of everyday life.

Focus on the Collective Struggles of African Americans

The African American community has faced and continues to face a variety of obstacles along the path to equity. Enabling texts neither ignore these struggles nor paint African Americans as merely victims of history. Instead, as Tatum (2009) argues, enabling texts challenge African American youth to examine critically the challenges that they face, whether those challenges are academic, social, economic, or personal. Enabling texts may achieve this focus through looking at historical African American struggles such as slavery, reconstruction, or the Civil Rights movement. For example, *The Rock and the River* (Magoon, 2009) explores the Civil Rights era through the eyes of a young man who feels torn between the nonviolent beliefs of his father and the Black Panther allegiance of his brother. Alternatively, enabling texts may deal with present-day civil rights struggles faced by African Americans. Tupac Shakur's poetry anthology *The Rose That Grew from Concrete* includes several poems that confront the economic and social ills of African Americans. Consider this untitled piece that implores readers to "Please wake me when I'm free / I cannot bear captivity / where my culture I'm told holds no significance / . . . / But now like a nightmare I wake 2 c / That I live like a prisoner of poverty" (Shakur, 1999, p. 15).

> African American youth need concrete strategies for confronting problematic issues in their own lives, and enabling texts can help provide such strategies.

Serve as a Road Map for Being, Doing, Thinking, and Acting

Despite an awareness of societal and personal challenges facing African American youth, enabling texts are positive in that they affirm the power of both the individual and the collective to improve one's life (Tatum, 2009, p. 68). These texts do not present miracle solutions to poverty, oppression, prejudice, or violence. In fact, if a novel resolves itself with such a magic bullet—a character wins the lottery and is transported out of poverty, or a gang member suddenly and without significant cause sees the error of his ways and reforms—this is a good indication that such texts are not enabling, in that they do not reflect the way that problems are solved in reality. As Tatum argues, African American youth need concrete strategies for confronting problematic issues in their own lives, and enabling texts can help provide such strategies. For example, in *The Rock and the River* (Magoon, 2009), the protagonist, Sam, decides to testify at a friend's trial, even though it will mean possibly endangering himself. Sam's brother tries to prepare him for what this choice signifies: "You have to understand what it means to tell the truth. . . . People are afraid to testify. It's a serious thing to stand up and say the cops are lying." Sam replies, "The easy choice is almost never the right one, right?" (p. 222). Enabling texts present difficult choices and genuine responses to issues—responses that readers can use as models when making similar choices in their own lives.

Recognize, Honor, and Nurture Multiple Identities

Just as real people can never be defined by a single trait, neither should book characters. As Tatum (2009) notes, characters should instead be portrayed as having multiple identities—academic, cultural, religious, gendered, social, national, etc. Such a nuanced portrayal is closer to reality and encourages readers to reflect on their own identities, as well as to realize that other people that they encounter in life should also not be defined or judged by a single characteristic. Two titles that illustrate this characteristic are *We Could Be Brothers* (Barnes, 2010) and *Bronx Masquerade* (Grimes, 2002). In *We Could Be Brothers*, the two main characters—young men who initially appear to be insurmountably different from one another—each discover hidden identities within the other, leading them to develop respect and friendship for one another. The students in *Bronx Masquerade* develop a love of poetry during a study of the Harlem Renaissance. When they begin to share their original poetry with each other on open-mic Fridays, they discover the individuals beyond the stereotypes. Tyrone explains:

> I look around this class and nobody I see fits into the box I used to put them in . . . Mr. Ward [the English teacher] says you have to take people one at a time, check out what's in their head and heart before you judge. Word. (Grimes, 2002, p. 86)

Demonstrate Resiliency

Whether an African American reader is growing up in urban poverty or in suburban affluence, developing resiliency—the ability to think critically, solve problems, and bounce back from negative events—is critical for long-term success. According to Tatum (2009), enabling texts can assist in this development by portraying characters who are self-reliant problem solvers. Seeing such a positive portrayal of African American youth can confer a sense of self-efficacy on readers. An example of a text that fulfills this criterion is *Bang* by Sharon Flake (2007a). The protagonist (a Black male) finds himself kicked out of his home and has to survive the violent streets of his neighborhood on his own. Despite a few missteps along the way, the protagonist ultimately finds a way to survive without resorting to the cruelty and lawlessness of those around him. While his particular path is not one that many adolescent readers would choose to follow, the overall positive portrayal of this young man as a determined, resourceful problem solver gives African American readers someone to look up to in literature and affirms the reader's ability to demonstrate those same character traits in the midst of adversity.

Interesting and Provocative

For Tatum (2009), a key component of literacy is the ability not only to read, but also to be able to express oneself in writing. Thus, enabling texts should provide positive reinforcement of the characteristics of strong writing. They should be engaging and fast-moving; they should be thematically rich; they should provoke deeper thinking from their readers; and they should awaken the intellectual curiosity of the reader. One example of such a text is *Shadowshaper* (Older, 2015). The novel is suspenseful and fast-paced, and it deals with weighty issues such as family, ancestry, and appropriation—all while the heroes are trying to escape terrifying, otherworldly creatures. The novel's plot provides fertile ground for the exploration and discussion of such questions as "How does art convey power?" and "How can people or groups appropriate culture from different communities?" Another example is Tupac Shakur's poetry. After reading the following poem, teens might be inspired to write their own poetry that addresses the "weeds" that they believe are holding back the growth of Black youth in the United States: "I find greatness in the tree / that grows against all odds / it blossoms in darkness / I was the tree who grew from weeds" (Shakur, 1999, p. 115).

Avoid Caricatures

Tatum (2009) notes that stereotypes of Black youth and communities are prevalent in disabling texts, where Black teen males are likely to be portrayed as "the hoopster, the fatherless son, the gang recruit, the truant, the dummy in need of remediation, and the purveyor of poor grammar" (p. 82), while Black teen females are depicted as welfare mothers or manipulative women who use their sexuality to control and exploit men. When Black characters defy the stereotypes, they are often mocked by others for demonstrating intelligence or for breaking the norms of their impoverished neighborhoods. A fact not mentioned by Tatum but equally important is that disabling texts also often stereotype non–African American characters as well (for example, the Asian nerd, the Hispanic girl with an attitude, or the cruel White teacher). Enabling texts avoid such caricatures, providing well-rounded and multidimensional characters instead. Often, such texts succeed in this regard by showing characters directly challenging stereotypes or realizing in the course of the narrative that the stereotypes that they hold are invalid. For example, the protagonist in Sharon Flake's poem "You Don't Even Know Me" rebukes his teachers, neighbors, and even his friends for making assumptions about his academic ability, his career aspirations, and his behavior based on stereotypes of Black male teens: "You know / I've been wondering lately / Trying to figure out just how it could be / That you can see me so often / And don't know a thing about me" (Flake, 2010, p. 4). In *The Freedom Writers Diary* (Freedom Writers, 1999), one female teen writer comes to discover that she cannot be defined by the labels that others place on her: "For the first time, I realized that what people say about living in the ghetto and having brown skin doesn't have to apply to me" (p. 203).

Include a Mentor or Role Model

One aspect of enabling texts that is not discussed by Tatum, but which we identified in many of the texts we evaluated, was the presence of a mentor or role model. This character is often, but not always, significantly older than the protagonist and passes along wisdom and advice in the course of the narrative. While the mentor or role model is often an African American adult, this is not always the case. In fact, sometimes the role model relationship develops unexpectedly, as in Walter Dean Myers's *Lockdown* (2010), where the mentor role is fulfilled by an elderly White character who at first seems openly hostile toward the protagonist. Nor does the mentor figure have to be physically present in the narrative; in *Jimi and Me* by Jaime Adoff (2005), the main character idolizes Jimi Hendrix, whose song lyrics and life story provide the guidance that the protagonist needs to navigate a difficult family situation.

A Word About "Nontraditional" Texts

In the discussion so far in this chapter, we have used traditional print resources to illustrate the characteristics of enabling texts. It is important to remember that other forms of media can also serve as enabling texts. For example, Morrell (2004) and his colleagues (Morrell & Duncan-Andrade, 2001) use hip hop as a way to teach African American youth. They have designed lessons that incorporate hip-hop music and culture into the traditional high school English curriculum, encouraging African American youth to see the connections between hip-hop artists and post-Industrial poets, as well as to investigate the parallels between hip hop and classic novels. Teen librarian Faith Burns sponsors a Music and Popular Culture Club, where the Black teens that she works with explore issues such as cultural appropriation in rap music and the stereotyping of Black youth in advertising, movies, and even TV news (personal communication, November 5, 2015).

After the acquittal of George Zimmerman for the murder of Trayvon Martin, a high school English teacher in Portland, Oregon, had her students listen to or read the transcript of President Barack Obama's speech about the court decision and critically examine it by considering questions such as: What do you agree with in the talk? What resonates most with you? What do you find problematic? What is missing? Who is the audience for this speech, and how do you know? The next day, the teacher had the students watch an interview with Professor Cornel West in which he criticized the president's speech. She challenged the students to analyze Dr. West's comments in the same way that they had President Obama's, and then to compare what Dr. West said with what President Obama said, and then with their own interpretations of each. In this way, she used nontraditional texts to engage the students in a complex literary analysis and writing experience (Christensen, 2013–2014).

Youth Voices

I think *Sunrise Over Fallujah* is a good book for African American males to read cause it's common for us to go to war without noticing really why. A lot of them they don't really join the military unless they think they have nothing . . . or because they think they don't have anything else to do.

—16-year-old Black male

This book [*Skeleton Key*] showed how [African American males] are always having to struggle for everything, and we really have to earn everything we get. And it really was a good way of showing how Jarett turned nothing into something. And he was able to do all these positive things in such a negative environment.

—16-year-old Black male

[*Bronx Masquerade*] . . . tells us that African American males feel like we do have a future, we just have to invest in it. . . . Me, for example, I don't live in a neighborhood in a community where I have problems like this. I'm sorta one of the luckier males. But these guys have to work hard day in and day out to make something with their life while people around them are constantly telling them they have no future, that they can't do anything with it. So these guys are really brave and courageous for going past what other people think is right in the African American community to make a future for themselves.

—16-year-old Black male

DISCUSSING ENABLING TEXTS WITH AFRICAN AMERICAN YOUTH

Not only should enabling texts be put into the hands of African American youth at every opportunity, but these texts should also be mediated by a teacher, parent, librarian, or other adult; that is, they should be utilized to "engage the students in dialogue about issues and concepts that matter in school and society," and to do so from "multiple perspectives and in relation to multiple identities" (Tatum, 2009, p. 90). According to Tatum (2009), the mediation or discussion of enabling texts is critical. He argues that without the chance to discuss their reading with others and to respond to the texts through writing, enabling texts cannot fulfill their true potential in the lives of these young people.

In his book *Reading for Their Life,* Tatum (2009) offers a framework for mediating texts that includes six components: identifying the appropriate literacy platform or developmental asset that will "allow them to benefit in racially segregated and racially integrated settings" (p. 41) by defining the self, becoming resilient, engaging others, and building capacity; selecting passages and vocabulary to introduce the text; developing framing questions to guide the discussion; establishing a writing connection; determining the format (small group, whole group, or individual) for the discussion; and evaluating the discussion and students' ongoing needs. Figure 5.2 illustrates how this framework might be used to guide a discussion of Andrea Pinkney's *Sit-in: How Four Friends Stood up by Sitting Down* (2010).

The most challenging elements of Tatum's framework are often selecting a passage to introduce the text and developing the framing questions. In Figure 5.3, we have provided suggested passages to capture readers and framing questions for two texts, *We Could Be Brothers* by Derrick Barnes (2010) and *Stella by Starlight* by Sharon M. Draper (2015).

Selecting the passage is like creating a booktalk—finding the right "hook" that will entice a struggling or reluctant reader to want to read and discuss the book. As Tatum (2009) notes, the attention of struggling readers is often not captured by the first pages (or even chapters) of many books. It might be a passage in the middle of the book, or even at the end, that motivates them to want to read it. Tatum illustrates this point by sharing the story of a young man who he observed one day during sustained silent reading sitting slumped in his chair, not even pretending to read. Dr. Tatum approached the young man with a copy of *Bang* and shared this passage from the middle of the book: "A black boy don't get a hundred chances to get it right. Sometimes he just gets one. That's it . . . You blow your chance, you blow your life" (Flake, 2007, p. 124). The young man immediately began to read the book, and when it was time for sustained silent reading to end, he did not want to put the book away (personal communication, June 10, 2012).

The framing questions are essential questions—questions that encourage youth to grapple with pressing issues they face in school and in society. A question is essential when it provokes "deep thought, lively discussion, sustained inquiry, and new understanding as well as more questions" (Wiggins, 2007, para. 7).

FIGURE 5.2 Sample Text Mediation Plan

Title: *Sit-in: How Four Friends Stood up by Sitting Down* by Andrea Pinkney (2010); illustrations by Brian Pinkney

Literacy Platforms
- Becoming resilient ✓
- Engaging others ✓

Introducing the Text *(getting students into the text right away)*
- Required vocabulary—[1–3 words]
- Text to introduce the book—use an excerpt to get the students involved right away

Write words on board–Segregation; Integration
Show book "trailer": Freedom Walkers; read first six pages of Sit-in; *ask kids for the definition of each term*

Framing Questions
1. *Is it better to follow what everyone is doing, or to do what you know is right?*
2. *What are the benefits of doing what you know is right? What are you willing to give up to do the right thing?*
3. *Are there things that are happening in our school or in your neighborhood that you would like to change? How could you start to make these changes? How could you get others involved?*
4. *Are there connections between standing up for what you know is right and becoming resilient and engaging others?*

Writing Connection *(calling attention to the text as a language model and helping students read as writers)*

Let's examine the first six pages of the text. What do you think about the author's:
1. Word choice—Is the author using words that invite the reader in or lock the reader out? *(Pinkney uses words related to recipes, which most children are familiar with; this invites readers in)*
2. Voice—Does it sound like a real voice? Is the author taking care to get a point across? *(Pinkney uses the students' names and repeats them throughout; there is a connection to a real place, Greensboro, NC)*
3. Momentum—Is the author able to keep the reader's attention? Why or why not? *(Pinkney uses short sentences; rhythm; illustrations; words/phrases in capital letters)*
4. Investment—Does the author seem to really care about what she is writing about? *(The inclusion of timeline and notes at the end demonstrates the care that Pinkney took to be accurate)*

Mediating Discussions Around One of the Framing Questions
In the whole group: Reread the first six pages; discuss Framing Question 1
In small groups: Read the rest of the book; discuss Framing Question 2 or 3; OR
Individually: Read the rest of the book; students write about something that they would be willing to stand up for

Evaluating the Discussion and Students' Ongoing Future Needs Going in Different Directions
1. Pacing. *Did the students have adequate time to absorb and respond to the text?*
2. Grouping. *Did students participate effectively in both small- and large-group discussions? Were the discussions substantive?*
3. Individual writing assignments. *Is there evidence that students defined themselves through their writing?*

FIGURE 5.3 Sample Starter Passages and Framing Questions for a Book Club

Title: *We Could Be Brothers*, by Derrick Barnes (2010)
Annotation: Two eighth graders from very different backgrounds, Robeson "Crease" Battlefield and Pacino Clapton, discover in after-school detention that they have a great deal in common.

Starter Passages
"I don't want other kids thinking I'm trying to be white or talkin' white like you do or calling me soft. You know."
"No, I *don't* know. And who says white kids have a monopoly on being good students . . . And I didn't know that using the English language like it's supposed to be used was a crime. *Talkin' white . . .* you don't know how stupid that sounds." (p. 39)
"You don't need to be hood to protect yourself, fool. He may want to hurt me, but I won't play into that stupid stuff. I'm about using my mind, not fighting." (p. 104)

Framing Questions
Is the view of school achievement as "something for Whites only" real or imagined?
Who has the authority to define your intellectual aspirations—you or society?

Title: *Stella by Starlight,* by Sharon Draper (2015)

Annotation: When the Ku Klux Klan reappears in Stella's segregated Southern town, the community unites to battle prejudice and injustice.

Starter Passages
"Stella stopped in her tracks, mouth agape. The horses were nearly upon her, but more terrifying were the horsemen. Each wore a white full-length robe. And a pointed white hood. And each carried a flaming torch in his left hand. The Klan." (p. 171)

Framing Questions
What are the alternatives when someone tries to stamp out the existence of others?
What does it mean to *truly* be free?

Students Carry the Discussion

It is also possible to teach students to mediate texts. The middle school librarian at Chewning Middle School in Durham, North Carolina, did just that, inviting students interested in facilitating book discussions to a workshop to learn how to establish and lead book clubs. In addition to sharing the guidelines shown in Figure 5.4, she taught students how to select a book for discussion, design a book "trailer" to motivate other students to want to read the

FIGURE 5.4   Eighth Grade Book Club Guidelines

Expectations for Student Facilitators	Expectations for Participants
• Select the book and design the plan. • Promote the club, recruit, and choose members. • Prepare for each meeting by reviewing the reading, writing discussion topics, and possibly planning activities related to the book . • Hold book club members accountable for participation and behavioral expectations. • Keep a notebook with your discussion questions and other preparation related to the book club. Share this notebook with the librarian on Mondays. • Keep the conversation focused on the book. • Encourage equal participation of all group members. • At the end of the meeting, review the next steps with your members. • Make sure that your meeting space is clean before you leave.	• Complete the sign-up form in the library. • Obtain permission and a pass from your third-period core teacher to attend meetings on designated days at lunch. • Return to class on time after each meeting. • Prepare for each meeting by reading the assigned section and thinking about what you can contribute to the discussion. • Participate by sharing and listening at appropriate times. • Ask questions when you do not understand. Offer help or ideas when necessary. • Honor your commitment to the group by attending meetings regularly. • Leave your meeting space clean.

Developed by Lara Will, Chewning Middle School, Durham, North Carolina

book, and develop a list of questions to guide the discussion. The student facilitators met with the librarian once a week to discuss their book group's progress. In a school that had many reluctant readers, the librarian soon found that she had more students wanting to join a book club than she could accommodate.

CONCLUDING THOUGHTS

The ultimate goal of literacy instruction is not simply to improve reading scores, but to support African American youth as they become agents of change in their own lives. Simply modifying the texts that we use in our literacy instruction will not achieve this goal, but it is an imperative first step in the process. Equally important is engaging Black youth in meaningful discussions about texts. When we do this, we motivate youth to want to read, we stimulate their intellectual curiosity, and we help them connect literacy to their lives—to see that literacy has a purpose beyond the four walls of the school. As librarians, we are not limited by the restrictions of standards and tests. We can be proactive and bold, and engage Black youth in dialogue about pressing issues that matter in school, in their neighborhoods, and in society. In this way, we can help close not only the literacy gap, but more important, the life outcome gap.

NOTE

This chapter is based on two previously published articles: Rawson, C. R., & Hughes-Hassell, S. (2012), "Rethinking the texts we use in literacy instruction with adolescent African American males," *The ALAN Review* 39(3): 21–29; and Hughes-Hassell, S., Rawson, C., et al. (2012), "Librarians form a bridge to books to advance literacy," *Phi Delta Kappan*, 93(5): 17–22.

Make It Happen in Your Library

Use these enabling texts to get started:

Elementary Picture Books

Blue, R. (2009). *Ron's big mission.* New York: Dutton. [Biography]
Copeland, M. (2014). *Firebird.* New York: Putnam. [Realistic fiction]
Deedy, C. A. (2009). *14 cows for America.* Atlanta: Peachtree. [Biography]
Grimes, N. (1997). *It's raining laughter.* New York: Dial. [Poetry]
Myers, C. (2000). *Wings.* New York: Scholastic. [Fantasy]
Myers, W. D. (2009). *Looking like me.* New York: Egmont USA. [Poetry]
Pinkney, A. D. (2008). *Boycott blues: How Rosa Parks inspired a nation.* New York: Greenwillow. [Historical fiction]
Pinkney, A. D. (2010). *Sit-in: How four friends stood up by sitting down.* New York: Little, Brown. [Historical fiction]
Pinkney, B. (1997). *The adventures of Sparrowboy.* New York: Simon & Schuster. [Fantasy]
Robinson, S. (2009). *Testing the ice: A true story about Jackie Robinson.* New York: Scholastic. [Fictionalized biography]
Shange, N. (2004). *Ellington was not a street.* New York: Simon & Schuster. [Poetry]
Steptoe, J. (1997). *In daddy's arms I AM TALL: African-Americans celebrating fathers.* New York: Lee & Low Books. [Poetry]
Weatherford, C. B. (2005). *Freedom on the menu: The Greensboro sit-ins.* New York: Dial. [Historical fiction]
Woodson, J. (2001). *The other side.* New York, Putnam. [Realistic fiction]

Upper Elementary

Amato, M. *Invisible lines.* New York: Egmont USA, 2009. [Realistic fiction]
Bryan, A. (2009). *Words to my life's song.* New York: Atheneum. [Biography]
Curtis, C. P. *Bud, not Buddy.* New York: Delacorte, 1999. [Historical fiction]
Freedman, R. (2006). *Freedom walkers: The story of the Montgomery bus boycott.* New York: Holiday House. [Nonfiction]
Grimes, N. (1999). *My man blue.* New York: Dial. [Poetry]

Harris, T. E. (2014). *The perfect place*. New York: Putnam. [Realistic fiction]

Levine, E. S. (1993). *Freedom's children: Young civil rights activists tell their own stories*. New York: Putnam. [Biography]

McWhorter, D. (2004). *A dream of freedom: The civil rights movement from 1954 to 1968*. New York: Scholastic. [Nonfiction]

Myers, W. D. (1998). *Me, Mop, and the Moondance Kid*. New York: Delacorte. [Realistic fiction]

Smith, H. A. (2003). *The way a door closes*. New York: Henry Holt. [Novel in poems]

Williams-Garcia, R. (2010). *One crazy summer*. New York: Harper Collins. [Realistic fiction]

Williams-Garcia, R. (2014). *P.S. Be eleven*. New York: Harper Collins. [Realistic fiction]

Woods, B. (2014). *The blossoming universe of Violet Diamond*. New York: Penguin. [Realistic fiction]

Woodson, J. (2003). *Locomotion*. New York: G. P. Putnam's Sons. [Novel in poems]

Middle School

Adoff, A. (1997). *I am the darker brother: An anthology of modern poems by African-Americans*. New York: Simon Pulse. [Poetry]

Adoff, J. (2005). *Jimi & me*. New York: Hyperion/Jump at the Sun. [Historical fiction]

Alexander, K. (2014). *The crossover*. New York: Houghton Mifflin Harcourt. [Novel in poems]

Barnes, D. (2010). *We could be brothers*. New York: Scholastic. [Realistic fiction]

Davis, S., Jenkins, G., Hunt, R., & Draper, S. (2005). *We beat the street: How a friendship pact led to success*. New York: Dutton. [Nonfiction]

Flake, S. G. (1998). *The skin I'm in*. New York: Jump at the Sun/Hyperion. [Realistic fiction]

Grimes, N. (1998). *Jazmin's notebook*. New York: Dial. [Realistic fiction]

Grimes, N. (2005). *Dark sons*. Grand Rapids, MI: Zondervan. [Realistic fiction, poetry]

Hansen, J. (1986). *Yellow Bird & me*. New York: Clarion. [Realistic fiction]

Johnson, A. (2005). *The first part last*. New York: Simon Pulse. [Realistic fiction]

Lewis, J., & A. Aydin. (2013). *March: Book one*. New York: Top Shelf [Graphic novel]

Lewis, J., & A. Aydin. (2015). *March: Book two*. New York: Top Shelf [Graphic novel]

Magoon, K. (2010). *The rock and the river*. New York: Aladdin. [Historical fiction]

Myers, W. D. (2000). *145th Street: Short stories*. New York: Delacorte. [Short stories]

Myers, W. D. (2004). *Here in Harlem: Poems in many voices*. New York: Holiday House. [Poetry]

Neri, G. (2010). *Yummy: The last days of a Southside shorty*. New York: Lee & Low. [Graphic novel]

Pearsall, S. (2008). *All of the above*. Boston: Little Brown. [Realistic fiction]

Shenkin, S. (2014). *The Port Chicago 50: Mutiny and the fight for civil rights*. New York: Roaring Book Press. [Nonfiction]

Smith, S. L. (2009). *Flygirl*. New York: Putnam. [Historical fiction]

Reynolds, J. (2015). *When I was the greatest*. New York: Antheneum. [Realistic fiction]

Robinet, H. G. (2001). *Missing from Haymaker Square*. New York: Anthenum.[Historical fiction]

Watson, R. (2015). *This side of home*. New York: Bloomsbury. [Realistic fiction]

Woodson, J. (1995). *From the notebooks of Melanin Sun*. New York: Scholastic. [Realistic fiction]

Woodson, J. (2000). *Miracle's boys*. New York: Putnam. [Realistic fiction]

Woodson, J. (2002). *Hush*. New York: Putnam. [Realistic fiction]

Woodson, J. (2008). *After Tupac and D Foster*. New York: Putnam. [Realistic fiction]

Woodson, J. (2014). *Brown girl dreaming*. New York: Penguin. [Memoir]

High School

Binns, B. A. (2010). *Pull*. Lodi, NJ: WestSide Books. [Realistic fiction]

Flake, S. G. (2004). *Who am I without him? Short stories about girls and the boys in their lives*. New York: Jump at the Sun/Hyperion. [Realistic fiction]

Flake, S. G. (2010). *You don't even know me: Stories and poems about boys.* New York: Hyperion. [Poetry, short stories]

Franco, B. (Ed.) (2001). *You hear me: Poems and writings by teenage boys.* New York: Candlewick. [Anthology]

Freedom Writers. (1999). *Freedom writer's diary: How a teacher and 150 teens used writing to change themselves and the world around them.* New York: Broadway Books. [Nonfiction]

Grimes, N. (2002). *Bronx masquerade.* New York: Dial. [Realistic fiction]

Harper, H. (2006). *Letters to a young brother: MANifest your destiny.* New York: Gotham Books. [Nonfiction]

Hefler, A. (2006). *A graphic biography of Malcolm X.* New York: Hill & Wang. [Graphic novel]

Houston, J. (2005). *New boy.* Boston: Houghton Mifflin. [Historical fiction]

Lester, J. (1995). *Othello: A novel.* New York: Scholastic. [Retold Shakespeare]

Magoon, K. (2014). *How it went down.* New York: Henry Holt. [Realistic fiction]

Mitchell, D. (2014). *Freedom summer murders.* New York: Scholastic. [Nonfiction]

Myers, W. D. (2006). *Autobiography of my dead brother.* New York: Harper Collins. [Realistic fiction]

Myers, W. D. (2010). *Lockdown.* New York: Harper Collins. [Realistic fiction]

Reynolds, J., & Kiely, B. (2015). *All-American boys.* New York: Simon & Schuster. [Realistic fiction]

Shakur, T. (1999). *The rose that grew from concrete.* New York: MTV Books. [Poetry]

Volponi, P. (2005). *Black and White.* New York: Viking. [Realistic fiction]

6

Characteristics of Effective Library Services for African American Youth

Casey H. Rawson and Sandra Hughes-Hassell

What would it look like for a library to critically examine and retool itself with the goal of providing not only equitable, but also powerful and meaningful, library services for African American youth? Thus far, we have explored this question theoretically, in terms of research-based frameworks including Critical Race Theory (Chapter 1), culturally relevant pedagogy (Chapter 2), racial identity development (Chapter 3), voice and agency (Chapter 4), and enabling texts (Chapter 5). Within these chapters, we have endeavored to consider not only the models and theories themselves, but the "so what" of each research domain—in other words, what do, and could, these frameworks mean for school and public librarians and for the African American youth they serve?

This chapter bridges the theoretical frameworks and research findings presented in Chapters 1–5 with the exemplary practice chapters that follow by presenting a model of effective library services for African American youth. The model synthesizes the research presented in Part One of this book, findings from our own research studies, and insights from library practitioners, African American youth, administrators, policymakers, publishers, and authors. The initial version of this model emerged from the Bridge to Literacy summit held in Chapel Hill, North Carolina, in June 2012 and was informed by summit keynote speakers, panelists, and participants, as well as relevant literature. Since the summit, this model has been revised and expanded in light of new research and innovative programs and services implemented by summit attendees and others (some of which are highlighted in the second half of this book). The model, summarized in figures throughout this chapter, accounts for library space, resources, and programs, as well as for librarians and library administrators and policymakers. It introduces and frames the practice chapters that follow, which provide specific examples of these characteristics in action.

USING THIS CHAPTER

As you read this chapter and examine the model, think about your library or libraries: your space, your resources, your programming, your staff, your users, and the broader community. In which areas does your library already exhibit characteristics of effective services for African American youth? In which areas might there be room for improvement? Once you have answered these questions yourself, ask these same questions to others—staff members, administrators, community members, and most important, African American youth themselves. Consider doing a formal, collaborative assessment of your library's space, resources, instruction, programming, and staff (for an example of what this might look like, see the Culturally Responsive Library Walk document at http://bridgetolit.web.unc.edu/?page_id=842). But don't stop there—once you have assessed your library's current services to, for, and with African American youth, take actions to improve them.

Characteristics of Effective Library Space

While some library services have moved beyond the library building itself (for example, online library resources and classroom-based school library services), the library's physical space remains a primary locus for resources, programs, and services, and thus for connecting with African American youth. "Library buildings," writes Anthony Bernier (2010), "represent and manifest ideals about who counts and what activities matter in a community" (p. 114). Unfortunately, because youth space in libraries is often unwelcoming, undersized, or poorly designed (ibid.), the message being conveyed to many African American youth by their library spaces is that they do not count, and that their activities do not matter. Many African American youth view the library as an unwelcoming, even hostile, place, a situation that seriously limits the opportunities that librarians have to engage and build relationships with these young men and women (Kumasi, 2012).

Student panelists at the Bridge to Literacy summit described libraries as quiet, dull, intimidating spaces, associated (for some of them) with punishment for unsanctioned talking or moving around. In contrast, these young men described their ideal library as collaborative and social—a space that fosters exploration, communication, and innovation through features such as group work areas, movable furniture, and interactive technology. Their ideal library would offer opportunities and spaces for both quiet and noise, work and recreation, independence and collaboration. It would be a safe space, fostering a sense of not only physical, but also emotional and intellectual security.

Effective library spaces also reflect, respect, and celebrate cultural diversity (Young Adult Library Services Association, 2012). This goes beyond ensuring a diverse library collection; it also includes showcasing cultural diversity in the library's artwork and decor, highlighting diverse resources in displays, and including diverse resources on recommended reading lists (Kumasi, 2012). The library's virtual "space" should also reflect these ideals. In the same way that the physical library should allow for exploration and interaction, the virtual library should aim not just to provide African American youth with information, but also to help them and other users develop their own voice and a sense of agency. This might be accomplished by incorporating elements of personalization and customization to the library website, allowing and encouraging users to submit content for the site, and including social interaction within the library home page (such as the option to chat with a librarian) or via an established social network like Facebook. Ensuring that the library's virtual content is accessible via mobile phone is particularly important for reaching African American youth, as many of them and their families use mobile devices to access the Internet (Lenhart, Ling, Campbell, & Purcell, 2010).

Effective library spaces take the developmental and family needs of African American youth into account. Anthony Bernier (2010) points out that typically, teen spaces in libraries are located as far away as possible from the children's area and are often also isolated from adult areas of the library. This practice ignores the fact that many young children may be visiting the library with older (teen) siblings, unsupervised by parents, which, as you'll read in Chapter 11, is indeed often the case for African American youth who live in urban communities. It also deprives youth of a "unique intergenerational social experience" that might result from interaction with and observation of adults in a noncommercial, information-focused environment (Bernier, 2010, p. 114).

Taking existing research, summit data, and existing exemplary library spaces into account, we have identified eight characteristics of effective library spaces for African American youth (for more detail, see Table 6.1):

- Nurturing: Physical and digital library spaces foster exploration and engagement in a safe environment.
- Respectful: The layout, design, and decor of the library's youth spaces are age-appropriate (for example, the teen space contains adult- versus child-size furniture); the youth space does not subject users to constant surveillance.
- Responsive: Youth voices and needs are considered and their ideas incorporated wherever possible in the design, layout, and decor of the space.
- Flexible: Furniture, room dividers, and materials are moveable and can accommodate a variety of programming needs; youth are allowed and encouraged to change the space to suit their needs. The space includes or can be made to include areas for work and play, quiet and noise, independence and collaboration.
- Comfortable: The library space invites prolonged visits by supplying comfortable furnishings.
- Welcoming: The library's displays and other decor highlight or include youth of color and their interests.

- Expressive: Youth can contribute to the library space via personal expression—for example, by contributing writing to an online poetry wall or displaying artwork in the library's youth area.
- Engaging: The library space encourages youth to interact with library materials, library staff, and other youth without unnecessary barriers (for example, technology that is locked away behind a counter or youth librarian offices that are distant from the youth area of the library).

Characteristics of Effective Library Resources

Research from several disciplines has provided evidence for a number of barriers to equitable access to relevant, meaningful, and developmentally appropriate print and digital resources for African American youth. One such barrier is the relative scarcity of material published by and about African Americans. For example, of 3,500 children's books published in 2014, only 179 (5.1%) were about African Americans (Cooperative Children's Book Center, 2015). While

TABLE 6.1   Effective Library Space

Goal	Characteristics	Actions
Provide a welcoming physical and virtual place for African American youth to increase, explore, and express multiple literacies.	• Nurturing • Respectful • Responsive • Flexible • Comfortable • Welcoming • Expressive • Engaging	• Create space within the library for movement, group work, and noise, as well as quiet work. • Keep the library brightly lit. • Offer or allow food and drink. • Choose comfortable furniture. • Offer a media lab. • Change library displays often. • Display visual examples of a wide variety of readers. • Ensure that the library's virtual space is accessible (particularly on mobile devices), interactive, and useful. • Provide a forum for youth to offer suggestions for improving the library's space, collection, or services. • Ensure that the library is accessible to youth when they most need it (e.g., before and after school hours, or during the summer). • Consider whether the library space facilitates intergenerational exchanges among children, teens, and adults. • Ensure clear sight lines to allow for unobtrusive staff supervision.

youth can use texts featuring characters of different cultures and races as windows to access ideas and situations beyond their personal experience, it is also important that they are provided access to "mirror" texts, in which they see themselves reflected in meaningful and empowering ways (Edwards, McMillon, & Turner, 2010; Gangi, 2008). Such texts may be relatively rare, but numerous resources are available to help librarians find these titles; a number of them are linked from the summit webpage (http://bridgetolit.web .unc.edu/?page_id=399). Chapters 1 and 13 also provide additional resources for building diverse collections. Beyond simply collecting these resources, however, librarians can also join the national conversation surrounding the issue of diversity in youth publishing, by blogging, promoting and patronizing publishers who show a commitment to multicultural authors and texts, or participating in social network conversations such as the #WeNeedDiverseBooks campaign on Twitter.

Digital resources, including hardware, should also be a focus for libraries working to improve their services for African American youth. Student panelists at the Bridge to Literacy summit expressed their desire that libraries offer "technology for everyone," including touch-screen computers and televisions, tablets, e-readers, music devices, cameras, and video games, as well as the wireless Internet infrastructure to support such technology. All resources, both digital and print, should be carefully selected to serve the library's unique user population, keeping in mind that the African American youth in any given library community are individuals with unique perspectives and needs. Whenever possible, youth input should be solicited and taken seriously when making collection development decisions; this input should come not only from current library users, but also from nonusers who may feel the library has little to offer them. Meredith Schwartz (2013) suggested several ways to reach and engage these nonusers, including meeting them where they are (for African American youth, this might include schools, sporting events, shopping centers, parks, and churches, to name only a few); sending out physical mail; and identifying a community insider who can serve as an ambassador for your library.

We have identified five characteristics of effective library resources for African American youth (for more detail, see Table 6.2):

- Relevant: They speak to the lives and needs of African American youth and reflect elements of their lived experiences.
- Meaningful: They have potential to be significant in the lives and literacy journeys of African American youth.
- Developmentally appropriate: Resources are carefully selected not only for reading level or text complexity, but also for appropriateness of the content for the targeted age level, *with high expectations* (see Chapter 1).
- Enabling: Resources are empowering; they encourage African American youth to take action in their own lives and communities (see Chapter 5).
- Provide counterstories: Resources highlight narratives that are counter to the prevailing stereotypes of African American youth (see Chapters 1, 4).

TABLE 6.2   Effective Library Resources

Goal	Characteristics	Actions
Nurture the resolve of African American youth; enable them to reconcile their multiple identities and to reimagine their place in the world.	• Relevant • Meaningful • Developmentally appropriate • Enabling • Provide counterstories	• Work with youth, parents, teachers, and administrators to select rich and enabling resources. • Write publishers to demand that they produce diverse texts. • Be intentional in recommending texts to African American youth. • Ensure that the collection development policy includes criteria for evaluating and selecting culturally relevant and enabling texts. • Feature culturally relevant materials in library displays, booktalks, and recommended reading lists. • Invest in technology (such as laptops, e-readers, and tablets) that youth can check out. • For school libraries, allow materials to be checked out over school breaks and in the summer. • Think beyond print and digital resources to include human resources in the community, such as civic and business leaders, artists, writers, etc. • Provide resources that facilitate student expression and cultivation of voice: blogging platforms, video and audio recording and editing software, word processing tools, etc.

Characteristics of Effective Library Programming

The National Council of Teachers of English (NCTE) has adopted a definition of literacy that goes well beyond traditional reading and writing to reflect the idea that students must now develop proficiency and fluency with a wide variety of tools for a wide variety of purposes. The NCTE definition holds that literacy is "inextricably linked with particular histories, life possibilities, and social trajectories of individuals and groups," and that to be a literate person, one must be able to "build intentional cross-cultural connections and relationships with others so to pose and solve problems collaboratively and strengthen independent thought" (National Council of Teachers of English, 2013). Effective library programs for African American youth recognize the personal, interpersonal, and cultural elements of literacy development and seek to enable

African American youth to see the value of literacy skills as a force for positive change in their daily lives, as discussed in Chapters 4 and 5.

To accomplish this, effective library programs honor and encourage the voices of African American youth by seeking and accepting their input regarding the library's programs and by giving them access to multiple tools and outlets for self-expression, such as music production, blogging, poetry slams, and open-mic nights. Effective programs are also collaborative, allowing African American youth and other young people to engage with and learn from one another, as well as from teachers, mentors, and other adults, to build the type of cross-cultural connections advocated by NCTE. Additionally, effective library programs set and communicate high expectations of success for African American youth. Dr. Ernest Morrell, one of the summit's keynote speakers, noted, "[I]f you do not expect success, they will not be motivated. Expect excellence, and excellence is what you will receive in return" (Hughes-Hassell et al., 2012, p. 16).

Effective library programs for African American youth also focus on families. Cabrera (2013) summarized the positive role that family relationships can have on the development of children and youth of color. Strong family relationships can support children in developing social competence, academic skills, self-esteem, and a positive outlook on their own race and culture that can protect them from some negative effects of prejudice and discrimination. Like all parents, African American parents and caregivers want their children to succeed. However, some African American parents and caregivers may lack literacy skills themselves or may have had negative experiences with schools. Responsive libraries recognize this and provide family and adult literacy programs in addition to programs aimed specifically at youth.

We have identified eight characteristics of effective library programming for African American youth (for more detail, see Table 6.3):

- Asset-based: Programming starts from and builds on the strengths of African American youth and their families and communities.
- Culturally relevant: Programming resonates with African American youth by incorporating elements of African American culture, youth culture, and popular culture (see Chapter 2).
- Challenging: Programming encourages youth to think critically and provides them with scaffolding to build on their existing skills and knowledge; it is based on high expectations for youth participants.
- Honors and promotes voice: Programming considers and integrates feedback from and opinions of African American youth; programming provides opportunities for African American youth to express themselves (see Chapter 4).
- Develops agency: Programming empowers African American youth to critically examine their local, national, and global communities and to take action to improve these communities and/or their own lives (see Chapter 4).
- Engaging: Programming is fun; it has both breadth (exposing youth to many different ideas) and depth (encouraging them to dive into ideas that are of personal interest).

- Authentic and relevant: Programming speaks to the lives and needs of African American youth and reflects elements of their lived experiences.
- Fosters community: Programming encourages relationship building among youth of all backgrounds, their families, and the wider community in which they live; programming connects youth to mentors.

Characteristics of Effective Library Instruction

Over the past several decades, the role of the school librarian has expanded to include a greater emphasis on teaching and learning, especially through collaboration with classroom teachers. As instructors, school librarians have the opportunity to participate directly in the literacy education of African American youth. Public librarians may also enact an instructional role to supplement, complement, or extend the literacy education offered in local schools. Effective library instruction employs asset-based instructional strategies that build on

TABLE 6.3   Effective Library Programming

Goal	Characteristics	Actions
Connect literacy and learning to the real world; support the development of multiple literacies; enable African American youth to act in their own lives and communities.	• Asset-based • Culturally relevant • Challenging • Honors and promotes voice • Develops agency • Engaging • Authentic and relevant • Fosters community	• Develop programming that cultivates youth voices (e.g., spoken-word performances, video contests). • Include programming specifically for African American youth. • Allow students to work socially and collaboratively. • Facilitate book discussions and other programs that center on essential questions of identity, racism, power, etc. • Connect programming to local concerns and issues. • Invite African American authors to speak, and provide opportunities during their visit for youth to interact with them. • Start or host a mentoring program. • Provide programs for families, keeping in mind the transportation and child-care needs and work schedules of parents. • Develop programs collaboratively with youth, parents, teachers, and other community members. • Set high expectations. • Incorporate pop culture, movement, rhythm or dance.

the strengths of African American students and lead to improved academic achievement, increased resiliency, and agency among these and all students. Boykin (2013) described asset-based instruction this way:

> Rather than schools functioning to identify and sort talent, their chief responsibility would be to develop talent. This capacity promotion stance would discern diversity in students' backgrounds and lived experiences not as reasons for their failure, but as sources from which to glean their assets. These assets would then be used to promote students to high-level academic outcomes. And when such assets are not readily available, the press is then to create assets for such students in the academic setting. (p. 14)

One model that facilitates asset-based instruction is Connected Learning, developed by Mimi Ito and her colleagues at the Digital Media and Learning Research Hub (also discussed in Chapter 4). Connected Learning is a framework for instruction that occurs at the intersection of students' interests, peer culture, and academic achievement. It emphasizes teaching and learning that is socially embedded, interest-driven, and oriented toward educational, economic, or political opportunity. One specific goal of Connected Learning is to "create more connections with non-dominant youth, drawing from capacities of diverse communities" (Ito et al., 2013, p. 4). Connected Learning is meant to bridge in-school and out-of-school learning, and thus could be used by school or public librarians as a framework for their instructional interactions with African American youth.

At the summit, Dr. Ernest Morrell discussed a number of projects that he has led or participated in with African American youth that illustrate some of the key principles of Connected Learning. For example, Morrell described his work with high school teens in California, who were introduced to rigorous research and media production techniques through an extensive project in which the teens investigated inequity within their local school system. The teens surveyed and interviewed local residents, searched statistical databases, learned filmmaking techniques, created Microsoft PowerPoint presentations and written reports that were delivered to city officials, and traveled in their community to spread the word about the inequity that they uncovered. This project was culturally relevant, authentic, cooperative, and interactive; fostered critical thinking; and set high expectations for the students. As emphasized by the Connected Learning model, the project was socially embedded into students' local communities, interest driven, and oriented toward educational, economic, and political opportunities for change.

In total, we have identified eight characteristics of effective library instruction for African American youth (for more details, see Table 6.4):

- Asset-based: It starts from and builds on the strengths of African American youth and their families and communities.
- Incorporates culturally relevant pedagogy: It carefully considers best practices for culturally relevant pedagogy in its design, implementation, and evaluation (see Chapter 2).
- Sets high expectations: Instruction challenges African American youth while providing them with the necessary scaffolding to reach instructor goals.

- Fosters agency: Instruction empowers African American youth to critically examine their local, national, and global communities and to take action to improve these communities and their own lives.
- Requires critical thinking: Instruction demands that students actively and rigorously evaluate, synthesize, and apply information before reaching conclusions.
- Authentic and relevant: Instruction speaks to the lives and needs of African American youth and reflects elements of their lived experiences.
- Cooperative, communal, and interactive: Instruction facilitates interaction and collaboration among youth, their instructors, and the broader community; instruction connects youth to mentors.
- Collaboratively developed: Instruction is planned, implemented, and assessed by school librarians working collaboratively with classroom teachers and other educational service providers in schools (e.g., counselors, special education teachers, or literacy coaches); public librarians collaborate with community agencies (e.g., social workers, universities, or local spoken-word groups) and authors/illustrators to plan, implement, and assess instruction.

TABLE 6.4 Effective Library Instruction

Goal	Characteristics	Actions
Employ asset-based instructional strategies and behaviors that build on the strengths and interests of African American students and that lead to improved academic achievement, increased resiliency, and agency.	• Asset-based • Incorporates culturally relevant pedagogy • Sets high expectations • Fosters agency • Requires critical thinking • Authentic and relevant • Cooperative, communal, and interactive • Collaboratively developed	• Emphasize writing as an essential element of literacy. • Create and sustain a dialogue between African American youth and their instructors. Be open to their honest evaluations. • Communicate high expectations to African American youth. • Gather data about youths' home lives and identify funds of knowledge that can be built on when developing instruction. • Utilize cooperative and collaborative groups and allow social interaction among youth participants. • Include culturally relevant images, examples, and texts in instruction. • Provide opportunities for youth to interact with African American professionals such as lawyers, doctors, and scientists, either face to face or virtually. • Involve parents in library instruction. • Situate instruction in local contexts. • Incorporate pop culture, movement, rhythm, or dance.

Characteristics of Effective Librarians

Describing their ideal library, the student panelists at the Bridge to Literacy summit stated that they want "happy, happy, happy librarians, not the grumpy ones"; "librarians who want to help, who are well informed and know how to answer your questions"; "librarians you can talk to and who want to talk to you"; and "librarians who aren't out to get us." Librarians who are effective in addressing the literacy needs of African American youth are caring, committed, and culturally competent. They reject the deficit-oriented perspective that represents the culture, race, language, and other characteristics of African American youth as limitations, and they similarly reject stereotypical views of African American youth that deny their individuality. Although the data on the need for improved literacy services to African American youth are clear, many communities may resist shifting their focus to this underserved group, and therefore effective librarians must be courageous in their advocacy for these children and teens and must fully embrace their responsibility to work with African American youth and their families. They engage in ongoing and critical evaluation of their library's resources, services, and programs, and use this data to develop responsive services and to advocate for additional resources—both monetary and human.

We have identified nine characteristics of effective librarians serving African American youth (for more detail, see Table 6.5):

- Culturally competent: Librarians are knowledgeable about their own cultural backgrounds and biases and the cultures of the youth that they serve.
- Accommodating of culture-based learning preferences: Librarians carefully consider their knowledge of African American youth culture when designing library programming or instruction, structuring or designing library space, and selecting library resources.
- Caring: Librarians genuinely care for African American youth as individuals and convey that care to them in professionally appropriate ways.
- Affirming: Librarians seek out and recognize the individual and collective gifts and talents of African American youth.
- Committed: Librarians are dedicated to closing achievement gaps and improving the lives of African American youth.
- Accountable: Librarians welcome positive and critical feedback from peers, administrators, and African American youth; they critically reflect on their own practice.
- Courageous: Librarians are willing to speak out for African American youth personally and professionally and to advocate actively for improved library services for these youth.
- Proactive: Librarians take action on issues and challenges related to African American youth without waiting for systemic change to happen first.
- Collaborative: Librarians recognize that they cannot effect systemic change for African American youth on their own; they work with other librarians, parents, educators, administrators, community members and organizations, and youth to plan for and provide library resources, programs, and services.

TABLE 6.5 Effective Librarians

Goal	Characteristics	Actions
Interact with African American youth as individuals; cultivate their voice and develop their agency.	• Culturally competent • Accommodating of culture-based learning preferences • Caring • Affirming • Committed • Accountable • Courageous • Proactive • Collaborative	• Examine your own practice and continually self-reflect. • Set high expectations. • Involve African American youth in library decision making. • Get involved in the community surrounding your library by attending events, reading community newspapers, attending school board meetings, etc. • Serve on diversity teams (at the library, school, or district/system level). • Participate in a Professional Learning Network–focused on equity; seek out additional professional development opportunities related to diversity • Join professional associations focused on diversity and equity, such as the Black Caucus of the American Library Association (BCALA) • Seek out and apply for grant money to be used specifically for African American youth. • Stay abreast of current research and best practices. • Conduct action research within your library; publish the results. • Maintain up-to-date community analysis documents. • Continually seek out new collaborative partnerships with a variety of stakeholders.

Characteristics of Effective Administrators and Policymakers

Many African American youth live in communities where school and public libraries are underfunded, with minimal collections and few full-time youth services librarians. For example, in New York City, where the public library system is the largest single provider of free broadband access in the city, circulation rose 59 percent and program attendance rose 40 percent from 2002 to 2011 (Center for an Urban Future, 2013). Young adults accounted for much of this increase, with teen attendance rising by 77 percent. However, over this same time period, city funding for public libraries fell by 8 percent. For the 2013–2014 school year, the Public School District of Philadelphia, with a total student enrollment of more than 150,000, employed only 15 school librarians (Segal,

2013). In order to address this issue of inequitable access to library services, resources, and staff, administrators and policymakers must be willing to make meeting the needs of African American youth a priority.

Effective library administrators and policymakers work to ensure adequate and equitable funding and employ dedicated and culturally competent staff members who are knowledgeable about the needs of African American youth and committed to meeting those needs. They also examine library policies to ensure that they are respectful of the needs and lived experiences of African American youth. As Dr. Morrell pointed out in his keynote address at the summit, many of the schools and libraries attended by African American youth "have become places where everybody is surveillanced [sic], places where there is punishment, where they are frisked before they walk onto campus" (Hughes-Hassell et al., 2012, p. 12). Effective administrators and policymakers recognize that this type of atmosphere is unwelcoming and counterproductive to literacy development goals. Instead, policies should be developed that emphasize and facilitate inclusion and community building. Administrators should ensure that all library staff members are provided with ongoing professional development to help them implement these policies, including training on the literacy needs of African American youth, cultural competence, social justice, collaboration, and evidence-based practice.

Administrators and policymakers may also play important roles in establishing partnerships with other agencies in their communities who are also working to address the literacy needs of African American youth. These agencies might include, but are not limited to, other schools or libraries, government agencies, religious organizations, local businesses, media outlets, and higher-education institutions. Finally, effective policymakers collect or synthesize data relating to school and public library programs in their communities and use that data to advocate at the local, state, and national levels for the urgent need to support and fund these programs.

We have identified five characteristics of effective library administrators serving African American youth (for more detail, see Table 6.6):

- Committed: Effective administrators are dedicated to identifying and addressing issues of inequity in the systems that they manage.
- Courageous: Effective administrators are willing to speak out for African American youth personally and professionally, and to advocate actively for improved library services for these youth.
- Proactive: Effective administrators take action on issues and challenges related to African American youth without waiting for systemic change to happen first.
- Attentive to and knowledgeable about the communities that they serve: Effective administrators gather rich qualitative and quantitative data about the communities that they serve, update this data continually, and develop and maintain personal connections to the community.
- Collaborative: Effective administrators work with a wide variety of other individuals and organizations to effect broad, systemic change and to implement innovative programs and services for African American youth.

TABLE 6.6   Effective Library Administrators

Goal	Characteristics	Actions
Provide the necessary infrastructure for developing and delivering high-quality library services to African American youth.	• Committed • Courageous • Proactive • Attentive to and knowledgeable about the communities that they serve • Collaborative	• Hire dedicated and caring staff. • Provide equitable funding. • Require research-based practices. • Develop culturally-responsive policy. • Collect quantitative and qualitative data about the communities served by the library system and make that data accessible to librarians. • Foster community partnerships. • Provide ongoing professional development. • Engage in courageous conversations. • Advocate at the local, state, and national levels.

CONCLUDING THOUGHTS

A library that effectively serves African American youth is one that looks holistically at its resources, programming, instruction, space, and staff in light of academic research findings, local community analysis and data collection, and input from youth themselves. Library resources cannot inspire African American youth on their own; they must be promoted, circulated, and mediated by culturally competent librarians. Engaging, culturally responsive library programs will not attract youth and their families if the library space is unwelcoming or inaccessible (for example, because library policies are restrictive). Collaborative, culturally responsive instruction will not become ingrained into school culture without endorsement and material support from administrators. While we have presented this model in separate categories in this chapter, it is important to note that all these categories—space, librarians, resources, programs, instruction, and library administration—intertwine with and rely upon each other. When you use this model to assess and set goals for your own library, ask yourself where these categories overlap and form links in your library and community.

The action examples provided in this model should be seen as jumping-off points for your own exploration of how best to transform your own practice, space, resources, and services. As discussed in previous chapters, and as illustrated by the chapters in Part Two of this book, the most powerful actions that you can take are local actions, created for *and* with the specific youth served by your library, taking into account their unique assets and challenges and the resources available in your library and community. Involving African American youth in the assessment and improvement of your library's space, resources, services, and programs is the best way to ensure that any changes that you make are truly in response to their needs, their voices, and their lived experiences.

NOTE

Portions of this chapter were first published in Hughes-Hassell, S., Kumasi, K., Rawson, C. H., and Hitson, A. (2012). *Building a bridge to literacy for African American male youth: A call to action for the library community.* Unpublished manuscript, School of Information and Library Science, University of North Carolina at Chapel Hill, United States. Retrieved from https://bridgetolit.web.unc.edu/?page_id=12.

Part II

Focus on Practice

7

Black Storytime: Empowering Children, Growing Communities

Kirby McCurtis

Connecting Research to Practice

As you read this chapter, look for the following characteristics of effective library services for African American youth:

- **Programming**—Culturally relevant, fosters community, challenging, engaging
- **Librarians**—Accommodating of culture-based learning practices, committed, caring, courageous
- **Resources**—Relevant, authentic, provide counterstories
- **Administrators/policymakers**—Courageous, proactive

Black Storytime at Multnomah County Library District (MCL), headquartered in Portland, Oregon, is a fun way to experience and celebrate African and African American culture at the library. Our storytime incorporates stories, music and movement, rhymes, and activities to help families build their children's early literacy skills, as well as promoting positive cultural images in order to affirm children's self-esteem and support growth of their Black identity. The goals are to culturally engage and support the African American community, support families as they prepare their children for school success, and to bring neighbors together. Former MCL Youth Services Director Ellen Fader and current Every Child Initiative Program Supervisor Renea Arnold were the driving forces behind Black Storytime, but the program idea initially came from the community.

HISTORICAL CONTEXT: RACE, POWER, AND PRIVILEGE IN OREGON

To understand better the reason such a program is needed here in Oregon, we will need to take a history detour. The first non–Native American settlers in Oregon were fur traders, trappers, missionaries, and eventually migrants from Missouri. Predominately White, these settlers brought prejudice with them and turned it into law, thus making sure that African Americans would avoid the region. In 1844, the first exclusion law directed at African Americans was passed by the provisional government of Oregon; "the temporary governing political structure set up by the first American settlers to reach the region over the Oregon Trail. This first law included a ban on slavery and a requirement that slave-owners free their slaves. African Americans who remained in Oregon after their freedom was granted, however, would be whip-lashed and expelled. If they were caught again in the Territory within six months, the punishment would be repeated" (McLagan, n.d, para. 3). While the new settlers did not favor slavery, it turned out that they were not in favor of inclusion either. This law was repealed in 1845, but in 1849, another exclusion law was passed. This allowed Black residents currently in Oregon to stay but prohibited new African American immigrants from settling in the territory (McLagan, n.d). In 1857, a new constitution was written due to the territory's impending statehood, and a third exclusion clause was included. New immigration was again prohibited, and also African Americans could no longer own real estate or enter into contracts. They were also denied the right to sue in court (McLagan, n.d). The law was repealed in 1927, but not removed from the Oregon Constitution until 2001 by legislators. It should be noted that Oregon was the only free state admitted to the Union with an exclusion clause in its constitution (McLagan, n.d). Oregonians made it clear from the beginning that Black people were not welcome.

In spite of this hostile environment, small waves of African Americans did eventually migrate to Oregon for job opportunities, beginning with the completion of the Transcontinental Railroad. Migration surged during two distinct periods, as African Americans found work first with the railroad industry in the 1880s, and then at the shipyards in the 1940s (Hottman, 2013). Oregon's adherence to Jim Crow laws "mandating 'separate but equal' status for Black Americans prevented African American residents from using existing services, so as the Black community grew, entrepreneurs built their own network of services, from barber shops to restaurants" (Hottman, 2013). Redlining, the "discriminatory pattern of disinvestment and obstructive lending practices that act as an impediment to home ownership among African Americans and other people of color" (Gaspaire, n.d., para. 1), kept African Americans in the community of Albina. For a time, residents were able to turn discrimination into something positive, building a small, close-knit community that flourished. World War II brought the need for more laborers, and with White young men drafted to fight in the war, African American workers were recruited. The number of African Americans in the Portland area tripled in size rapidly, but there was no place for these new workers to live due to restrictions about where Black residents could live and Albina being too small to house these new workers (Geilig, 2015). Unlike in most cities affected by war industry, the housing authority in Portland did not build public housing for this new influx of workers. Shipbuilding magnate Henry Kaiser's answer was Vanport, a temporary housing structure outside the city's limits. Vanport was built in 110 days using federal funds and cheap materials; it quickly became the second-largest city in Oregon, with almost 40,000 people living there, including at least 6,000 African Americans (McGregor, 2003).

Although many African American workers left Portland as shipyards were shuttered after the war, those who remained could not find new housing—Black residents still could not purchase homes in most parts of the state. People living in Vanport remained in the housing complex, but shoddy construction and unemployment turned the "city" into a slum. In 1948, on Memorial Day, the Columbia River flooded through a dike, washing away Vanport and leaving 18,000 people homeless, 25 percent of whom were African American (McGregor, 2003). With nowhere left to go, the majority were forced to find shelter in Albina. Overcrowding, chronic unemployment, and institutionalized racism started to chip away at the small Black district.

Smithsonian Magazine reports, "By the 1960s, four out of five Black Portlanders lived in Albina—an area that would suffer years of disinvestment and backhanded home-lending practices by city officials. By the 1980s, the median value for a home in Albina was 58 percent below the city's average, and the neighborhood became best known as a hotbed of gang violence and drug dealing" (Gellig, 2015). Urban renewal programs began in the historic Black neighborhoods, followed by White takeover. Gentrification in Portland has been so rapid that the original community is no longer recognizable. Research conducted by the local newspaper *The Oregonian* finds that the core of the city—particularly the inner northeast—has become significantly Whiter since 2000. While in 2000, there were 10 census tracts in Albina that were majority Black, in 2010, there are none (Hannah-Jones, 2011). The safe culture space has disappeared. Black businesses are gone, Black churches see dwindling membership, majority-Black schools have been closed, and the community at large is displaced. The African Americans who left "didn't move to nicer areas. Pushed out by gentrification, most settled on the city's eastern edges, according to the census data, where the sidewalks, grocery stores, and parks grow sparse, and access to public transit is limited. As a result, the part of Portland famous for its livability—for charming shops and easy transit, walkable streets and abundant bike paths—increasingly belongs to affluent whites" (Hannah-Jones, 2011).

With this historical context and an understanding of the history of race-based policies designed to benefit only Whites, it is easy to understand why few African Americans choose to call Oregon home today. Currently, just 2 percent of Oregonians are Black; and 6 percent of the residents of Multnomah County, Oregon's most populous county and home to Portland, are Black.

Youth Voices

Black Storytime is our Saturday morning ritual. We plan our day around it. We've been going since Davide was two. Now, every time I see my 4-and-a-½-year-old point to the little boy in one of his books he got to take home from Black Storytime and say, "Mommy, is that me? He looks like me!" I smile as big as he does. I think to myself, finally, maybe he won't have to constantly convince himself that being Black and at a mostly White school, White neighborhood, and White city is "OK." Instead, he will know as innately as he knows how to run or play, that he is valuable, he is beautiful, and he is worthy of being seen and heard. Just like the kids [in] his books. I just love it. And for my 2-year old, who is the only black child in his daycare, Black Storytime is huge for us. It's his time to connect with people little and big who come in all shades and all hair types. For once he is not the different one. He's just his perfect little self. And he LOVES books.
—Raina Croff Mbaye

I was so relieved to find people that looked like my daughter at a public storytime. Kirby's leadership during storytime is super interactive and nurturing—it makes even the shyest kid smile and want to participate. The collection of FREE children's books with black and brown faces and main characters, are affirming; and everything I always wished for as a child, myself.

—Tiffany Kirkpatrick

IMPETUS FOR THE PROGRAM

A number of agencies have produced and continue to update reports calling for action to improve policies toward, and increase services to, Black Portlanders (see the Urban League's State of Black Oregon, Coalition of Communities of Color's An Unsettling Report, and Ifanyi Bell's essay and video). In 2010, responding to a series of reports issued about Black students' graduation rates and the social and economic health of Black families in Multnomah County, the library set out to make a targeted effort to help get children ready for school and for a lifetime of success. MCL used a Library Services and Technology Act (LSTA) grant to perform an in-depth community assessment project focusing on the achievement gap in African American children. The goal of the project, Preparing African American Children for Kindergarten, was to gather information to develop a community-driven, culturally appropriate, and effective action plan to help African American children be ready to learn to read by the time they enter kindergarten. There were three key recommendations:

- Design and implement an innovative **community engagement-pilot project** in collaboration with one or more African American community organizations.
- Enhance outreach efforts to increase awareness of and participation in current library programs supporting the efforts of African American families to prepare their children for school.

- Implement systems change strategies to reduce or remove structural barriers that prevent African American families from realizing the full benefit of library programs designed to support school success. (Jones, Sohl, and Woodward, 2011)

The recommendations were developed with input from African American parents and grandparents, community-based service providers, government officials, business and foundation leaders, and library staff, managers, and supervisors. An advisory committee played a key role in processing input and advising the consultant team throughout the development of the recommendations. Each recommendation included strategies for the library and a call for some form of early literacy-based programming for young children and their caregivers. With this feedback, Black Storytime was born.

Six months after the report was released, I was recruited and hired, becoming the second person—and first youth librarian—at MCL to have a special designation on my position that focuses on the need for specific outreach and program development targeted to attract those in the African and African American communities. The designation, called Knowledge, Skills, and Abilities (KSA), is one strategy that MCL identified in 2005 to place on specific positions. This allowed MCL to focus on recruiting and hiring staff that have specific knowledge, skills, and a passion for providing linguistically and culturally specific services. During my interviews for this unique position, I was asked what a storytime for African Americans would look like; little did I know when I answered that many of the aspects I highlighted were similar to the recommendations from community members.

Planning the Storytimes

With no standard or template for Black Storytime already in existence, Youth Services Director Ellen Fader gave me the freedom to create. She identified an age group (0 to 6 years old) and set a launch date that gave me about six months to design and execute the plan. My planning process involved three sets of information—my personal style and experience, recommendations from the community, and feedback from a limited-duration internal task force that was organized prior to my arrival. Knowing that I needed to be comfortable and have fun in order for the program to be successful, I knew I wanted to play on my strengths and the things I enjoy most during storytime: music, movement, and interactive storytelling. I also wanted to build on research about developing culturally responsive programming for African American youth. Notable strategies from community input, as listed in the final grant report (Jones, Sohl, & Woodward, 2011), include:

- developing and promoting explicitly Black culture-focused storytime and programs at libraries, including program activities that engage children and families through movement, music, dance, and art (p. 13);
- redesigning children's spaces within libraries to include space for fantasy play, dress up, and hands-on manipulative activities (p. 14);
- providing tips on how to teach your child while doing everyday activities such as shopping, cooking, driving, or getting ready for school (p. 8);

- scheduling parent/child-focused events in the evening or on week-ends, as well as during weekday times (p. 13); and
- further developing early childhood and primary-aged collections to include more "cool things to read," including sports, pop culture, and African American culture, with special emphasis on items of interest to boys and men (p. 14).

Thinking about all of these factors, I set five goals for the program:

1. Books can be a mirror or a window. During each storytime session, I want Black participants to see themselves in the books.
2. After hearing about or attending Black Storytime, displaced Black Port-landers will begin to see my branch library as a resource hub for the Black community in East Portland.
3. Black neighbors will have an additional community space to connect with each other.
4. Non-Black attendees will recognize the value and beauty of Black culture.
5. Participants will have fun.

Next, the material selection began.

Choosing Books to Share During Storytime

The community input suggestion about collection development prompted me to investigate the library catalog, in an attempt to identify gaps. Prior to start-ing at MCL, I was responsible for youth and teen collection development for a large system and worked to include titles that would reflect all my young patrons. I knew about the low number of books written by and about African Americans from resources such as the Cooperative Children's Book Center (https://ccbc.education.wisc.edu/). At MCL, I found a significant collection of items with an African American cultural focus, thanks to great librarians and a healthy materials budget. However, it is not easy for patrons to find these things within an overall collection of millions of items, so one of my goals was to find ways to highlight our rich collection.

Although I needed to be sure that Black Storytime would expose families to the quality literature that the library already owned, I felt the need to set par-ameters. I decided I would not share any books about slavery or books with racism and oppression as sole themes during storytime. While this informa-tion is important for understanding Black history and the Black experience in the United States, I did not want to push my beliefs about at what age to have these conversations with children. In addition, I wanted to include titles that focused on positive, empowering events and characters. Unfortunately, those guidelines drastically diminished my material selection. I knew there were many picture books about the Civil Rights movement, but looking at my pile of "not a good fit for storytime" books was truly alarming. I was forced to widen my scope to include books that feature a multiracial cast of characters and books without humans. For books about animals or food, I knew the importance of

FIGURE 7.1   Storytime Favorites

Allen, Kathryn Madeline. *A kiss means I love you.* Chicago: Albert Whitman, 2012.

Isadora, Rachel. *Peekaboo morning.* New York: G. P. Putnam's Sons, 2008.

Lewis, Kevin. *Chugga chugga choo choo.* New York: Hyperion Books for Children, 1999.

Pinkney, Sandra L. *Shades of Black.* New York: Scholastic, 2000.

Hughes, Langston. *My people.* Photographs by Charles R. Smith, Jr. New York: Atheneum Books for Young Readers, 2009.

Tarpley, Natasha Anastasia. *I love my hair!* Boston: Little, Brown, 1998.

Schofield-Morrison, Connie. *I got the rhythm.* New York: Bloomsbury, 2014.

Wilson-Max, Ken. *Where's Lenny.* London: Frances Lincoln Children's Books, 2013.

Marsalis, Wynton. *Squeak, rumble, whomp! Whomp! Whomp!* Somerville, MA: Candlewick, 2012.

Marley, Cedella. *Every Little Thing.* San Francisco: Chronicle Books, 2012

approaching storytime with a cultural sensitivity. I would need to avoid books that included negative stereotypes. Weekly storytime book selection is still a laborious process because there are just not enough books published featuring Black children with "normal" childhood experiences, but I stick to this list: books about Black or Brown children; books with a multiracial cast of characters; books by Black authors or illustrators; animal books; books about inanimate objects; and books about nature. I have also started adapting longer books for storytime depending on the participants that week, or simply putting new and noteworthy titles on a table for families to check out and explore on their own. Figure 7.1 shows a list of storytime favorites.

Adding Music, Rhymes, and Movement

An internal task force compiled a list of youth CDs that the library owned that had an African American cultural focus. Classics from Ella Jenkins and Sweet Honey in the Rock were included in this list; I added artists that I loved, including Aaron Nigel Smith and Ziggy Marley, whose work I had used successfully in past storytimes. I also looked for songs that could be used with felt pieces to add the hands on elements the community suggested. Popular on many of the CDs were call-and-response songs, and this helped me quickly create a playlist for rhymes. While I wanted to include traditional rhymes that many families are familiar with, I wanted to take action rhymes and fingerplay to a new level by incorporating classics from the Black community that might not ordinarily fall into this category. "Miss Mary Mack" and "Loop de Loop" are two rhymes that immediately came to mind.

Planning for movement was by far the easiest and most fun thing to do. Music and dance are important to Black culture, and I had no doubt that this storytime group would be ready to get up and move! I made a playlist with songs that I normally did in storytime, added a few that involved circle work to promote the neighbor interactions, and then sought out traditional African American favorites, African chants, and Caribbean dance numbers for children. Putamayo had several great albums that I was able to incorporate. Instruments and props were ordered so that the types of movement in each storytime could be varied. The Black Storytime prop collection now includes beanbags, bells, small drums, a parachute, rhythm sticks, sandpaper blocks, scarves, shakers, and a shekere (a percussion instrument made from a hollow gourd).

Organizing Storytime

In many ways, Black Storytime looks like the traditional storytimes we already offer at our libraries. I deliver early literacy messages to parents and caregivers based on Every Child Ready to Read guidelines, I answer questions about books and library services and model different ways to interest and engage children in books and reading. Unique to Black Storytime are the selection of materials that I share and the culturally responsive approach I take to planning, organizing, and delivering storytime. I tailor early literacy messages and use culturally appropriate examples and activity suggestions (see Figure 7.2).

Black Storytime is a family storytime, so the age range varies widely. I share three books each storytime—two that I read aloud, and one board book that each family reads to their little one, lapsit style. We have a rotating collection of board books that are shared among the branch locations that offer Black Storytime. If I am sharing a book that does not have children of color, but instead has animals or imaginary creatures, I try to make the story interactive with flannel sets or individual participation activities like clothespin wheels. This allows children to feel a part of the storytelling experience and promotes the early literacy practice play in a way that is an enjoyable learning experience for both adults and children.

In addition to books, I typically share five rhymes or fingerplays and five songs, at least two with props. Studies have made headlines recently showing that Black students are more likely to be disciplined and suspended in school, as early as preschool. When picking movement activities, in addition to selecting culturally appropriate music, I include at least one song and one rhyme that work on executive function and self-regulation. If I can help children get prepared for school by practicing listening, paying attention to directions, and sitting, then storytime is helping them be more successful in school and hopefully will prevent unnecessary discipline that could later lead to dropout.

The Program Launch

MCL launched Black Storytime as a pilot program at Midland Library on June 23, 2012, with a plan to add two additional locations by fall. The marketing plan had a number of different components, including print and media.

FIGURE 7.2   Sample Books, Activities, and Parent Messages

Book: *Jazz on a Saturday Night* (Dillon, Leo, & Dillon, Diane. New York: Blue Sky Press, 2007)
Our next book is about jazz music, and we, as the readers, get to watch the excitement build as the audience is captivated by the sheer magic of an unforgettable night.

Activity: Instruments
Now let's pretend that we are in a band of our own. Everyone can pick up an instrument; grownups, you might need to select for the younger children and help them play.

Action Song: "Play Your Instruments." The great children's artist Ella Jenkins has a great song for kids to play instruments.

Parent Message: Grownups, when you give your child opportunities to explore music through singing, dancing, and playing musical instruments, you are actually helping them work on their listening skills and building their phonological awareness. This will help them become a good reader because they are unconsciously hearing words and beats broken down into parts, which is a skill they need to sound out words!

Song: "Hip Hop Simon Says" (It's Hip Hop Baby)

Song: "Turn-A-Round" (Hap Palmer)

Rhyme: Hands on Shoulders
Hands on shoulders/hands on knees/hands behind you if you please/touch your shoulder/now your nose/now your hair/now your toes/hands up high in the air/ down at your sides and touch your hair/hands up high as before/now clap your hands/one, two, three, four

Parent Message: Grownups, when we do songs and rhymes like this, we are working on body control (also known as *executive function*) and self-regulation. According to research from Harvard University, executive-function and self-regulation skills provide critical supports for learning and development. Executive-function skills allow us to retain and work with information in our brains, focus our attention, filter distractions, and switch mental gears. Try incorporating physical development activities at home to get your child physically ready to learn.

The Marketing+Online Engagement division at MCL did a photo shoot featuring me and a family that were regular patrons at my branch interacting with books, music, and puppets. The photos were used on a high-quality postcard and on a standard flyer with a description of the program, date, and location. The postcards were mailed out to local Black-owned businesses, including barbershops, hair salons, corner markets, and real estate offices. The flyers were sent to every branch location and neighborhood school. The library division Every Child Initiative (formerly Early Childhood Services) does regular outreach

Black-culture focused storytimes incorporate stories, songs, rhymes, activities, and movement from the African and African American experience to help families build their children's early literacy skills.

to Head Start, preschools, day care centers, Healthy Start, and at various Multnomah County clinics. Outreach specialists included flyers and postcards during their visits prior to the launch. I was interviewed by the local, Black-owned newspaper *The Skanner* and featured in the library's monthly e-newsletter. KBOO, a community-supported radio station, also aired a spot about the program. I attended end-of-the-school-year nights and parent education programs, where I promoted the program and left flyers. Youth Services Director Ellen Fader made an FAQ document for all library employees, and branch staff shared the flyers and invited families whenever possible. Then we waited. The first storytime had 25 children attending with their parents and caregivers and was deemed an immediate success. Since that initial session, two more staff have been trained to present Black Storytime, and MCL now offers the program at three branch locations.

Community Response

Community response has been positive for the most part, with families that attend loving the program. Quotes from happy parents include:

- "Thank you for being forward-thinking and creating a space for children of color" (personal communication, June 5, 2015).
- "Coming to Black Storytime gives our toddler the time to stretch his imagination with singing, dancing, and being playful with his peers" (personal communication, June 5, 2015).
- "My favorite quote from Frederick Douglass is 'Once you learn to read, you will be forever free' and sharing a reading experience with a diverse group of storytime goers is powerful. [It is powerful] to see kids walking out of storytime chanting a familiar song or picking up on a new word from Black Storytime" (personal communication, June 5, 2015).

Unfortunately, there have been, and continue to be, negative responses. During the week of the initial launch, a conservative talk-show host criticized the program, asking on Facebook, "Does anybody think this is a good idea, paid for with your tax dollars" (Larson, 2012)? Many commenters on this post responded by questioning whether White children would be welcome at Black Storytime; for example, one woman wrote, "So if I were living in the area, and I brought my caucasion [sic] daughters to 'black storytime,'[sic] would we be asked to leave?"

Thankfully, MCL Director of Marketing+Online Engagement Jeremy Graybill anticipated such reactions and made sure to emphasize in the program's marketing materials *all* families who were interested in experiencing books, songs, and rhythms from the African American experience were welcome to participate in storytime. Now the biggest question/complaint from staff and patrons alike is over the

> Community engagement is more successful than community outreach because of its participatory nature.

name—"Why is it called *Black* Storytime?" We bounced around a few ideas, and even recently had another conversation about the name and if it still worked. The other name ideas were always rejected because they were unnecessarily complex, confusing, or both. Calling it "Black Storytime" is simple, straightforward, and makes it all-encompassing for the complete diaspora. The storytime should speak to all people who are Black, not just African Americans. I am always open for a conversation about the name—and my questions remain the same, rooted in the practical: Will I need to go into an explanation on what the program is with the new name? Will it still be catchy enough to market?

ADVICE FOR STARTING YOUR LIBRARY'S BLACK STORYTIME

Black Storytime is a fun and informative way to experience African and African American culture at the library. Black-culture focused storytimes incorporate stories, songs, rhymes, activities, and movement from the African and African American experience to help families build their children's early literacy skills. However, it may not be exactly what your community wants. Community engagement—"the process of working collaboratively with and through groups of people affiliated by geographic proximity, special interest, or similar situations to address issues affecting the well-being of those people (CDC, 1997)"—is more successful than community outreach because of its participatory nature. I would urge all public librarians to move away from information delivery or one-way conversations (this is what the library can do for you) and shift the focus back to your community. Understand what the community wants and needs, try to figure out if the library is the best partner, and then, together, create something new. If storytime is what the community decides is the best program, the good news is that you have resources in Oregon and you don't need any extra funding to start and maintain the program. Having a commitment from the youth services director and library director is essential to the program's success, as is being able to communicate the importance of the work that you are doing to both patrons and staff. A pilot project needs everyone's buy-in and support in order to get off the ground and make an impact.

Know the End Goal

The LSTA grant and subsequent launch of Black Storytime was only the beginning of a systemwide look at how we can attract and retain African American staff to reflect the community in which our libraries exist. Since the start of Black Storytime, the library has also added a culturally specific programming team and formed a formal workgroup of public service African American staff to identify trends, recommend services, and nurture key partnerships. Our ultimate goal is to strengthen our ability to serve the African American community and support full and vibrant engagement.

One of the challenges facing librarianship is the lack of diversity and underrepresentation of people of color in our institutions, and MCL is no exception. Another idea from the grant that has continued to gain traction is that the library needs to hire more African and African American staff so that the library becomes more welcoming. While 6.9 percent of county residents identify as African American, only 1.8 percent of library staff identify as African American. While MCL has work to do to have our staff fully reflect the community—and is committed to doing that work—a broader effort must be made to remedy the national shortage of librarians of color.

Naming the Storytime

I think that the name needs to feel comfortable for everyone, so if you are starting your own Black Storytime and feel strongly about a different name, go for it. Be prepared for questions and complaints no matter which name is chosen, and be ready to defend your choice clearly and concisely. Staff at MCL can look at the Black Storytime FAQ as a resource when trying to help patrons understand; creating your own as well would be helpful in educating and supporting front-line library staff. Remember that the goal is to create a community of learning, so make the name choice best for your neighborhood.

CONCLUDING THOUGHTS

As a public librarian, I know front-line staff become the face of the library, and a positive interaction can be the difference between people loving their library and avoiding the place. Black residents in Portland did not feel that the library was a welcoming place for them, so MCL has made, and continues to make, deliberate efforts to change this perception. Creating Black Storytime was one successful programmatic way to improve the experience that Black families had at the library and to address

> "I was so relieved to find people that looked like my daughter at a public storytime."

the achievement gap between Black and White children. Designed to culturally engage and support Black residents, an added benefit has been the creation of community. Public libraries everywhere must be open to transforming their services to best suit the community in order to remain valuable and empowering to all residents.

Make It Happen in Your Library

1. Secure the support of the youth services supervisor and library director.
2. Engage the community in gathering information to develop a community-driven, culturally appropriate, and effective action plan for library programming.
3. Ground your programming in current research on culturally relevant pedagogy.
4. Clearly articulate the goals of your program and tie them to concrete learning outcomes for youth.
5. Connect your programs to the strategic plan and mission of the library and the municipality.
6. Be prepared for responses, both positive and negative, from the community.

8

Writing and Reading That Reflects the Lives of Our Students

Teresa Bunner

There is no greater agony than bearing an untold story inside you.
—Angelou (1969, p. 22)

Connecting Research to Practice

As you read this chapter, look for the following characteristics of effective library services for African American youth:

- **Instruction**—Cooperative, communal, and iterative, sets high expectations, fosters agency, authentic and relevant
- **Resources**—Relevant, authentic, provide counterstories

I believe in story. I believe in the power of story. As an educator of 25 years, I can cite research and give you a list of books and articles to read that support sound practice. But what drives me to keep learning, to keep thinking and to stay in the field, are the stories. The stories that I remember of young people who have allowed me the privilege to teach them and to learn from them. My work with young people has been driven by the desire to help them find their stories, to help them find other people's stories and see the connection to their own, and to discover the power their stories have to influence others and the world.

When I moved into the role of academic support specialist with the Blue Ribbon Mentor-Advocate (BRMA) program for the public school system in Chapel Hill, North Carolina, I lost my daily classroom and school contact with students, but I still was driven to consider the role of literacy in our students' lives, especially now that I was working with the BRMA participants, students of color in 4th through 12th grade. Chapel Hill Carrboro City School's student achievement data look good. But like many districts, when you disaggregate the data, students of color are not achieving at as high a rate. In working with our students, we have come to understand that for many of them, their school experiences do not draw on their strengths and reflect their life experiences. This can make school an alienating environment.

In my quest to support these young people's literacy development, I read Alfred Tatum's work around his African American Male Summer Literacy Institute. His book, *Reading for Their Life: (Re)Building the Textual Lineages of African American Adolescent Males* (2009), confirmed for me the power that enabling texts and writing could have for students of color. (For more on enabling texts, including a definition, examples, and programming ideas, please refer to Chapter 5.) I also realized that while I could continue to tutor students or help find others who could tutor, attend parent-teacher conferences and IEP meetings, and visit students for pep talks when grades dropped, it would not be enough. Dr. Tatum's work made me realize that our students needed a time and space that drew on their strengths and their lived experiences and offered them a chance to share their voices.

At that time, BRMA held a summer program for middle school students based on research that supported the need for students of color to develop a positive racial identity to achieve academic success (Hanley & Noblit, 2009). This summer opportunity taught students to confront stereotypes through the arts and to write their own counternarratives. Students came to understand that through the support of allies, they could face negative stereotypes and define for themselves who they would be. After that one week in middle school, however, BRMA offered no other direct, arts-based, identity development programming for our high school students. With Dr. Tatum's work in hand, I approached our program coordinator, Graig Meyer, about developing a high school writing institute that would build on students' learning about allies and continue the development of positive racial identity through the use of mentor texts, writing experiences, and interaction with local and national authors to enable students to continue to create their own counternarratives.

I was able to travel to Chicago and spend two days at Dr. Tatum's African American Male Summer Literacy Institute. The "brother authors," as Dr. Tatum calls them, were engaged in their activities every minute of my time there, even to the point of not wanting to step away from their writing when lunch was announced. Dr. Tatum made sure that his high expectations extended even to guests in the room, making sure that I completed the same activities and writing as his young authors. These young men were fully engrossed and engaged in the act of writing. Each day, there was a time for the brother authors to share their writing. What these young men shared was poignant and powerful. This time that they were given to write truly allowed them to find and share their voices.

My passion for literacy, the use of Dr. Tatum's program as a guide, and the support of Graig culminated in the birth of the Blue Ribbon Mentor-Advocate

Summer Writing Institute in July 2012. In this program, 10 high school students of color, a writing coach (a creative writing student from the University of North Carolina), and I gathered on the University of North Carolina at Chapel Hill (UNC-CH) campus for four days, armed with a plethora of notebooks and pens.

At the end of those four days, students completed a reflection about our time together. When asked what feedback they had that might improve the program, every student replied, "More time." Guided by this feedback, my own reflections from the experience, and the continued support of Graig, I reenvisioned the summer institute into a three-week program, and we secured a grant to fund it.

While each summer brings different participants and experiences, there are key tenets that create the power of the program to affect young people. Some are pedagogical; others are logistical. I am indebted to Dr. Tatum for sharing his work, as it has provided the basis for our program.

PEDAGOGICAL TENETS

The three key pedagogical tenets are asset-based instruction, time to read and write, and connections to authors.

Asset-based Instruction

I believe that there is much that we currently get wrong in our schools when it comes to reading and writing instruction. Too often, it is dictated by skills instruction and the need to only write in genres listed in the standards. I would argue that this practice stifles our students' abilities to see themselves as readers and writers, especially our students of color, who see very little of themselves represented in the school curriculum. Asset-based instruction recognizes that the knowledge that students bring to schools from their personal and cultural experiences is central to their learning.

In school, writing has unfortunately become something that is directed by the teacher in which students merely respond to what they are told to write. They are not encouraged to connect writing to their lived experiences or to be creative and explore new genres or formats. That very first writing institute presented a scenario that drove home the negative impact this approach has on students. Because we had only four days, I felt a rush to get the students writing on their own as quickly as possible. The first day, we watched two TED talks: Sara Kay's "If I Should Have a Daughter," and Chimamanda Adichie's "The Danger of a Single Story." Students took notes and wrote in response to those pieces. We completed a few other short writing activities, and then lunch arrived. After lunch, I told students "Now it is time for you to write!" Ten faces. Ten blank stares. A student responded,

> They were so conditioned to view writing as what the teacher tells you to do that they had no idea that writing was an act of expression, of conveying thoughts and ideas that are our very own, or at the very least, how to find their own voices.

"But what do we write?" Heads nodded. "Anything you want," I replied. "But what's our prompt, Ms. B?" another student queried. Sensing their panic, and not wanting to scare them off the first day, I pulled out an autobiographical poem frame and a list of thought-provoking journal prompts that I had copied in case of emergencies just like this.

After handing these out, I realized how quiet the room had become. I looked around and saw 10 heads bent over tables, 10 pens scratching across paper. I realized that this is what they expected writing to be. It was a worksheet, a formula, a predetermined prompt that told them what to write and how to write it. I was dumbfounded. They were so conditioned to view writing as what the teacher tells you to do that they had no idea that writing was an act of expression, of conveying thoughts and ideas that are our very own, or at the very least, how to find their own voices.

> The power of an asset-based approach comes in valuing students' knowledge and experiences and drawing it into the classroom.

The next day, I shared my thoughts with them. I told them that in here, writing was whatever they wanted it to be—no right or wrong. I explained that as writers, the only way to learn and grow and improve is to start by getting something down on paper to work with. I then shared with them a mentor text (text used as examples of good writing for students) from Sharon Flake, who would Skype in with us later in the morning. It was the poem "You Don't Even Know Me." We read the piece and talked about the themes and big ideas that we saw in the piece and related them to our experiences. The students then wrote their own "You Don't Even Know Me" pieces. Sharon's visit with us could not have been any better timed, as she echoed what I had been trying to help the students understand about writing. She was so gracious with the students and even invited them to share a piece of their writing with her. She offered positive feedback to each student who shared.

Lunch time came again, and I was prepared to continue guiding the work after that. When we reconvened, one of the students raised her hand and said "Mrs. Bunner, would it be okay if we just spent the rest of the time writing?" There it was—exactly what I had hoped for them. They were ready to find their voices, and it was time for me to get out of the way for a bit. The power of an asset-based approach comes in valuing students' knowledge and experiences and drawing it into the classroom. There is time to get to the "academic writing," but we must first empower students with the knowledge that they have a voice as a writer and help them see the act of writing as an act of expression and creation.

But asset-based writing instruction is not just turning students loose. It is also about showing them what is possible within themselves by sharing writing from authors whose lives and stories and complexions are similar to theirs. It is offering them texts that are the windows they so often get in their school classes, but also showing them pieces that are mirrors and help them reflect back on themselves. In our second year of the writing institute, our theme was "Writing Our Stories, Changing the World," drawn from the following quote from James Baldwin: "You write in order to change the world, knowing perfectly well that you probably can't, but also knowing that literature is indispensable to the world . . . The world changes according to the way people see it, and if you alter, even by a millimeter, the way people look at reality, then you can change it" (quoted in Watkins, 1979, p. 3). Imagine my surprise when the students told me that they did not know who James Baldwin was. How could students of color not know one of the most influential writers of color? How can they see themselves as writers if they don't know those who came before them? There is great literary history represented by writers from many backgrounds. When we help our students find and explore those texts, we are calling on and building from these strengths.

The mentor texts that the students in the four years of our program have read are varied (see the box "Sample Mentor Texts" for examples). Each year, I choose a few texts ahead of time, but I also leave room for texts that are dictated by the interests and backgrounds of the students who walk in that summer.

Sample Mentor Texts

"Fish Cheeks" by Amy Tan
"Only Daughter" by Sandra Cisneros
"Names" by Sandra Cisneros
"I Am Offering This Poem" by Jimmy Santiago Baca
"You Don't Even Know Me" by Sharon Flake
TED Talk—"The Danger of a Single Story" by Chimamanda Adichie
"If I Should Have a Daughter" by Sarah Kay
"Theme for English B" by Langston Hughes
"Still I Rise" by Maya Angelou
"The Giver" (poem) by James Baldwin
The Counting Rope by Jacqueline Woodson
Ellen's Broom by Kelly Starling Lyons
"Discovering Books," from *Black Boy* by Richard Wright
"Learning to Read" by Frances E.W. Harper
Night by Elie Wiesel
"Behind Bars," an excerpt from *Monster* by Walter Dean Myers
Freedom on the Menu: The Greensboro Sit-ins by Carole Boston Weatherford
"Learning to Read" from *The Autobiography of Malcolm X*

Youth Voices

Beaner, Wetback, illegal alien.
You scream at me,
You deprive me of my dreams
My voice my thoughts and my self-esteem.

You never stop to think of me
You judge us all with ease.
But when that day comes,
When you need my help
I will extend my hand
Despite what you said back then.
And hopefully you will change your mind
about this Beaner, Wetback, illegal alien.

—José

"Guess What"

Guess what y'all?
I'm black
African American
I'm 16 years old
but,
I've never been in a gang
I don't know what it feels like to live with one parent
I've never dealt drugs
I don't really know what it feels like to need something

I'm 16 years old,
without any kids
I don't have a record
Actually,
I'm on my way to graduating high school
I'm part of a family,
with a mother and a father.

Did you know?
I can speak proper English
I can enunciate my words
My daddy has never been to jail
He is there when I need him most
My mother has her Master's degree in Psychology
My daddy has a high school diploma

Guess what y'all
I'm black
An African-American girl who doesn't fit your stereotypes.

—Kelli

In addition to the mentor texts, the students get to choose books to read on their own. The books are mainly those written by our visiting authors (this part of the program will be explained in more detail later in this chapter)—authors who look like the students, with stories that serve as both windows and mirrors for them to explore. Books are purchased by BRMA, and students are allowed to choose at least one title from each visiting author. These are works that they access on their own. I do not "teach" them the books. I do strongly encourage the students to read as much as they can before the author comes to visit. Otherwise, though, these are their books to explore at their pace, in their own way.

The writing tasks that we complete over the three weeks are there as a guide, not a mandate. Some of the students come with an idea of who they are as a writer. They are ready to work on their own almost from day one. So, the tasks are designed to stretch them as writers, to challenge them to try a new genre or style, and to deepen their understanding of writing as an act of social justice and change. Those very same tasks help those who do not see themselves as writers to find their voice, to play with words and ideas, to offer a structure for imitation and the freedom for experimentation, and to realize their voices have agency in the world.

Words, phrases, and sentences are the building blocks of writing. Before we ask students to write or to share their writing, before we assign essays in our classes, students need to feel comfortable with language. They need to know how to play with words before they can revise and play with ideas. So we build those skills in a way that draws on what they already know. We start with lists like "Ten things that irritate me," and play with words through activities like "Masterpiece Sentences." This has become one of the students' favorite activities, even resulting in a "Best Masterpiece Sentence" competition each year.

Time to Read and Write as a Community

If we are truly using asset-based literacy instruction, then we must provide students the time and freedom to explore and build their literacy skills within the context of our scheduled instructional time with them, whether that be the school day, or as in the BRMA case, the 15 days of the writing institute. Certainly I want students reading and writing outside the school day or our institute time. However, when we consistently relegate "free reading" or "free writing" time to outside of instructional time, then we send the message that these acts really have no value. If my expectation is that **you are** a reader and a writer, then I will offer you that time during our day to read and to write because I value those skills and abilities.

Not only is there time within our institute day to read and write, but there is also time within our day to discuss with each other what we are reading and writing. We also have time for students to booktalk, share what they are enjoying about the book, or even ask questions of others who are reading the same book. Many times, I have had students ask if I have copies of a title that they can borrow because what their peers have shared makes them want to read the book.

Of course, there is time to write. The students usually end up demanding more time as the days progress and they are immersed in the pieces they are writing. Students have writer's notebooks and a variety of writing utensils. They also have access to laptops if working on the computer is their preferred method of writing. Writing coaches, usually university students studying creative writing or communications, are invited to be mentors to our students. These students volunteer their time to work with student writers so that they can gain experience and, if our budget allows, receive a small stipend for their time. Access to these coaches provides students with more intensive support and feedback on their writing and allows more support for students with special needs or those students who are struggling to find their voices.

While students may work alone, this writing time also can become collaborative and communal. The student writers begin to use the language of writers as they support and challenge each other. A perfect example of this is a conversation between two young women, both at the institute because they had failed English and chose to take advantage of the option to participate for credit recovery (more about this aspect later). One of them was reading the other's piece. She turned to her and asked, "What is it you want your reader to understand here?" She went on to coach the second writer into revising a section of her piece so that it was clearer to her readers. She was a writer, with a writer's language. How can we not celebrate that?

Time to Interact with "Real" Authors

The opportunity to visit Dr. Tatum's literacy institute gave me much to reflect on and helped to cement what has become a key component of our writing institute—the opportunity for students of color to connect with authors who look like them. As I watched Dr. Tatum interact with his students, I realized that his identity as a Black male enhanced his ability to facilitate a writing institute for young Black men who looked like him. I do not have that advantage. In fact, as a White female, I look like the people whom my students see every day in their schools. I realized that even if I found a cofacilitator, that would not be enough because our institute is open to Black, Latin@, Burmese, and Karen students. I was confident in my ability to teach writing, to guide students, and to provide them enabling texts, but I also realized that the students needed to see writers—to hear from people who looked like them, had similar life experiences as them, and who were sharing their voices with others through story. To meet this need, we ensured that our funding for the program included a budget line to bring in guest authors.

> There is incredible power in connecting students with people whose names grace the covers of the books that they are reading. There is even more power when those authors look like them and reflect back the reality that they, too, can be writers.

I have referred to these author visits as "magic" (Bunner, 2014), and they truly are. There is incredible power in connecting students with people whose names grace the covers of the books that they are reading. There is even more power when those authors look like them and reflect back the reality that they, too, can be writers. The first year of the institute, our funds were extremely limited, and I planned it very last minute. Sharon Flake, author of *The Skin I'm In* (2010) and other books, graciously agreed to Skype in to our institute.

She talked about her journey as a writer and how she writes, and at the time she had just finished writing *Pinned* (2012), so she shared a sneak preview of the novel with us. The students were thrilled to get a peek at something not everyone could read yet. Sharon invited the students to share some of their writing and provided them with thoughtful, encouraging feedback. Since then, the students also have been able to work with Mitali Perkins via Skype and in person with Matt de la Peña, Kelly Starling Lyons, Jacqueline Woodson, and CJ Suitt, a local spoken-word poet. These authors were our "rock stars." The students have awaited each visit with eager anticipation and have willingly participated in writing and sharing, as these expert craftspeople have helped them on their journey as writers. They have also avidly read their books. Something about the immediacy of meeting authors provides a motivation to explore their books (and others as well).

LOGISTICAL TENETS

The pedagogy and practice employed motivates students and invites them as active participants in our time together. But in studying Dr. Tatum's program, I realized there are some key logistical aspects that need to be in place in order to allow students access to an opportunity like this.

Space

It would probably be easy to secure space in a school in our local school district. But if part of my goal was to create an atmosphere unlike what the students already encounter in school, then it seemed counterproductive to hold it in that very space. Through a partnership with the local university, we were able to secure classroom space there. By having students attend the institute on a college campus, we also send the message that we see a future for them. Sometimes we often underestimate the power of the subtle, implicit messages that we send.

Not only did we have classroom space, but we had space that was ours for the time that we were there. We could create anchor charts (charts that make thinking visible by recording content, strategies, processes, cues, and guidelines during the learning process), post student work, and make the room feel like a working environment for our entire time. The classroom that we were allotted also allowed the use of technology, which expanded our options for mentor texts beyond the written word to TED talks, videos, advertisements, and other media.

Transportation

Too often, due to our privilege, we forget about lack of access to resources like transportation. It is vital to a program like this that students be able to get there. Part of Dr. Tatum's program included providing the brother authors with

Metro cards so they could access public transportation to attend each day. For our part, holding the institute at the university ensured that students had access to the public bus system, which is free in Chapel Hill. I made sure that students had access to route maps and helped them figure out which buses to take if they were unsure. For many participants, it was the first time that they had used public transportation, and it opened up many possibilities far outside the realm of our summer writing institute.

Breakfast/Lunch

Not all of my student writers live in poverty. But some do. Summer months mean the loss of school-provided breakfast and lunch. To this end, I made sure that we provided breakfast snacks (granola bars and juice) and a good lunch each day for everyone. This need was also addressed through the grant. Lunch was delivered each day from various local establishments. Something powerful is created in the community when sharing a meal. Consistent meals are not the sole reason that students attend, but I am sure that the knowledge that a good lunch would be provided each day may have helped some wake themselves up in the morning and make the trek to campus via public transportation.

Stipends or Credit

Dr. Tatum's program offers students a stipend for attending the summer literacy institute. To be honest, I was unsure how I felt about this aspect at first. I do not believe in incentivizing reading and writing. Upon further reflection, however, I realized that many of my students might not choose to participate because they need to get summer jobs. Their participation might affect the number of hours they would be able to get at work as well. I also considered the message that it would send for students to earn money as writers. What better way to convince students to consider this as a career option? In light of this, I opted to offer a stipend. No student is getting rich from participating, but the stipend—around $125—certainly provides some financial independence that they might not otherwise have.

When we advertised the first writing institute, one student was disappointed that he would not be able to attend, as he had failed a class and needed to attend summer school. With numerous other summer events and programming, I was unable to figure out a schedule that would not interfere with summer school. In our district, summer school credit recovery means that students are placed on a computer and they work alone to complete an online curriculum. There is no teaching involved and, based on the students' assessment of their time, very little learning takes place. The students are simply meeting an hourly and minimum score requirement to regain their credit.

I worked with our district curriculum personnel and submitted a proposal to allow our BRMA students who failed English to enroll in the summer writing institute for credit recovery. I aligned what we did in the institute with state standards and shared research about the efficacy of students reading and writing every day to improve skills and increase critical thinking. It was approved. Now students have an option of a stipend *or* credit.

There are requirements to receive either the stipend or the credit. Per our school district summer school guidelines, students cannot miss more than one day or they do not receive credit. So we adhere to this guideline for our writing institute. Our guidelines also state that students must actively participate each day, they must read at least one book, and they must produce two pieces that they have taken through the writing process and submitted for inclusion in an anthology of student work. In four years, I have only denied one student a stipend. It was a difficult call, but in consultation with his mom, we agreed that not giving him the stipend would send a much stronger message to him than rewarding his almost complete nonparticipation during the three weeks. I believe that the stipend might be enough of an incentive to make students enroll, but in the end, I do not believe that it is the sole motivation that brings them back for three weeks. Over the years, I have had several students who had to miss a second day who said, "I know I can't get the stipend any more, but can I keep coming?" The answer, of course, is yes! And I have allotted them the stipend, as each case was that of a young person who needed to work or help family and was dealing with circumstances out of his or her own control.

Program Schedule

Our summer institute meets four days a week for three weeks. I tell students that in college, they will get "reading days" before exams. I explain that we don't meet on Fridays because that is their "reading and writing" day. I expect that they will read their book or work on their writing on those days. I do not check up on them, though. There are no logs or parent signature sheets to corroborate what they do with their time. High expectations are set, and students realize that if they do not use this time, they likely will not finish a book before the author visits or be able to get two pieces of writing into a publishable state.

Each day session is four hours long. The first year, since we had so few days planned, we met for five hours. That was a lot for the students and, to be honest, for me as well. Four hours allows a little cushion for students in the morning to grab a snack and to roll in if buses are late.

CONCLUDING THOUGHTS

It is hard to capture in words just how powerful this experience is for students. I have watched hesitant students walk in the first day questioning their ability to write, only to watch and listen and read the powerful words and ideas that they create. I have seen students return consecutive summers because they value the experience. I have been privileged to introduce a student to one of her author heroes. There is incredible power in allowing our students of color space and time to find their voices and opportunity to share it with others.

Make It Happen in Your Library

1. Connect reading and writing to the students' lived experiences.
2. Adopt an asset-based approach that builds on the strengths of students.
3. Focus on reading and writing as tools of expression that allow students to act in the world.
4. Set high expectations and provide the support that students need to meet those expectations.
5. Connect students to mentors, including authors of color.

9

Let the Sun Shine: "Maker Jawn" at the Free Library of Philadelphia

Theresa Ramos

Connecting Research to Practice

As you read this chapter, look for the following characteristics of effective library services for African American youth:

- **Programming**—Develops agency, asset-based, honors/promotes voice, fosters community
- **Administration**—Committed, proactive, attentive and knowledgeable
- **Instruction**—Fosters agency, cooperative, communal, and iterative, authentic, relevant

The Free Library of Philadelphia is a major urban library system serving 1.5 million people within the city of Philadelphia through 49 branch libraries, three regional libraries, a Central Library, the Regional Library for the Blind and Physically Handicapped, and most recently, the Rosenbach Museum. When I began working at the Free Library many years ago, one of the first things I was introduced to was the "sunshine law"—a law designed to ensure that every resource, service, and program *is equitably available to everyone,* regardless of economic status, gender, ethnicity, belief, or age. For example, when we first began providing public access to computers in the mid-1990s, the "sunshine law" became particularly relevant to the issue of age, so that preference was not given to adults for their "serious" work over kids who just wanted to "play."

Although the Library offers some paid programs such as author events, there are many programs that specifically target underserved populations—including immigrants, youth in especially impoverished neighborhoods, and young children. For example, the Field Family Teen Author Series gives away free copies of books to students in schools and gives them the opportunity to meet authors. During my time at the Free Library, I have had the privilege of managing several initiatives that were specifically designed to provide resources to and amplify the voices of nondominant populations. While none of our programs are exclusively intended for African American youth, in the spirit of equity, many elements are specifically designed to close the opportunity gap in Philadelphia, and, in a small way, begin to level the playing field.

This chapter profiles several Free Library teen programs, including the Bits & Bytes program, which is focused on technology; a Wallace Foundation grant, focused on positive youth development; the Literacy Enrichment After-school Program (LEAP) and Philadelphia Youth Network teen employment programs; and a blend of employment opportunities, mentoring, and youth development in our current Maker programming. Throughout the past 15+years, we have incorporated learnings to scaffold sustained "changed practice." In every instance, a small pilot project has evolved through a combination of public and private funding, and most of them eventually became integrated into the Library's core services. The most important factor in this sustained and targeted approach has been the commitment and vision of the administrative and public service staff, particularly Hedra Packman, who continually supported the staff's efforts to dream big, fail, and try again with an even bigger vision. The current Maker Jawn program, the focus of this chapter, represents a culmination of the philosophies and practices developed through these programs and their impact on the participating youth and their underserved communities.

WHAT IS "MAKER JAWN"?

In September 2014, the Free Library of Philadelphia Foundation received a grant from the Institute of Museum and Library Services (IMLS) to implement Maker Jawn: an intergenerational library STEAM initiative to create on-the-floor maker spaces in libraries. Maker spaces enable local residents to gain access to technology and participatory education and encourage creative applications and collaborative projects. Mentors guide multigenerational community members as they create cross-disciplinary, interest-driven electronic art projects; build interest and knowledge in science, technology, engineering, art, and mathematics (STEAM) fields; use tools and skills to create and share artifacts that reflect their identities and communities; and gain key 21st-century skills.

Maker Jawn spaces are situated within some of the most underserved communities in the country. For example, North Philadelphia, a predominantly African American and Hispanic neighborhood served by the Widener branch of the library, has been decimated by poverty (with a 47.9 percent poverty rate and a 20.6 percent unemployment rate) and crime (with 1,058 violent crimes and 2,514 property crimes reported in 2015) (Crime in Philadelphia, 2016).

Many youth lack home Internet (an estimated 55 percent of Philadelphians were without home Internet in 2012) (Kirk, 2012) and attend underfunded, "no-frills" public schools. In 2015, there were just 11 school librarians employed in Philadelphia's 218 public schools (Graham, 2015).

Maker Jawn experiments with creating replicable, scalable spaces and programs that prioritize the creativity, cultural heritage, and interests of diverse communities, embedded directly within the fabric of the library. The program endeavors to spark a do-it-yourself spirit and encourages participants to become critical creators and innovators instead of passive consumers. While working to provide access to and training with technology tools, Maker Jawn also places an even greater emphasis on relationship and community building. The program is staffed by Maker Mentors, who support self-directed projects and help develop key skills such as resilience, problem solving, and collaboration. Mentors nurture interest-based learning and creative exploration with a wide range of materials—including everything from sewing machines, three-dimensional (3D) printers, and iPads to markers, glue sticks, and recycled cardboard.

The roots of Maker Jawn go back to 1997, with the Bits & Bytes program (see Figure 9.1). Like many libraries, the Free Library had employed teens to shelve books, but Bits & Bytes looked at teen employment in a way that combined work with learning experiences and youth development. As part of an $18 million, three-year Model Urban Library Services for Children renovation grant from the William Penn Foundation, the Free Library hired Teen Leadership Assistants (TLAs) and college students to help communities become comfortable with and competent at using computers. In 1998, a Public Libraries as Partners in Youth Development (PLPYD) grant from the Wallace Foundation added an important element of youth development to the Library's teen employment program. Positive youth development sees teens as resources to be developed rather than as problems to be solved, and recognizes that a combination of opportunities and supports can help teens successfully make the transition to adulthood. Combining teen employment with positive youth development enhanced and strengthened the Library's work with teens.

Concurrently, LEAP, the Library's after-school program, provided homework help, computer assistance, workshops, and mentoring for students in grades 1–12. The TLAs, who represented the diverse ethnicities of their neighborhoods, acted as role models and informal mentors to the younger children in the library. They also benefited from being mentored themselves by adults in their libraries and from taking monthly workshops on topics as diverse as healthy relationships, personality assessment, multimodal literacies, and college prep.

Early on, we realized that although most TLAs indicated that they were going on to college, it didn't turn out that way in reality. It became apparent that as potential first-generation students, they did not understand the pathways to college, had not taken the Scholastic Aptitude Test (SAT) or completed financial aid applications, and in some instances believed that you were assigned to a college in the same way that you were assigned to a high school. An intensive SAT/College Prep program dramatically increased the number of TLAs who actually made the transition to college. Later, a program that hired them as college students kept them connected to the Library and proved to be a powerful example to younger youth in their neighborhoods. From 2002 to 2009, the Philadelphia Youth Network funded an additional twenty low-income youth who worked as TLAs in the LEAP program and received extra mentoring and training.

In 2010 and 2011, the Free Library was awarded additional grants by the Philadelphia Youth Network to hire and train 120 teens as literacy coaches for a summer reading program. Teens were trained to carry out literacy-based, tabletop activities with children at libraries throughout the city. Teens met once a week at the Parkway Central Library, where they explored an aspect of early literacy development, developed activities for their libraries, and received books and supplies that they could use for informal programming on reading tables on the floor of the library. This program actively supported academic achievement while helping teens develop leadership and work readiness skills to ensure postsecondary success. The program design provided opportunities and supports that were customized to the particular needs and interests of each participating youth. Not only were teens guided to develop confidence in their own literacy skills, but they were also encouraged to think critically by analyzing and facilitating the activities through the curriculum provided. Each teen was also encouraged to develop their public speaking abilities, particularly during the weekly trainings, when they were invited to share their accomplishments as well as any challenges they may have faced.

Developing maker programming at the Free Library was the logical next step in an organic process of teen development and empowerment, and it was supported by crucial staff that were deeply committed to participatory design. In the spring of 2011, a team of digital resource specialists began "Teen Media Week" as part of the Library's Hot Spots initiative, a project funded by the Knight Foundation that supported computer labs embedded in community centers as a way to engage teens. Young people were introduced to animated Graphic Interchange Format (GIF) files, cinemagraphs, green-screen video, beat making, and more. Staff started working informally with Dr. Yasmin Kafai at the University of Pennsylvania's Graduate School of Education, doing e-textiles workshops where teens sewed light-emitting diodes (LEDs) into clothing and other objects they created.

In January 2012, the Library received an IMLS/MacArthur planning grant to design a learning lab at the Central Library. Although that lab is still in the planning phase, we have taken the concept out into neighborhood libraries. One of the most important outcomes of that grant has been the opportunity to connect with and help build a network of over 30 other libraries and museums nationally that are looking at ways to better serve teens. (K-Fai Steele, one of the original Hot Spot digital resource specialists, now manages the YOUmedia Learning Labs Network and Community of Practice through the National Writing Project.) The opportunity to share ideas (and failures) with other organizations has been key to our ability to grow programs in a way that reflects the best and most current national focus. (It also helps make sure we are relevant when applying for funding!)

In the summer of 2012, 35 teens from low-income families worked as Teen Programming Assistants for the Library's summer program funded by the Philadelphia Youth Network. From Monday to Thursday, the teens worked at their

FIGURE 9.1 The Roots of Maker Jawn: Youth Employment/Youth Development

Initiative	Description	Benefits to Teens
LEAP: **1989–Present**	One of the Library's core services, providing homework help and programming for neighborhood youth. Teen employees have become progressively more integral to the program.	Employment opportunities are critical for low-income youth. The Library provides opportunities for personal and professional development in a supportive and challenging environment.
Bits & Bytes: **1997–2000**	TLAs (teen employees) and college students provided support in accessing newly installed public computers.	TLAs were quick to learn with the support of near-peer college students as mentors; they became invaluable to their neighborhood libraries and saw themselves as integral to library services.
Public Libraries as Partners in Youth Development (PLPYD): **1998–2000**	Combining teen employment with positive youth development enhanced and strengthened the Library's work with teens. Teens had the opportunity to participate in national conferences.	Youth voice was amplified as TLAs participated in trainings and took on leadership roles.
Philadelphia Youth Network: **2002–Present**	An after-school and summer youth employment program, the network provided an opportunity to pilot new programs.	Provided leadership opportunities for teens to design and implement innovative programs.
Knight Foundation Hot Spots: **2011–2013**	Computer labs within neighborhood organizations were customized to meet the needs of unique communities.	Teens had access to exciting new technologies and the support of mentors.

local library sites completing daily assignments in the form of action research—for example, creating Google Maps illustrating the need for more teen services in their neighborhoods, polling teens in an interactive way (using sticky notes, stickers, audio and video interviews, and blogging their reflections through a Tumblr site) about whether they liked or attended programs currently offered by the Library, and designing an ideal library space for teens. A Team Leader (a college student/near-peer Mentor) rotated around branches, guiding students with work and helping with any technical or organizational questions. On Fridays, teens convened at the Parkway Central Library, where they formed small groups to collaborate and discuss their findings, as mediated by an outside presenter. Each project group went on to present their work at the summer-end celebration in front of approximately 200 teens and library staff members, and a representative group of teens presented their project at a culminating event at the Pennsylvania Convention Center.

Dr. Kafai introduced staff to a Maker Ed opportunity in early 2013, which provided an opportunity to expand maker programming and secure additional funding, particularly a Library Services and Technology Act (LSTA) grant in September 2013. The learnings from that grant directly informed our development and implementation of the current Maker Jawn program, which is described in detail in the remaining sections of this chapter.

Youth Voices

Khaleef Aye

I'm not a special case. There's nothing outstanding about me. I am representative of the investments of time and wisdom from several people that I was fortunate enough to meet, many through my experience at the Free Library of Philadelphia. More than any training or other preparation, Audrey Roll, Solomon Steplight, Theresa Ramos, Hedra Packman, and Jean Byrne exercised great patience, gave me the tools, and (most importantly) they believed in me.

The Free Library created an environment that provided access to technology that I simply could not have obtained on my own. I'd always been a fan of music and enjoyed watching videos, but the idea that I would be able to actually create seemed so far from possible that I found myself limiting what I thought that I could do. High expectations and support built my confidence. Getting paid for my work was critical. It meant that instead of trying to find ways to make money for necessities, I could focus on finding ways to get better at what I loved while mentoring others. Every project I was involved with at the Library, from teen worker to Maker Jawn Mentor, followed the same winning combination of resources, mentorship, confidence building activities, autonomy, and (eventually) the transition of participants to Mentors. Seventeen years later, I am still closely involved with the Library as Production Manager for 900AM-WURD, the only African American–owned and—operated talk radio station in Pennsylvania.

In 1998, I was going into my senior year in high school when I was offered a job as a summer teen worker at the Cecil B. Moore Library through Work Ready Philadelphia. That fall Audrey Roll hired me as a Teen Leadership Assistant (TLA), helping patrons with computers and mentoring young people in my neighborhood. Everything I was learning, I tried to pass on to the young people in my neighborhood library. The young teens I had mentored became TLAs and continued to mentor a new group of youngsters who started their own group, "Young Bull Entertainment" or "YBE." Their focus was music, audio, photo, and video production. There were youth as young as 10, essentially running their own studio sessions!

Both the Digital Dragons and YBE worked because youth were having fun, someone was giving them tools and believing in them. Additionally, it was important that every youth there have some level of engagement with the production.

YPE became huge, especially after kids started bringing home DCs of their music. The continuation of the project meant the world to many of the teens. Consistency is critical to building trust and success. Unless there is a sustainable system intact, or the kids have been conditioned to seek out information and opportunities, ending a program that has that much of an effect on the community could be devastating to the participants and hamper future opportunities with the group.

The Nuts and Bolts of Maker Jawn

Nontraditional Staffing Model

Maker Jawn staffing is built on a model that differs from many traditional youth service programs. Maker Mentors are artists, musicians, engineers, designers, and educators from the Philadelphia community, who are managed by a part-time, nonlibrarian project coordinator. The Maker Mentor position is part-time/temporary and is funded through a combination of city and grant funding. Mentors are supported by work-study students and interns from local universities. Maker Mentors work 20 hours a week in library locations, teaching community members how to combine technology with crafting and storytelling. Alongside planning and facilitating programs, Maker Mentors divide administrative tasks among themselves and actively participate in various aspects of running the program. They develop curricula; run collaborative professional development sessions; create blog posts, reflections, and public-facing resources related to the program and maker curriculum in libraries; participate in meetings with community partners; and represent the initiative nationally through conferences (e.g., ALA, PaLA, ULC's NEXT conference, and DML) and through participation in the YOUmedia Learning Labs Network Community of Practice site.

> Literacy goes beyond the ability to comprehend and express oneself through written language; it is about the ability to construct meaning through a wide range of platforms that includes things like YouTube videos, fabrication, and social networks.

The Mentor model takes pressure off librarians by establishing a dedicated role for nonlibrarian staff with specific areas of expertise to develop programming, familiarize themselves with technical skills, handle administrative duties, and connect to the outside library and educator world through blogging, presentations, and social media. One of the important aspects of Maker Jawn and the way that the Maker Mentors work with youth is how young people develop literacy skills in ways that are meaningful to them. The Maker Jawn concept of literacy goes beyond the ability to comprehend and express oneself through written language; it is about the ability to construct meaning through a wide range of platforms that includes things like YouTube videos, fabrication, and social networks. Much of the value in the near-peer relationship that the Free Library fosters through this nontraditional staffing model occurs through spending time with young people and slowly developing a relationship. In fact, the primary focus of Maker Jawn is on mentorship and giving nondominant youth in Philadelphia the opportunity to connect to interesting, creative, and caring adults who are invested in their goals and interests. Over time, Maker Jawn creates a culture not only of making, but a culture of mentorship. Building a trusting relationship with young people happens naturally over time through imagining and working on projects together; it cannot be forced or rushed.

In addition to Maker Jawn program staff, everyone from neighborhood library staff to executive staff supports the work being done for and with teens. A security guard at one of the libraries in North Philadelphia, for example, had seen a group of teens who were working throughout the week on green-screen projects. Curious, the guard asked if he could be shown how it worked. The teens encouraged the guard to step in front of the camera, and afterward showed him how to edit the image. All this was done informally, and with a lot of laughter. This guard, although a library employee, was not required to engage in this program. He was not required to even speak to the teens at his library. However, he connected with this group of teens by being willing to learn from them, and through his participation, acknowledged that their program was interesting and meaningful. Now, instead of being a potential obstacle to youth workshops, he understands what they are doing and can encourage other staff to engage as well.

Maker Jawn Programming

Programming at each site is designed to fit available space and to be responsive to the needs and interests of each library's community. This model allows for continuity and reliability for young people who frequently turn to their public libraries for after-school activities and a safe place to be. Maker Jawn programming starts from and with the population served. This engages participants in a participatory design process that ensures more authentic learning and engagement, directly reflects their voice and interests, empowers them to recognize that their opinions are powerful and meaningful, and democratizes the informal learning process (i.e., a teen can teach another teen, a Mentor, or a librarian). Maker Jawn workshops are interest-driven; the Mentor is there to introduce new materials and to cheerlead makers as they play with tools and explore concepts, ultimately shaping the program's direction.

Ideally, when participants first enter a library maker space, they see people actively engaged in a wide variety of creative projects. They hear people communicating respectfully and collaborating on projects. They feel welcome, stimulated, and excited. They leave with an idea and want to come back and work on a project. Maker Mentors work hard to actively welcome and engage potential new participants. When someone new shows up, the Mentors give them an overview of the space and program, introduce them to the regular participants, show them the various tools and materials, and try to give them a sense of the possibilities available in the space. Regular program participants give new ones this "tour" and ask the regulars to show off their projects with the goal of inspiring the newcomer.

Current programming happens across five different neighborhood libraries in North Philadelphia. As discussed in the Youth Makerspace Playbook (Maker Ed, 2015), "programming is very flexible space-wise and changes to fit the needs of library staff, mentors, and participants. The space in each library is different. In some libraries, materials share space with library books on the shelves and programming happens directly on the library floor. In others, programming occurs in a separate room that is shared with other programs, or in outdoor space" (p. 14). Participants know that once they are "involved and working on projects, they can do so in whatever library space makes most sense" (Maker Ed, 2015, p. 14).

Materials are organized by mentors' discretion at different sites, generally in "boxes and bins since designated shelving is often not available. At some sites, program participants help to organize and label the storage of tools and materials—this is helpful in getting everyone familiar with where supplies are located as well as in giving patrons a sense of ownership and pride in the space" (Maker Ed, 2015, p. 39). There is an office in the basement of one of the library sites where larger equipment that is shared among sites is stored (e.g., projectors, 3D printers, vinyl cutters, video cameras, etc.). Maker Mentors maintain an inventory of tools and supplies, have a checkout system for shared equipment, and collaboratively create order lists of needed supplies on an ongoing basis.

Maker Jawn has several pieces of equipment that are brought to various program sites for specific projects. Maker Mentors who have experience using these pieces of equipment have run professional development sessions overviewing their use and have created written guides that can be used by other Mentors and program participants. The Maker Mentors also work with interns and work-study students to create video tutorials about using this equipment.

Although the maker space at each library site is different, all the Maker Mentors strive to create a supportive, engaging, and welcoming environment. They display participant work to celebrate achievements and inspire new projects. They generally tend to set up a few different project types for people to engage in if they are not already working on a self-initiated project, with the understanding that starting this type of project can sometimes feel intimidating. On a typical day, a Maker Mentor might set out a laptop and Makey Makey (a kit that turns everyday objects into Internet-connected touch pads) for computer-based projects, a wind-powered-car challenge, and a few examples of cut-paper projects to interest participants. Someone might engage with one or all three activities, work on an unrelated self-initiated project, or just sit, chat, or draw. Maker Mentors provide a range of possible activities, with different access points, while also making space for more long-term, open-ended engagement. They encourage participants to take ideas or suggestions and inventively flip them upside down. Programs range from video production to gardening, from printmaking to sewing (hand, machine, and e-textiles), from copper-tape circuitry projects to audiobook recording and stop-motion animation.

Maker Mentors encourage participants to use recycled materials whenever possible, which provides a teaching opportunity to think about the maker movement not only in terms of "creating" things, but "fixing" things and repurposing items to become new objects. They often work with cardboard boxes, scrap paper, and other materials accumulated from the rest of the library staff, who know that their trash will be transformed into something more exciting. One Maker Mentor came up with "The Sculpture Challenge," a creative activity that uses various scraps that tend to accumulate in the maker spaces. She places these random items in envelopes and hands them to program participants, who then have to use all the pieces to create a sculpture. In this way, recycling goes beyond using up old leftovers; it raises consciousness about consumption, and the reasons for "making."

Maker Mentors maintain daily logs that list participants' names and ages, along with the projects that each participant worked on and for what amount of time. They also track individual participants' progress through the compilation of monthly reports. Success is not only measured by project completion: "the mentors understand that learning happens even if a project gets abandoned somewhere along the way. Another way to measure success is by paying attention to whether participants feel ownership of the space and are working well with one another. When someone excitedly suggests an idea or a project, mentors know they have succeeded in creating a space for exploration, creativity, and learning" (Maker Ed, 2015, p. 63).

Although the Maker Jawn program operates on a drop-in basis and the participants are not the same each day, each program site has developed a core group of committed regulars. These participants have worked on collaborative projects that give back to the library and surrounding community. In the spring of 2014, youth at one site built and maintained a hay-bale garden in the library's parking lot. They grew sunflowers and pumpkins, and some even took extra seeds home to plant with their families. At another site, a nine-year-old participant who is very passionate about animal rights created a video and held a bake sale to raise funds to adopt a wildcat at a nature preserve. She then went on to work with a Maker Mentor on writing a grant to raise awareness about animal rights issues in her own neighborhood and started an animal rights club that held regular meetings.

These regulars who take ownership over the space and tools become informal mentors for newer participants. Over the past year, the program has been working primarily with youth who have participated in a wide range of projects, which include making movies, music videos, and animations; creating an interactive welcome sign using the Intel Galileo development board; making comic books and zines; building art-making robots out of toothbrush motors; sewing; and creating a digital badging system. In January 2015, Maker Jawn began expanding programming to an intergenerational audience. Projects that have already been created by the new participants include a 3D-printed, cookie-cutter lending library, with unique shapes designed and printed by adult participants. Adult participants have also been developing job-seeking skills that include personal branding, using social media, and gaining digital media literacy.

CONCLUDING THOUGHTS

Although the initiatives described here were supported by grant funding, this is not to say that successful programming depends on outside funding. Rather,

FIGURE 9.2   The Chain Reaction of "Maker Jawn"

The Library provides a safe space for teens to gather. → *Teens develop trusting relationships with mentors as they engage in low-barrier maker activities.* → *Teens are drawn to more complex projects as they develop expertise.* → *Teens express their unique voices through their work.* → *Teens share their voice with ever-larger audiences.* → *For some teens, "making" opens up academic and/or career opportunities.*

the progression of responsive services to teens was always driven by a few staff members who were committed to getting youth meaningfully involved at the Library, especially through the lens of creative technology. The most valuable learning and community building at the Free Library have not happened because of an expensive dedicated teen center with multiple 3D printers and dozens of new laptops loaded with software. As Figure 9.2 shows, it has happened because the library system as a whole has a vested interest in teen learning. It has opened up positions that can help point teens in the direction of articulating their interests and connecting those to school, jobs, or some way of enriching their lives, whether it is creatively, intellectually, or socially. This type of job requires hiring responsive, creative people who can think in innovative terms and ask questions rather than give answers.

> Maker Jawn has the potential to move towards a future where libraries don't *have* maker spaces, but where the entire library *is* a maker space—where everyone is a learner and a teacher, where the line between staff and community member is blurred and porous, and where every young person, irrespective of race, age, gender, economic status, or education, has a voice.

One of the best things about the current Maker Jawn approach is that it encourages and promotes a certain level of self-exploration, collaborative learning, and creativity that, in the end, can be a life-changing event for program participants and program Mentors alike. It also has the potential to move towards a future where libraries don't *have* maker spaces, but where the entire library *is* a maker space—where everyone is a learner and a teacher, where the line between staff and community member is blurred and porous, and where every young person, irrespective of race, age, gender, economic status, or education, has a voice.

Make It Happen in Your Library

1. Focus on engaging youth in a participatory design processes that ensure authentic learning and engagement, directly reflect their voice and interests, empower them to recognize that their opinions are powerful and meaningful, and democratize the informal learning process.
2. Expand the concept of literacy beyond the ability to comprehend and express oneself through written language to the ability to construct meaning through a wide range of platforms.
3. Provide opportunities for nondominant youth to connect to interesting, creative, caring adult mentors who are invested in their goals and interests.
4. Place an emphasis on relationship and community building while working to provide access to and training with technology tools.
5. Prioritize and embed the creativity, cultural heritage, and interests of diverse communities directly within the fabric of the library.
6. Pilot and revise projects through a combination of public and private funding prior to integrating them into the Library's core services.
7. Build on the passion of library staff who are committed to getting youth meaningfully involved at the Library, especially through the lens of creative technology.

10

African American Teens as Community Change Agents: Unlocking Potential with Pearl Bailey Library Youth Programs

Demetria Tucker and Sonya L. Scott

Connecting Research to Practice

As you read this chapter, look for the following characteristics of effective library services for African American youth:

- **Librarians**—Caring, affirming, proactive
- **Space**—Respectful, responsive, nurturing, welcoming
- **Programming**—Asset-based, honors/promotes voice, develops agency, fosters community

Pearl Bailey Library (PBL) was established in 1985 and named after the famous African American singer and actress Pearl Bailey, who was born in Newport News, Virginia. The library is located in the southeast community of the city and has the highest number of youth aged 12–18 visiting the library daily in the Newport News Public Library System (NNPLS) during after-school and out-of-school

159

breaks. Prior to the programming overhaul described in this chapter, the majority of the youth who came to the library used very few of the services that we offered. Youth were primarily using library computers for gaming and web-based social networking. It is crucial to note that the library has always played a major role as a central meeting place for the youth living in southeast Newport News because of the limited number of "for free" after-school programs and computer services offered in the area. The core youth customer base at PBL consists of African American youth, particularly young men aged 6–18, who come to the library daily after school from about 3 p.m., with many of them staying until closing at 9 p.m. They look to the library as a safe haven from the violence and gang activity that plagues this part of the city.

> The team recognized that the youth of the Pearl Bailey Library were an untapped community asset. We wanted to provide library programs and services that would enable them to assert their identities as intelligent young people who can, and do, contribute in positive ways to their schools, families, and neighborhoods.

With the continued increase in popularity and use of the Internet and social media, PBL became an even more popular hangout for tweens and teens. To provide additional structure and programming for the increase in youth attendance, major changes to both the physical layout of PBL and its programming schedule were implemented in 2008. Two youth librarians, Sonya L. Scott and Joy Jackson, spearheaded the initial effort by first rearranging furniture and shelving to create a separate teen seating area. The Youth Services staff then worked to establish a teen advisory committee and to create the "Chill Spot," a dedicated area of the library for holding programs for youth aged 12–18. The Chill Spot was envisioned as a space that would not only encourage tweens and teens to feel like they belonged at the public library, but also to support positive social interactions among the youth.

After these initial changes, a formal Youth Services team was established under the direction of the new senior family and youth services librarian, Demetria Tucker. Tucker recognized that the team would need to take a hard look at all current PBL tween and teen library programs and services, as well as conduct research to find out what other after-school programs were being offered in the community. A grant writer, Judy Condra, was hired to work with the team since the library staff anticipated that the necessary changes would require additional funding.

The new Youth Services team developed an approach that:

- established community partners that included veterans, college students, and both civic and fraternal organizations;
- developed relationships with our youth to engage them in the development, implementation, and evaluation of library programs and services; and
- created a safe and collegial environment through innovative methods that sustained learning, literacy, and youth leadership beyond the standard scholastic curriculum of a classroom setting.

The team recognized that the youth of PBL were an untapped community asset. We wanted to provide library programs and services that would enable them to assert their identities as intelligent young people who can, and do, contribute in positive ways to their schools, families, and neighborhoods. We also vowed that PBL would not only bridge the digital divide, but also enhance literacy enrichment through our new youth-driven programs and services.

In 2013, the PBL Youth Program was selected as a National Arts and Humanities Youth Award winner, the highest honor for an after-school and out-of-school program. During 2013–2014, the library and its staff received numerous other national and city awards for its excellence. In this chapter, we explain how we achieved this success. We also discuss our continued efforts to enable our youth to reach their full potential and become empowered members of their community.

STAFF: AN ESSENTIAL COMPONENT

As with any successful youth library, it takes skilled, compassionate, and dedicated paraprofessionals and professionals who value working with youth. Our Youth Services team included:

- *Demetria Tucker—Senior librarian for family and youth services.* Her primary responsibilities included collection development, reference services, readers' advisory, and planning and implementing library services and programs for children and teens of all ages.
- *Sonya L. Scott—Senior youth information services specialist.* She developed programs and services that are educational and entertaining for children and teens of all ages. She also assisted with collection development and provided both readers advisory and reference services to young adults and adults.
- *PBL Teen Advisory Committee Executive Board*
- *For Kids Only (FKO) Advisory Committee*

Other people who were instrumental to the success of the PBL youth services program included:

- *Izabela Cieszynski—Newport News Public Library System Director*
- *Anita Jennings—PBL Supervising Branch Manager*
- *Watina Smith—PBL Senior Information Specialist/Adult Programs*
- *Judy Condra—former staff/grant writer (2010–2013)*

NECESSARY SUCCESS FACTORS

Prior to the first meeting of the Youth Services team, we reviewed several City of Newport News documents, including the now-defunct Keeping Our Kids Safe initiative that strived to make the community a safe place for youth to live, grow, and thrive. We also looked at the strategic plans for the city and for the NNPLS. Additional resources that we reviewed included the American Library Association (ALA) and the Young Adult Library Services Association's (YALSA) best practices for urban public libraries serving children and teens. These documents indicated that young people in general, but especially those who live in urban communities, need a safe place to interact socially, to learn about jobs and volunteer opportunities, and have reliable, safe public transportation. Our next step was to identify the necessary success factors. What did we need to do to best support our youth? What behaviors did we need to change in order to reenvision our youth services program? What issues did we need to address? Based on our research and our previous professional experiences, we identified the following factors as critical to the success of our new youth engagement efforts.

Get Personal

We knew that success depended on the Youth Services staff being approachable and forming interpersonal relationships with each child and teen that entered PBL daily. It was especially important for us to get to know the key neighborhood teen leaders and trendsetters, and to gain the trust of the broader community. It was also critical that the other PBL staff establish and gain trust from the youth.

Change the Way That We Maintain a Safe and Welcoming Environment

For a variety of reasons, youth who live in at-risk neighborhoods often have adversarial relationships with adult authority figures. For many, their past experiences have led them to mistrust adults and to challenge rules and regulations, especially if they view them as arbitrary or unfair, and to view adult interventions as harassment. Our emphasis on supporting positive youth development meant that we needed to change how we engaged with our teens and to change how our teens viewed and interacted with adults, and with each other, in the library. We needed to establish clear rules and expectations to not only make the library a safe and welcoming space, but also to support our teens in learning to monitor their own actions and behaviors. We also knew that we needed to work with the library security guards and the Newport News police officers who patrol the neighborhood to encourage them to develop interpersonal relationships with our teens—relationships that would allow the teens and the adults to get to know each other as individuals, thus reducing the potential for conflict and tension.

Get Youth Buy-in/Ask for Feedback

Designing programs *with* our youth, not for them, would be a necessary step in enabling them to be change agents in the community. A key factor in getting buy-in from the teens would be asking for, and honoring, their ideas and opinions—to solicit their feedback on proposed library services and programs. We knew this could be accomplished by conducting informal oral and written surveys, and also by hosting open forums focused on questions such as: How could PBL best serve you? What PBL services or programs did you like best and why? Does PBL provide a welcoming atmosphere?

Set Benchmarks

One of our key goals was to help our teens be healthy, caring, and responsible members of the community, which meant that we needed to set benchmarks to guide our programs and services. We selected the Search Institute's "40 Developmental Assets for Middle Grades" and "40 Developmental Assets for Adolescents," which identify "skills, experiences, relationships, and behaviors that enable young people to develop into successful and contributing adults" (Search Institute, 2016, para. 1).

Get and Communicate Results

We knew that we also needed to develop or select a tool to record outcome measures for the new youth-driven programs and services. Simply measuring outputs, such as the number of teens attending a program, would not be enough. We needed to be able to measure the outcomes—how the new library programs and services were making a difference in the lives of our youth and in the community.

Youth Voices

My name is Sierra Hamilton, and I have been a volunteer for Pearl Bailey Library for three years now. Being new to the area when I first came here, I didn't find anyone or anywhere I could go to express myself and have fun doing it. I was introduced to the library by accident and from there just kept coming back. I don't know what about the library made me want to come back, but when I really think about it, I think I kept coming back because the entire library staff was so welcoming. By the end of the first day, everybody knew my name. Two people in particular helped me become the WOMAN I am today, Ms. Sonya and Ms. "T"ucker. If it wasn't for them pushing us teens to finish school and come up in the world, I don't think it would have been as easy as it was. They made sure grades were up and up by having routine report card and interim checks EVERY SINGLE semester. Offering help to those who need it, and pushing the ones who did good to do great. I was 17 years old then. I'm 19 now and I'm proud to say that with the help of Ms. Sonya and Ms. T and the rest of the Pearl Bailey staff, I was a high school graduate in 2011. With that being said, I'm also the first member in my family to graduate. From seeing me struggling and watching me come across the stage, my grandmother went back and got her high school diploma.

Hearing her achievement made me realize that I motivated someone, and I realized no matter how old someone is if they have dreams, they can be accomplished.

—Sierra Hamilton

At first I used to go to the library just to have access to the computer. But the more I came, the more invited I felt. I met a lot of good people here. I made a lot of friends. At the library I feel safe. I feel that the librarians, three in particular, help me the most. I'm always at the right state of mind. They have so many activities to do. I even joined the TAC committee. I ♡ Pearl Bailey.

—Katherine Diaz

THE TRANSFORMATION BEGINS

Once we had had reviewed all the youth-based documents and developed our list of key success factors, we were ready to develop an initial plan and put it into action. Our first step was to hold a meeting with all the PBL staff to explain the new concept of "youth engagement." We needed all staff members to understand the goals of our teen programs, to recognize the positive impact that the programs could have on our teens' lives, and to join us in our efforts. We especially needed to encourage a change in attitudes and behaviors toward youth—to help staff adopt an asset-based stance that would allow them to focus on the potential that our youth have, rather than on the problems they sometimes present.

Because we knew that teen input was essential to developing responsive and successful programs and services, we asked teens to complete a survey (see Figure 10.1). Many of them were hesitant about participating in the survey because they felt that no one really cared about what they wanted. The Youth Services staff stressed the importance of getting their input and promised that they would see their suggestions implemented. In the end, 44 teens completed the written survey, and 22 responded to an oral version of the survey. The reasons that they gave for visiting the library included that they wanted to access computers, the library was a safe gathering place, and the staff were friendly .

We then conducted two open youth forums to get additional feedback from our youth and as a way to jump-start the development of an informal Teen Advisory Committee (TAC). During both sessions, the Youth Services staff shared the results of the teen survey and explained the benefits of having an advisory committee. We also requested that the teens help us create rules of conduct for the library and suggest how we might address the computer short-age problem that we faced after 3 p.m. on school days. Computers are a main draw for our youth, which means that every day, library staff see 30–40 (or even more) names listed on the computer sign-in sheet for one of the four pub-lic computers located in the Youth Services area. All PBL library customers are allowed to use the computers for two hours per day. While children and teens are allowed to use computers in the adult computer lab, our teens had indi-cated to the Youth Services staff that they felt more comfortable using the ones

FIGURE 10.1   Sample Teen Survey

"IT'S YOUR LIBRARY—TELL US WHAT YOU THINK!"

TEEN SURVEY

PEARL BAILEY LIBRARY

We would like your input on the library in order for us to best serve YOU, so if you are between the ages of 13 and 18, please respond to this brief survey. After you have completed the survey, please return it to the Youth Services Desk for a ticket to be entered into a prize drawing to win a "jump drive."

1. Please circle if you are male or female
   Male   Female

2. How old are you?

3. Is the library staff friendly, approachable, and knowledgeable?
   Yes   Sometimes   No

4. Are the print books/material and non-print books/materials (CDs, DVDs) plentiful, and up to date?
   Yes   No   Sometimes   I don't know

5. How often do you come to the Pearl Bailey Branch Library? (Please circle one)
   Every Day   1–5 times a week   1–5 times a month
   More than 5 times a month   Never

6. Why do you use the Pearl Bailey Library? (Please circle all that apply)
   To use the Internet   To do homework/research
   To hang out with friends   To read books/magazines
   To borrow books, music, DVDs, etc.   To get help from a librarian
   To attend library programs/events   Other:

7. Do you attend teen events and programs? If no", why not?
   Yes   No   Sometimes

8. How often do you attend the teen events and programs? (Please circle one)
   Never   1–5 times a week   1–5 times a month

9. In 2008, Youth Service sponsored more than 25 events and programs for teens, ages 12–18. How many of the programs did you attend? (Please circle one)
   None   1+   5+   15+   20+   25+

10. Please list your top three favorite teen programs for 2008.

11. Are you a member of the Pearl Bailey TAC (Teen Advisory Council)? If "no",
    why not?
    Yes   No

12. How would you describe the "Chill Spot"? What do you like or dislike about it?

13. Which of these programs/topics would make you want to use the library
    more? (Please circle <u>three</u>)

Having a comforting and welcoming space for teens	Music Center
Computer technology classes	Crafts
Fashion/beauty	Poetry Slam
Homework help	Leadership skills
College life	Health/fitness
Community awareness	Politics/current events
Video games/gaming	Traditional board games
Job opportunities	Writing

Thank you! Your Opinion Counts! ☺

---

in the Youth Services area. Because of this preference, the Youth Services area often became overcrowded, with young people gathered in small and large groups, waiting for their computer time. The situation often caused disturbances for other patrons, especially adults, and we wanted to find a solution. We stressed to the teens that it was important for them—especially the "key leaders"—to help brainstorm solutions, to help establish procedures, and to be change agents in the process.

One of our first priorities was to continue to strengthen our personal connections with the teens. We did this in two ways. First, every young person who entered the Youth Services area was greeted by their first name. (We learned their names from sign-in sheets and from our day-to-day interactions with them.) We also asked the teens about their days at school and if they needed any assistance with their homework. Soon, many of the "key" youth leaders and players began hanging around the Youth Services service desk just to talk to staff. As the teens and Youth Services staff members became more comfortable with each other, the teens began to share more information about their personal lives and goals.

Second, to engage our teens, the Youth Services staff promoted the use of three-dimensional puzzles, card games, and board games (such as Monopoly, Connect Four, and Scrabble and other word games) as fun activities not only to play with their peers, but also to challenge the Youth Services staff. By being approachable and available to engage in daily game challenges with the teens, we not only earned their trust, but quickly became both socially and emotionally connected.

Staff also created "READ" posters, similar to ALA's posters, that featured TAC members as a means of encouraging other teens in the city to read, as well as a way of publicizing PBL programming. The posters were displayed in Newport News public schools, City Hall, and at PBL. In addition to promoting our youth programs, these posters provided a voice and presence for our youth. We wanted to show that our teens are the stars of our library! The response from both the young adults and the public was enthusiastic. We continue to print new posters each year.

Building Our Teens' Leadership Skills

Our TAC meetings were typically well attended with 15 to 20 teens, making these meetings the major vehicle for our teens' voices to be heard and for us to cultivate their leadership skills. The teens suggested programming ideas, recommended new policies, and suggested materials for the library. Our PBL TAC has been recognized at a Newport News City Council meeting for their contributions to making a difference in the southeast community. And the program sees results: 79 percent of former PBL TAC members are enrolled or have graduated from college, are serving in the military, or are participating in professional apprenticeship programs. Many of the teens who have been TAC officers have gone on to take leadership roles in school and beyond. Katherine Diaz, a former member and TAC Vice President, for example, was named the 2009 Mayor's Youth Citizen of the Year.

> The program sees results: 79 percent of former PBL TAC members are enrolled or have graduated from college, are serving in the military, or are participating in professional apprenticeship programs.

Based on youth feedback from our surveys and TAC meetings, we implemented a variety of new activities in the Chill Spot, including a Teen Urban Lit Club, Wii games, Homework Help, karaoke, and even a teen version of the 2009 presidential inaugural ball with fun activities. After the success of a few programs, we realized that we needed to offer programs more frequently and on a regular basis. We realized that one way to do this was to solicit assistance from our teens—to have teens help staff the Chill Spot in the afternoons. We asked teens to submit written proposals to conduct a program (craft, chess, writing club, etc.) and to lead this program in the Chill Spot. The Yu Gi Oh card club, Chess Club, and Craft Day are examples of programs that were led by teens who submitted written program proposals.

Having teen input on the rules of conduct for the library has been instrumental in reducing behavior problems. Since 2010, the staff has seen a significant decrease in the number of reported disturbances inside the library due to more approachable library security and the "ownership" and buy-in for the conduct rules by our teen patrons. We have found that members of our TAC have been key to helping us implement library rules. As leaders, many of the TAC members have taken it upon themselves to explain the official library rules of conduct to new individuals, as well as to teens who are ignoring them. If teens continued to display disruptive behavior, we spoke firmly to each teen individually, away from friends, about the established rules and consequences. Anyone who continued to be disrespectful and display inappropriate behavior was banned from the library for a specified time period.

Recognizing that many of our youth had not had experiences outside their immediate surroundings, Joy Jackson spearheaded community outings or field trips for our TAC members. This programming component allowed youth from southeast Newport News to have nonschool life experiences outside their neighborhood boundaries, including cultural and civic outings. To counteract the lack of transportation, we used Newport News City vehicles. Small groups of TAC members have attended People to People/Meeting of the Minds monthly meetings. People to People, a civic organization, meets monthly with teens to brainstorm ideas for how to stop the violence in the Newport News community. In addition, our TAC members have attended theater productions, participated in regional library "Tech It Out" events, and visited a Disabled American Veterans chapter.

Our Work Continues

We continue to work with TAC members to evaluate the quality of programs and services offered using immediate teen feedback, surveys, and program requests. We track both current program participation and the progress of former TAC members. The following programs are offered to tweens and teens at PBL on a consistent basis after school. PBL also hosts special themed programs that are offered throughout the year—taking advantage of our PBL staff or teen talent whenever possible.

- *Youth Enrichment Program (YEP)*—Teens aged 13–17 who live in southeast Newport News can apply to participate in this internship program. The program allows teens to explore a career, gain job readiness skills, learn leadership and interpersonal skills, and gain an opportunity for them to give back to their community. Participants in the program are required to commit to a minimum of 10 hours of service learning per week and receive a monetary stipend as an incentive at the end of each month. The YEP's primary duties include shelving and filing both book and nonbook materials. They also assist with events, including helping presenters, greeting and directing attendees, and doing setup and tear-down. This program is funded annually by the NNPLS Friends of the Library.
- *Male Mentoring Program*—Big Brothers Big Sisters and Zeta Lambda Chapter of Alpha Phi Alpha Fraternity Inc., in conjunction with PBL, host a Male Mentoring Program for boys and young men ages 9–18. The sessions are held monthly and last about two hours. The program empowers the participants to aspire toward higher education through self-creation, avoidance of risk-taking behaviors, and participation in positive activities. All participants must register and complete a Big Brothers Big Sisters application form.
- *Homework Assistance in Math and Science*—We were not able to find an adult volunteer to lead this program, so we chose to use an asset mindset by taking advantage of the strengths of our teens. Teens who

excel in math and science volunteer as tutors. Our teen volunteers are excellent, assisting many of their peers and young children with their homework. We award the volunteers at the close of the school year with gift cards. For the past three years, we have also partnered with pharmaceutical students from Hampton University, who assist students weekly with their math and science homework.

- *Teen Urban Lit Club*—Teens select the featured books and participate in book discussions, crafts, online activities, and movie outings.
- *Anime and Manga Club*—This club is conducted by an expert volunteer. Teens are given an opportunity to vote on three anime selections per month. Additionally, games and Japanese-themed crafts are incorporated into the monthly programs. Members assist with the annual ToshoCon Convention hosted by the NNPLS. Several members of the club along with Youth Services staff attend the annual NekoCon Convention held in Hampton, Virginia.
- *Chess Club*—An adult volunteer and/or a senior teen member of the chess club conducts these monthly sessions where participants learn to play the game of chess and discuss strategies.
- *High School Graduation Celebration*—Held annually during the June TAC meeting, we provide special recognition to all graduating high school seniors. Each graduating senior receives a Microsoft PowerPoint presentation on a flash drive of assorted personal pictures of their participation in library programs. This event is so popular that many former members return to participate in the celebration and show support for their peers.

CONCLUDING THOUGHTS

We feel that the keys to providing successful youth-based programming and services is establishing an interpersonal relationship with each of the youth that we serve, valuing their input by involving youth in our initial planning process, providing a consistency of programs, and finally being accessible. We also note that it is very important to be open and honest with youth about what is doable. We shared our departmental budget and involved our youth and teen advisory members. Finally, we equipped our youth with the organizational skills needed to participate in the process of making the difficult choices due to limited resources and for purchasing of library resources and program materials.

Make It Happen in Your Library

1. Keep the library director, grant writer and the entire Library branch family informed during your initial planning process and actively seek their ideas. This allows them to understand your goals, your need for Youth Services staff, the necessity for time for planning and execution, but most of all their support and buy-in for what you do.
2. Provide high-quality staff. Hire youth services staff and recruit volunteers who are passionate about working with young people and who have friendly, approachable personalities.

3. Don't let your programs "grow whiskers." Tweak them! We have learned from past experience that it is okay when a program we thought was great flopped. Learn to be flexible.
4. Actively recruit and engage your teens in the planning and programming process. Allow teens to lead programs.
5. Befriend your grant writer and public information officer.
6. Track the success of your programs and services using measurable goals.
7. Seek partnership and alliances with community partners. Take every opportunity to talk about your programs and services that you offer. It is important to have your youth formally acknowledge community partners, library boards, Friends groups, and staff with thank-you cards.
8. Take the time to make a concerted effort to understand your community and the citizens that you serve.

11

Outreach and Community Partnerships at Stanford L. Warren Library

Sarah Alverson and Heather Cunningham

Connecting Research to Practice

As you read this chapter, look for the following characteristics of effective library services for African American youth:

- **Librarians**—Caring, collaborative
- **Programming**—Engaging, authentic, fosters community, challenging
- **Resources**—Enabling, provide counterstories, developmentally appropriate

The Stanford L. Warren Library, a branch of the Durham County Library system, is a small community library in Durham, North Carolina. The library was originally established in 1916 as the Durham Colored Library and was the second Black library in the state. The original mission of the library was to provide books, resources, and a community meeting space for Durham's Black community. It served as an important community resource, especially during the Civil Rights era.

> Providing equal access to information and resources is one of the most important aspects of public library service.

In 1966, the Stanford L. Warren Library merged with the larger Durham County Library system ending the segregation of public libraries in Durham. The Stanford L. Warren Library benefited from joining this larger system but still maintained its unique history as a meeting space, resource center, and safe haven for Durham's Black community. Today, the demographics of this library location are still largely African American. However, due to economic and political changes in the city, the once-thriving community now experiences high unemployment rates and increasing crime. Like many youth who live in urban communities in the United States, the youth in this community attend schools that are underfunded and classified as low performing. These youth want a safe place to socialize and relax, access technology, and explore their personal interests and passions, especially during the summer months. To grow up healthy, caring, and responsible, these youth, like all youth, also want additional positive adult mentors to both encourage them and set appropriate and high expectations for their behavior.

Providing equal access to information and resources is one of the most important aspects of public library service. In a low-income community, like the one that Stanford L. Warren serves, this is especially significant, as some families experience financial barriers that prevent youth from participating in extracurricular activities or accessing technology at home. The schools too lack the resources to provide adequate access to technology or enrichment activities. A small, public, community library is the perfect place to meet the needs of youth, as it can be one of few safe, free places for them to hang out after school hours. At Stanford L. Warren in particular, many children and teens frequent the space from the time school ends until library closing time, providing a great opportunity for librarians to engage with these youth through innovative programming.

In this chapter, we describe the goals that we have established for the youth services programs at Stanford L. Warren and strategies that we use to overcome some of the challenges we face. We then describe two specific programs that we have found successful in addressing the literacy needs of the African American youth in our community.

GOALS OF YOUTH SERVICES PROGRAMMING

We have three goals for our library programming. The first is basic—to create a library space where African American youth feel welcomed, accepted, appreciated, and safe. In our work, we have found that it is important to first establish a positive environment and build trust with youth before focusing on further goals. Youth in our community do not always see the library as a welcoming and safe place, free of bullying and harassment, where they can express themselves, learn, and grow. Too often, as described in Part One of this book, African American youths' experiences with formal institutions such as schools, libraries, and law enforcement have been negative. Getting to know kids in the library by greeting them by name, finding out about their interests, and simply acting as a friendly mentor goes a long way in establishing a positive foundation for library programs. We create this atmosphere by developing a designated space for kids and teens, building rapport with youth, and ensuring that *everyone* working in the library understands the best ways to work with our youth.

Our second programming goal focuses on youth empowerment. Research shows that the community library as a "third place" (a public, social space that is neither home nor work or school) can help youth discover their abilities, develop a positive sense of identity and self-concept, and acquire positive social competencies. This goal is especially important for our library, since many of the kids in the community use the space as almost a "second home," spending significant amounts of time within its walls. While some might view their almost continuous presence in the library as problematic, we see this as an opportunity for library staff to develop positive mentor relationships with the youth and to give them ownership over their own learning and development.

According to the Search Institute (2016), social and emotional skills are an important aspect of human development and play a role in success throughout childhood and later in life. A community library, like Stanford L. Warren, is an ideal place to reinforce these skills through engaging and purposeful activities and programs. Through empowerment of youth, librarians can simultaneously teach these skills and proactively establish behavior expectations. For example, at the beginning of our teen programs, we establish the "rules" together by discussing the rights of the youth in the space—the right for individuals to be heard and the right for individuals to express themselves free of judgment. This simple change in wording gives youth a sense of ownership of their actions and encourages them to be responsible for their behavior.

Our third programming goal involves introducing youth to new ideas, providing access to technology, and teaching them to access, create, and share information. As previously stated, the youth in our community do not necessarily have access to a variety of resources within the home or at school. They do not always have the opportunity to explore their interests or expand their worldview via travel or participation in extracurricular activities. Their schools offer some limited electives or enrichment opportunities during the school day, but many of the youth lack access to technology in their homes and are thus inadequately prepared to compete in a technology-rich world. The kids passively use technology but are not necessarily creating, understanding, or developing skills. Library computers are used mainly to play games, watch videos, and interact on social networks. Many struggle with accessing library resources to find credible information for school papers and projects. They also have difficulty using information to form new ideas and make connections.

Stanford L. Warren Library provides computer tutoring to teach Internet skills and Microsoft Office programs, three-dimensional printing workshops, robotic-programming events, and "Donuts for Database" exploration programs. In the robotic programming events, teens and children have the opportunity to use the Wonder Workshop robots Dash and Dot to learn visual, hands-on programming on iPads. The youth code Dash and Dot to interact with their environment and with each other, manipulating various objects and obstacles, all the while, encouraging the creativity of the youth programmer. Another example of how we integrate new concepts and technology directly into library programs is our Teen Anime Club, a program developed upon youth request that often incorporates Japanese history and culture into entertaining events. Teens share their love of anime while also participating in Japanese tea ceremonies or sushi-making workshops. Teens gain new technology skills by creating personal avatars or learning basic programming to develop their own animations. The idea is that after a brief introduction to new ideas and technology, youth will continue to pursue their interests, and in the future, the library can provide more in-depth programming on these topics. By exposing youth to new ideas and information, and by improving their information literacy and technology skills, our library can act as an information equalizer within the community.

OVERCOMING PROGRAMMING CHALLENGES

In an effort to ensure attendance at library programs, we struggle with the age-old question that all youth librarians face—how to provide programs that are both enjoyable and educational. After a long day in school, rarely do youth want to come to a program that screams "information and education." Instead, they much prefer programs that are fun, engaging, and stimulate their senses, thus providing them with a break from the formal educational system. This is especially true for our youth, who often have not had positive experiences at school and have been subjected to low expectations and even discrimination.

A unique challenge that Stanford L. Warren faces is that teens, and even older elementary aged children, in our community often have younger siblings with them when they visit the library. Both the older youth charged with baby-sitting and their younger siblings are held accountable to Library Courteous Conduct Policies. Unfortunately, this means that the younger siblings must have direct supervision, making it difficult to offer age-specific programming; that is, programs that require teens to be in one part of the library and children in another. Opening programs to all age groups can be chaotic, as it is necessary to balance a wide range of developmental levels, interests, and attention spans.

In an effort to overcome this particular challenge, we often work together to develop youth programs. By working together, we are able to split the youth into age groups after an initial introduction and icebreaker. The theme for both groups is the same, but each of us tailors the program to fit the age level and needs of the participants. Our first such program was a joint Poetry for Pizza Workshop for children and teens. The program began with a shared icebreaker (using an adjective that starts with the first letter of your name), followed by a period of separate writing prompts led by each librarian. At the end of the program, the entire group joined to share personal "I Am" poems and eat pizza. While this method worked incredibly well, the new challenge becomes coordinating two busy schedules to plan, prepare, and facilitate library programs.

At our library—as is true with many public libraries—it is also often more difficult to ensure program attendance than it is to create, plan, and prepare a library program. While we tend to see many of the same faces every week, attendance at programs is sporadic, though we do have regulars who visit every day. Many of our youth must also walk to the library from the surrounding community since their parents or guardians are not at home to drive them, making their attendance dependent on the weather.

To help us overcome the challenges of low attendance numbers and lack of interest, we actively engage in outreach, establishing connections with individuals and groups in the community who can help us work better with the youth who are regular library users, as well as those we rarely see. In the library world, outreach is typically seen as taking a service or program out into the community, but it can also signify bringing an organization or resource into the library space. Both forms of outreach require intentional efforts to meet the needs of library users, and perhaps even more importantly—nonusers.

While creating community partnerships has always been encouraged within the public library sphere, it is not always an easy task. Time constraints, challenging interpersonal relations, and a plethora of community organizations to choose from can be daunting. From our experience, however, we have found that once formed, good partnerships are mutually beneficial. These partnerships help increase awareness about library services, provide additional resources for library users, and expand the library's reach within the community. Partner organizations often benefit from free advertising and free programming. While we are sometimes approached by outside agencies wishing to collaborate, more often it is necessary to reach out to groups ourselves. Some of our partnerships have worked and others have failed. Success is usually determined by youth interest, program attendance numbers, and ease of communication between both parties. There is obviously no one-size-fits-all criterion for every library, but our main objective is to work with community organizations to meet the library's goals, while also serving the needs of the youth in our community. Next, we describe two community partnership programs that have been successful and address the literacy needs of our youth.

Youth Voices

"I Am"

I am outgoing like the sun shines in the sky.
I wonder if I will ever be an artist.
I see me being free.
I want to go home.

I am friendly.
I pretend not to be mean.
I feel trapped like a dog in a cage.
I worry if my people doing okay.
I cry inside but not outside.

I am intelligent like my friend
I understand I have to serve my days.
I say I'll be out in no time.

I dream to become a tattoo artist.
I try not to go insane in that little room.

—15-year-old African American female

Durham Youth Home Book Club (Heather)

In May 2014, an outreach program was established with a local youth detention center—The Durham Youth Home (DYH) book club. This residential facility houses youth ages 12–17 serving court-ordered time for various transgressions. These teens conduct their schoolwork within the building during school months and community-based organizations partner with the home to provide additional educational activities for the residents. The center houses 10–15 adolescents at any given time with limited access to books and resources, and there is no teen librarian to work directly with the youth. Most of the youth in the facility are African American.

The idea for the partnership began after information about the detention center was shared at a library staff event. DYH is a drop off site for Durham County Library's OASIS program, a service that provides resources to those in the community who are unable to access the library directly. I also heard through word of mouth about youth in our specific community who had spent time at the DYH; this fact alone reinforced the idea that this was a place where I needed to be. Once contacted, the director of the facility was eager to collaborate with the library in a greater capacity and was open to different program ideas. After some brainstorming and discussion, we settled on the idea of a book club.

The DYH book club initially met twice monthly for one-hour sessions. The teens at the detention center come and go, but for any given program, there were usually four to eight teens, both male and female. The general atmosphere of the facility was very prisonlike, with several security doors to enter, guards on duty, and the youth in matching, scrublike attire. The tense atmosphere did not seem conducive to building connection and encouraging active participation.

I was admittedly nervous for my first session. Would the teens even be interested in reading? How would they respond to my presence? I had no idea what to expect. I soon learned that every session began the same way: The teens were always quiet until they learned my expectations; my casual, yet energetic facilitating style contrasted greatly with the strict atmosphere of the home. As is usual when working with teens, but even more so in this environment, it was necessary to break the ice.

The program was generally divided into four parts—Introduction/Icebreaker, Book Discussion, Writing Activity, and Wrap-up (see Figure 11.1 for a sample program plan). The Introduction gave me a chance to explain the purpose of the club, define the rights of the space, learn names, and help the teens loosen up. I discovered that in this type of workshop, it was important to set the tone for the session before leaping into any activity. Defining the teen's rights within the space helped to create an environment of mutual respect where youth felt safe to express personal opinions without fear of judgment. The Icebreaker was

FIGURE 11.1 Sample Durham Youth Home Book Club Plan

Circle up/Introductions (5 min)—purpose of book club (read, share, write, reflect)

Icebreaker (10 min)—Pig Personality Test
Hand out sheets of white paper and have each youth draw a picture of a pig and give it a name. Then follow the directions found at http://teachingthem.com/2011/02/18/draw -the-pig-personality-test-icebreaker to discuss what their drawings say about them and whether they think it is accurate.

Discussion of Book Club Book (15 min)—*The Absolutely True Diary of a Part-Time Indian* by Sherman Alexie.
Questions to prompt discussion:
  • Junior straddles two worlds—the Indian world of the Wellpinit reservation and the White world of Reardan. Do you know anyone who has had to this, and how did they cope?
  • Junior uses cartoons to express feelings that he can't express in words. What ways do you express your feelings?

Writing/Drawing Prompt (15 min)—In *The Absolutely True Diary of a Part-Time Indian*, Junior uses cartoons and humor to illustrate his feelings and cope with tragedy. On page 57, he draws himself as two people, White and Indian. Have you ever felt like there were two sides to who you are? Who would you be if you achieved your dreams? On a sheet of paper, draw a picture of who you are when you feel happy and hopeful. On the other side, draw a picture of who you are when you feel sad or discouraged. You can also write this out on paper.

Select New Book Club Pick (10 min)
Fist, Stick, Knife, Gun by Geoffrey Canada (1995)
Bronx Masquerade by Nikki Grimes (1998)
Divergent by Veronica Roth (2011)

Closing Circle (5 min)—circle up and share your writing thoughts

simply a lighthearted activity to get the teens talking, laughing, and making connections. In one session, for example, the teens wrote three things on a sheet of paper to describe themselves, balled it up, and had a 30-second paper ball fight. Afterward, they had to guess which paper belonged to whom. This was an excellent way to get the teens engaged in the program from the start and to create a more relaxed atmosphere for discussion. In this type of environment, breaking the ice was essential since the teens did not interact regularly within the home. As a result, they often did not even know each other's names.

The heart of the program was book discussions. As covered in Part One of this book, the discussions focused on the important ideas or themes in the book, poem, or story that we had read and how the teens related to the story rather

> I found that when we read culturally relevant and enabling texts, the teens could relate to them, and their own personal thoughts and stories began to flow.

than analyzing content for literary merit. My goal was to engage teens in thinking critically about events or situations in the book, to share their thoughts with the group, and to experience reading as an enjoyable act.

My hope was that the teens would connect situations in the story to their own lives and thus develop a greater understanding of themselves and their own struggles and aspirations. I found that when we read culturally relevant and enabling texts, the teens could relate to them, and their own personal thoughts and stories began to flow.

The activity portion of the session typically consisted of a writing or drawing prompt connected to the book or story that was discussed. This was a huge hit with the teens, as it gave them a chance to express what they were feeling in a creative way. After the first few sessions, I decided to let the teens choose between writing or drawing, so long as they kept to the general theme. I was so impressed at the quality and thoughtfulness that went into their work, and over time, this segment was extended for longer and longer periods because they were so focused. At the end of the program, we would circle back up, share our work on a voluntary basis, and determine the next reading selection. Sometimes I would show book trailers to stimulate interest or simply book talk a few titles. During this time, I found that many teens were eager to make personal book requests, which was encouraging. Forms of entertainment within the DYH were limited and as a result, these teens were reading like crazy! I had varied requests for everything, from biographies to science fiction to chicklit to horror. The situation that these teens were in was far from ideal, but this circumstance was an opportunity for the library to make a real impact on their lives. These teens in turn made an impact on me, and I left every single session feeling inspired.

Overall, the collaboration with the youth home was a huge success. I made personal connections with teens who had been labeled "difficult" or "troubled." Many opened up to me about their personal lives. They freely discussed their love lives, struggles with their families, their experiences in gangs, and the hardships they faced within their communities. Most had the desire to make their lives better but felt stuck in a cycle of low societal expectations and their own inability to control their reactions. Using culturally relevant and relatable reading material, the youth were able to safely express their feelings about important controversial topics, and as a facilitator, I was able to guide the conversation in a way that hopefully encouraged the teens to think critically about their lives. The book club was an outlet of expression for them within a restraining space, as was made evident by the remarkable work that they produced.

In terms of instruction, there were books that the teens devoured and there were books that flopped. There were writing activities that produced thought-provoking work and activities that the teens showed no interest in. For me, each session was a learning experience and flexibility was essential. I often altered the program depending on how many new teens were present, or just based on the dynamics and interest of the group. I found that some books just did not resonate with the teens. There were other books that everyone loved and felt they could relate to, such as *Yummy: The Last Days of a Southside Shorty,* by G. Neri (2010). Any misconceptions about reading interests were tossed aside, as their choices were varied. Some enjoyed reading about teens in similar situations, while others preferred escapist fiction or popular titles like *Divergent* (Roth, 2011). It was impossible to please everyone, but engaging them in conversations about what they did and did not like helped me with selection and in determining which activities would be most engaging.

Book Babies (Sarah)

In 2013, Heather came to me with a proposal for a partnership with Book Harvest, a Durham-based nonprofit organization that provides books to low-income households (http://bookharvestnc.org/). Throughout the year, Book Harvest collects donated books in new or gently used condition, putting them into the hands of children who have little to no books in their homes. The goal is to provide children with a home library, and in the process develop the literacy skills that are so important for academic success. Book Babies, a program offered by Book Harvest, provides age appropriate books to select Medicaid eligible babies every six months from birth to age five. Over the course of early childhood, this program provides participants with over 100 books in the home. By the time that a newborn reaches kindergarten age, the goal is that he or she will enter school with a solid preliteracy background. As soon as we heard about Book Harvest, we wanted to get involved. The goals of this nonprofit organization fit perfectly with one of the most basic goal of libraries—to get books in the hands of underserved youth!

The schools surrounding Stanford L. Warren Library have received some of the lowest School Performance Grades in Durham County. The Performance Grades make it apparent that children and teens struggle within the school system, which in turn affects post–high school education and job performance. In an effort to turn children into lifelong learners, Book Babies endeavors to reach children at the earliest possible time and begin the process early, helping them to develop their learning skills into life habits while still babies. Going beyond simply delivering books to families, Book Babies seeks to foster a home environment that encourages reading through home visits and additional parental training. Parent modeling and involvement is a driving force in the success of children in school, and Book Babies hopes to start this cycle early. Through home visits, reading tips sent out via text messages, early literacy training, and Book Baby celebrations, Book Babies instructs parents in how to be their child's first literacy teachers.

It was encouraging to find a partner organization so closely tied to the library's mission. Through the Book Babies Task Force, the library was given a voice in an important local initiative. I now meet monthly with a group of individuals dedicated to fostering reading in young children and providing opportunities for low-income families in our community. Together, we collaborate and develop methods and practices that are in turn shared with parents. We discuss book selections to ensure that both diverse and age-appropriate materials are introduced. We constantly discuss how to serve the community by instilling reading practices that promote lifelong learning in these young families.

My favorite part of being a librarian on the Book Babies task force is that every six months, Stanford L. Warren hosts a celebration to bring Book Babies participants and families together (see Figure 11.2 for a sample schedule). The library provides a free event space for this celebration, as well as trained library professionals to facilitate literacy activities. In turn, the celebration allows the library to spotlight programs and services within the community. Families who might have hesitations about visiting the library due to the unfamiliar layout, language barriers, or lack of knowledge about children's programs can be reached through the established relationship with Book Harvest. The library

FIGURE 11.2 Sample Book Babies Celebration Schedule

10:30—Greeting from Book Harvest and Book Babies staff

10:35—Networking, brunch, literature, and information tables
- Parents are encouraged to interact with Book Babies staff, librarians, and each other as they wait for storytime to begin.
- Library Card sign-up tables with Spanish translators are set up, registering entire families for library cards.

11:00—30-minute storytime, geared toward babies (from birth to two years old); stories, songs, and commentary are translated by a Spanish translator
- Storytimes are heavily song-based, encouraging parent-baby interaction. Books are simple, with the librarian demonstrating to a parent how to point to colors, count, etc. during the storytime.
- The librarian has a running commentary through the storytime, instructing parents how best to facilitate reading time.

11:30—Age-appropriate interactive activity tables, sensory bins, literature, and information tables
- Parents and children participate in diverse activities that encourage parents to interact with their babies, building on the storytime lessons.
- Sensory bins filled with rice, sand, and water beads allow children and parents to play while simultaneously stimulating the senses, encouraging children to explore the environment and listen to their parents talking to them.

12:00—30-minute storytime geared toward toddlers (two to four years old); stories, songs, and commentary are translated by a Spanish translator
- With the older group, the librarian demonstrates to parents how to challenge their children beyond the words on a page, fostering development in comprehension and learning levels.

12:30—Final words from Book Harvest and Book Babies staff provides library card sign-up for entire families, as well as information on checking out books, attending programs, and utilizing library resources.

Working collaboratively with Book Harvest, we encourage early child literacy through the Book Babies program and Book Babies celebrations. Through storytimes, parents learn how to read to their children and how to foster learning in everything that they do with their child. In addition to a typical library storytime, the librarian also demonstrates how to interact with children while reading, how to expand learning beyond the pages of a book, and how to use speaking, playing, and singing to produce kindergarten-ready children. Working collaboratively with Book Babies staff, parents receive reading advice and age-appropriate developmental tips about their young children.

With the mutual goal of providing resources and services to the Durham community, our library partnership with Book Harvest has been a huge success! As of fall 2016, 160 children and their families were enrolled in Book Babies. While the program is being formally evaluated by researchers at Duke University, anecdotal evidence suggests that it is affecting children's lives. One mother of an 18-month-old explains it this way: "Book Babies is an excellent resource for getting a jumpstart on my daughter's education. She loves to walk around the house with the books and bring me books to read to her. She's already turning the pages and pointing at the pictures she likes the most" (Book Harvest, 2016, pullout quote). With the right tools, children have a better chance of success upon entrance to kindergarten. Book Babies seeks to teach parents these early literacy techniques and skills as they become their child's first teacher. Our long-term goal with this partnership is to guide the children to become lifelong library users who will pass down a love of reading and learning with future generations.

CONCLUDING THOUGHTS

Meeting all our library goals and objectives is still a work in progress, but focusing on the specific needs of the African American youth in our community has helped us to establish a firm foundation for library programming. Our first goal of creating a safe, welcoming space for youth has been achieved incredibly successfully. In-house programs like Book Babies have enabled us to develop a positive rapport with individuals in the community; children, teens, and adults alike. Youth are now not only coming to the library for free computer access, but also because they are interested in our fun (and free) after-school events. Many kids and teens know us by name and actively seek us out to ask about special activities. The library is seen as a space that is free from violence in a high-crime area, and a space where adult mentors approach youth with genuine interest and mutual respect. By making an effort to reach out to library youth and local families, we not only gained many new (and future) library users, but also established an open and accessible community atmosphere.

Our second goal of youth empowerment was woven into general programming to address the specific barriers and stressors that African American youth face. In our community in particular, we noticed that youth were often unaware of their potential, burdened by outside stressors, financial or otherwise, and lacking positive coping strategies. These deficits act as major impediments to personal achievement and growth and can result in hard consequences, such as spending time within a youth detention center. Our programs in no way solve these issues, but instead give youth the opportunity to express themselves in an accepting environment, develop a positive sense of self, and engage in self-reflection. Our main objective is to foster self-worth in a way that encourages continued personal development for community youth.

> Children and teens who feel safe and empowered are more likely to engage in discovery, self-improvement, and lifelong learning.

In our experience, children and teens who feel safe and empowered are more likely to engage in discovery, self-improvement, and lifelong learning. Our third goal of introducing youth to new ideas and technology was more successful once we had established real, positive connections within the community. Youth were more willing to participate in programs when they felt free to express themselves without fear of negative consequences. The African American youth that we work with defy the stereotypes that they are not interested in learning or in certain types of activities. Book Babies children and parents were excited about learning early literacy skills and using library resources. DYH teens enjoyed reading and exploring new ideas. As a whole, the youth in our community are willing and eager to explore everything, from storytimes to book clubs.

Make It Happen in Your Library

1. Partner with local community organizations to make African American youth and other groups who are often marginalized feel more positive about visiting the library.
2. Maintain communication with community organizations. Do not just send e-mails or make phone calls. Meet face to face on a regular basis.
3. Visit local churches, community centers, and other non-profit organizations serving youth. Be persistent. Attend events after work hours.
4. Focus on how your collaboration will benefit the community partner. Are you addressing one of their key goals, such as improving the literacy of African American youth? Can you include their logo/info on flyers to spread the word about their work?
5. Get creative—how can a local community agency's expertise be integrated into a library program?
6. Set concrete and measurable goals—what do you want the children/teens to gain from the experience? How will you and your partner measure the success of the program?
7. Discontinue programs/partnerships that are not working.

12

Changing the Library and School to Meet the Needs of African American Students

Anna Teeple

Connecting Research to Practice

As you read this chapter, look for the following characteristics of effective library services for African American youth:

- **Space**—Flexible, comfortable, welcoming
- **Librarians**—Culturally competent, accountable, courageous
- **Resources**—Enabling, relevant
- **Administrators**—Committed

OUR JOURNEY BEGINS

Five years ago, North View Junior High—an International Baccalaureate World School—was visited by a British consulting group. The state of Minnesota had hired the consultants because of the school's low test scores and the significant achievement gap between our White students and our students of color. We were a school with a population of 89 percent students of color, and at least 75 percent of our students were eligible to receive free or reduced lunches. It was an extremely stressful period, as the staff knew that our school was failing our students of color, and the British consultants were less than friendly. The report came back from them, and we were devastated: We were put on a list of "priority" schools—the 25 worst schools in the state. Morale was at its lowest, and rumors were flying about what might happen. Would all the teachers be fired? Would the entire administrative team be replaced? Would they close down the school and move the students to the other three junior high schools?

None of these rumors came to pass. Instead, the district chose us to be a *turnaround school.* Staffing changes were made: Our principal was replaced, and we were assigned a turnaround officer charged with keeping track of student data. We also applied for and received a School Improvement Grant (SIG) of over $2 million for training and materials.

The next school year started with two extra days of preservice training for school staff. The district's superintendents and curriculum directors were also in attendance. Suddenly, everyone was telling us their vision for North View, including the need for us to utilize culturally relevant pedagogy and culturally relevant texts. During hall duty one day after the preservice session, I asked a former assistant superintendent of curriculum and instruction what culturally relevant texts were exactly, and received a blank stare. I point this out, not as a criticism of that person, but to point out that no matter who we are in education and what title we might hold, *we don't know what we don't know,* but so long as we admit these gaps in our own learning and continue to ask questions, learn, and build skills, our students will benefit.

In this chapter, I introduce some of the changes that we have made at our school and in the library program in order to support our students of color. Included in the discussion will be a description of my own racial equity journey as an educator. As Melissa Katz and Molly Tansey said in their recent blog post *Teaching While White* (http://www.tolerance.org/blog/teaching-while -white), "as white educators, we have to step outside our comfort zones and have these conversations [about race and privilege]—embrace feeling uncomfortable and push ourselves to stay in this place and have conversations that matter. These issues affect the everyday lives of students, but even further they impact the very way that students are able to engage in the classroom."

My Racial Equity Journey

The first year of our priority status, the principal requested that all staff take the Intercultural Development Inventory (IDI). The IDI is a 50-question survey that assesses how individuals view and understand cultural differences between themselves and others (http://idiinventory.com). There were a few teachers at North View who scored quite high, and I was one of them. The IDI measured my intercultural development, and my score indicated that I was at the "acceptance" level, meaning that I had an intercultural and global mindset. That score gave me false confidence—I thought I knew what needed to be done. However, I realized later that it did not assess what really needed to be examined— my own Whiteness. I have come to understand that becoming more culturally competent or racially conscious can happen for White educators only if they learn about systemic racism and examine their own privilege.

The next year, we had a leadership change in our Department of Equity, and the new director brought in Beyond Diversity, a nonprofit organization that provides diversity programs for individuals, communities, and organizations (http://beyonddiversity.org) to work with us. During a two-day workshop, we covered topics such as the following:

- How and why our perceptions are shaped by early messages that we receive about race.
- How institutions in the United States are shaped by Whiteness and White privilege.
- The history of race in the United States and how that history has affected culture, mindsets, and behaviors.
- How beliefs about race influence not only individual behaviors, but also the structure and operation of institutions such as schools.
- How attempts to address racism have been hindered by internalized racial superiority and oppression.

Those two days were a defining moment in my racial equity journey. The first day, I experienced so many emotions, ranging from shame, to guilt, to sadness, to anger, as we learned about White privilege and how it affects individuals and institutions. As I unpacked my invisible knapsack of White privilege, I felt ignorant for not seeing it

> As I came to confront my White privilege, I knew that for real change to occur, for our school to address the racial achievement gaps that existed between our White students and our youth of color, I had to be willing to admit what I did not know and be comfortable asking tough questions of myself and of others.

and angry that I had not been challenged to think about my own advantage. I was outraged to learn about the systemic nature of the discrimination that people of color, including our students, experienced every day and to know that I was one of the oblivious "White folks" I heard them complaining about.

The second day of the training, we discussed the below-the-line information about Rosa Parks. Below-the-line information is the story that is usually not written in textbooks and is often not taught in most schools. Again, I felt anger—anger that I had not learned the complete story. I had been taught only the "whitewashed" version—the version that portrayed Rosa Parks as a tired, helpless seamstress who refused to give up her seat on a bus instead of as a dedicated civil rights activist purposefully selected to take on this role (c.f. Theoharis, 2014). But more important, I was angry that our students were receiving an ethnocentric view of American history—one that reinforced the dominant narrative and marginalized the "role of ethnic and cultural groups in U.S. society" (Banks, 2015, p. 60).

My exploration of my own Whiteness and the privilege that my skin color affords me did not end with that workshop. Our school equity team continued to examine the topic during the school year. Eventually, all our staff meetings had an equity component. It is important to point out that I was fortunate that all our workshops and training sessions were led by facilitators who understood the courage that it takes to engage in conversations about race, power, and privilege. They knew the range of emotions that we would feel and prepared us for the discomfort and internal conflict that we would experience. As I came to confront my White privilege, I knew that for real change to occur, for our school to address the racial achievement gaps that existed between our White students and our youth of color, I had to be willing to admit what I did not know and be comfortable asking tough questions of myself and of others. I had to grow and learn so that our students could succeed.

A FIRST STEP: ADDRESSING BASIC COLLECTION NEEDS

I had been at my school for three years prior to the turnaround status. In building my collection, I followed what I had learned in graduate school—build your collection according to the racial makeup of your students. For example, if 20 percent of your students are African American, then 20 percent of your books should be about the African American experience. Put another way, I have 1 percent Native American students at North View. According to the model of collection development that I had been taught in library school, in a collection of 10,000 books, only 100 of them should be about Native Americans. In schools with 70 percent White students, they should have 7,000 books about White people? It just does not make sense. As I have become more racially conscious, I see that this model normalizes Whiteness, privileging the White experience over that of communities of color. The model also assumes that students should not or would not be interested in reading about individuals from different racial or ethnic groups than their own. All youth should see a wide range of lives and experiences reflected in literature. Teens and adults can—and should—have crucial exposure to other people, cultures, and viewpoints through reading books to prepare them for real life.

During this time, North View participated in the federally funded Reading Is Fundamental (RIF) program, which three times a year provided funds to purchase approved RIF books at a lower cost to give away to students. I dreaded buying books for the RIF giveaway. With the money that I received from RIF, if I wanted every teen in our school to receive a book, I could spend only approximately $2 per book. The selection at that price was subpar at best, and anything that featured African American protagonists was a title that my Black students had read already. It pained me to lay these books out for students, only to see them throw the books away as they left the library.

I vowed that this year would be different. I asked my principal for money from the school improvement grant to increase the amount of money that I could spend per book for the RIF giveaway. He granted my request, and I was excited for a RIF giveaway for the first time. At this time, I still did not fully understand what culturally relevant texts were and why they were so important. I only knew I wanted and needed to get more books that represented the students at my school. I knew that I did not have much, if any, current fiction for my students of color. I had books about slavery, Martin Luther King, and

Rosa Parks—what I now consider the "typical" multicultural, nonfiction texts—but not much else.

As I was perusing the catalogs to make my RIF purchases, I found a street-lit series entitled *Drama High,* by L. Divine, that I thought my students might enjoy, and I was able to purchase it. I had never seen my African American girls so excited about RIF books before. Those books were the first ones to go. My principal picked one up, read the series title, and looked at me doubtfully. All I said was, "The kids love them." An English teacher who brought his class in told me he knew that the kids like "those street-lit books," but he was no fan of them. When I asked why, he said because they are not written in "proper English and they don't help the kids learn how to write or speak." I was just happy that they were reading. This continues to be a point of contention between some English teachers and school librarians. When it comes to our collections, I strongly believe that we need a variety of books in order to hook our students. Once we get them excited about reading, then we can introduce them to other genres or authors. It is also important to remember that, as Stephen Krashen points out, it is the *amount* of reading that drives reading success and achievement, *not* the specific titles.

After the success of the street lit at the RIF giveaway, I ordered several series for my fiction collection, and they flew off the shelves. The following year, we ordered several copies of the first book in each series because we discovered that often students would check out the first book and hold on to it for a while to read during Reading Zone (our school's name for sustained silent reading), or it would get lost. Without the first book in a series, though, the entire series lost its appeal; hence, extra copies of that book were vital. Again, I was thrilled that we had struggling and reluctant readers checking out books. The library was busy, and the circulation statistics were going up.

I attempted to have a conversation with our former director of equity about the success that we were having with street lit; however, it turned out to be frustratingly unsuccessful. He basically shut down the conversation with his body language by turning away and did not let me explain the students' increased reading interest. At that time, I was not aware of the importance of culturally relevant texts in empowering students of color. I just knew that I was fulfilling one part of my role as school librarian, and that was to help kids find books that they wanted to read. I felt successful, but the interaction with the director of equity left me feeling confused. I figured out much later, after the director and I had built a relationship, that he didn't like street literature because he did not want his own daughters reading it. So, he had a personal dislike for the genre from a parental standpoint.

While I understand that some people see street literature as reinforcing stereotypes of African American students, teens do not see it this way, nor do street-lit writers. Instead, the teens and the authors view street lit as providing realistic representations of "the harsh everyday realities of lower class and lower-middle-class inner-city neighborhoods and the various dramatic activities that occur in the name of survival" (Morris, 2010, p. 56). So while the authors of street lit might be criticized for telling a single story of urban youth, their intent is not to perpetuate stereotypes, but to share the lived experiences of communities that are not often found in mainstream young adult literature.

IMPROVING THE PHYSICAL SPACE

During the school improvement process, our teachers worked with a "Healthy Classroom" consultant on school and classroom climate. One major project was to create cozy reading spaces that were conducive to curling up with a book. One of the final projects was the library redesign, and the consultant helped the literacy coach and me come up with a plan. Since she consulted at a variety of buildings, she took pictures of fabulous libraries in the metro area from which we could garner ideas. The literacy coach and I did our own research as well. We designed a "pie in the sky" plan that included splitting up our extra-long shelving into smaller sections so that we could create different spaces within the library—new furniture that was comfortable, moveable, and more student friendly; paint to liven up the stark, off-white walls; a chalkboard wall that has endless uses; a display area for student work/pictures; and a new display area to showcase new books. Our total remodel cost would be almost $15,000. (We were lucky to acquire funds for this remodel, but ideas from our library design could be adapted at low or no cost, particularly the all-important student display spaces.)

> Our school mantra during this time of change for improvement was "what's best for kids." Designing a space around an adult meeting space was not what was best for the kids at North View—or anywhere.

The one caveat about our new design was that we would be removing most of our square tables and chairs to make room for the new furniture and shelving layout. Without those tables and chairs, we would no longer be able to hold our monthly staff meetings in the library. I have always disliked the idea of libraries keeping a certain large space available for whole-school meeting areas, especially when those meetings required closing the library to the students. Our school mantra during this time of change for improvement was "what's best for kids." Designing a space around an adult meeting space was not what was best for the kids at North View—or anywhere.

We now had two humps to get over—securing funding for our project and getting approval from our principal. We already were guaranteed $4,000 from Central Office. Our consultant recommended that we apply for the Lowe's Toolbox for Education grant and request the maximum amount of $5,000. She also said that she would talk with our principal about the plan to remove the tables, and suggest another option—to use an oversized classroom for our meeting space. It would be a little snug for 65 staff; however, we would be spending only an hour a month there, which would be doable. That's one thing I've learned as a librarian: Always troubleshoot the situation that you are bringing to your principal. It shows initiative and that you are able to think "big picture." Not only did our principal approve the plan, he said that if we received the grant, he would give us any additional money needed to complete the project. It was an exciting day when we received the check from Lowes.

We worked all summer on the remodel, and when we opened in the fall, the students were so excited. Their faces lit up when they came in and saw the couches, chairs, and beanbags. Some students wanted to sign their names and draw on the chalkboard wall; others commented that it felt like a coffee shop. Still others piled the beanbags on top of each other and threw themselves on top. During conferences, we had older students come back with their younger brothers and sisters and ask why we made it "so cool" after they had left.

My goal was to make the library feel welcoming and be a space where everybody belongs. And we succeeded! The library has become a gathering space before school where kids play Yu-Gi-Oh!, finish homework, play guitar, listen to music, print their papers, chat with their friends, and of course, *check out books*. One of the most welcome changes was the reorganization of our fiction collection into a bookstore model, I made this change to help my struggling readers find books. A teacher new to our building this year recently commented about how substitute teachers that come to our building always talk about how student friendly our library is and the number of teens that use the space.

Along with the physical space change, I have also had the opportunity to teach others about the change in philosophy of what a library can and should be to meet the needs of students of color. Each school in our district has an instructional coach, and ours was in the library one day when a group of African American students was collaborating on a project. They were a lively group, moving around and talking among themselves, but also focusing on the project. The instructional coach pointed at the group and asked me if I was okay with the noise level and activity. I assured him that I absolutely was, telling him that the days of the shushing librarians were gone—at least at North View. I explained that not only was this how modern libraries were meant to be, but that research suggests youth of color learn best when learning is structured to be "variable, energetic, vigorous, and captivating" (Hale, 2001, 117). If we are serious about closing the achievement gap, then we need to rethink our instruction to take advantage of the learning styles of our youth.

IDENTIFYING AND PURCHASING CULTURALLY RELEVANT TEXTS

As part of our improvement plan, I was given $10,000 in addition to my regular book budget to purchase more culturally relevant books for the library. As I mentioned, *culturally relevant* was a term that had been thrown around frequently at our professional development sessions, but never clearly defined. I began searching online and found "Building a Bridge to Literacy for African American Male Youth: A Call to Action for Librarians" (http://bridgetolit.web.unc.edu). It was exactly what I had been looking for: validation for some things that I had already been doing, a more complete explanation about culturally relevant texts and their purpose, and direction for librarians seeking to meet the needs of youth of color. I had been reflecting on my White privilege and new understanding of systemic racism, but up to this point, I had not changed my collection development practices.

After reading "Building a Bridge to Literacy for African American Male Youth: A Call to Action for Librarians," I began to have a deeper understanding of exactly what culturally relevant texts were and how they could be used to improve literacy and empower youth of color. I had also started following organizations and individuals on social media, such as We Need Diverse Books, Lee & Low Books, Teaching Tolerance, Color of Change, Tu Books, Diversity in YA, Latin@s in Kid Lit, and Justice Advocate, to name just a few. Now that I had a clearer understanding of what kinds of books I needed for the library, I started exploring and continue to explore, with the goal of improving my knowledge of diverse literature beyond street literature.

I usually purchased most of my books from Barnes and Noble. I liked physically going into the store and choosing the books that I wanted by cover appeal and wandering into different genre sections to discover titles that I may not have found otherwise. The Barnes and Noble that has the account with my district is one located in a suburban, predominantly White area. As one would expect, they do not stock a large variety of diverse books. I have had many conversations with the staff that specialize in young adult literature, and though they understand my plight, they have explained that they have no control over what titles are stocked at their store. The suppliers in New York are the ones who make the decisions—if they do not think that a book will sell in a community, they will not stock it. The staff can always order books for me from the Barnes and Noble warehouse, and I do order a significant number of books that way because I cannot find them on the shelves.

But now, I have another option. While I was searching for alternative sources to purchase multicultural literature, I came across a Kickstarter campaign in 2013 to open Ancestry Books—the first bookstore that focuses on literature written by and about people of color in North Minneapolis, a traditionally Black and racially isolated community. Chaun Webster and his wife, Verna, opened the store in 2014, and I have been working with them in a variety of ways. For example, North View participates in a program called Dial-A-Story, where young children can call into a main number at our school, and student volunteer readers will read children's books to them over the phone. The literacy coach and I invited Mr. Webster to come to our school to talk to our classes of struggling readers, who would have an opportunity to volunteer for the Dial-A-Story event. He shared his passion for operating a bookstore in North Minneapolis and brought a selection of children's books featuring people of color and shared the importance of these counterstories with our students. The students seemed captivated by the idea that this Black man in hipster clothes and a hat owned a bookstore in North Minneapolis, a place to which many of our students of color could relate. When the students were perusing the books, they were excited to see so many books with Black kids on the cover. As they knew they could choose the books they wanted to read and we would buy them for the library, they had a hard time deciding on their books!

One of our teachers and I also set up a field trip to Webster's store, along with a stop at the café next door for refreshments and to talk about the experience. We ended up with a small group, all females. On the way there, the girls talked about who they knew in the community. They seemed excited to share their familiarity with the neighborhood with adults from their school. Webster talked to the girls about why he started the bookstore and how difficult it is for authors and illustrators of color to get their books published. He showed them some specific books he thought they would like and booktalked the titles. The students loved them. The teacher had arranged for each student to be able to choose three books to take back to North View to keep in their classroom library. One girl commented that it was "really cool to see all the books with people that look like me."

After Ancestry Books opened, I put together an order of diverse titles that included books I had seen at the store, as well as other titles from the We Need Diverse Books Tumblr blog. The order totaled almost $1,500—and that presented a problem. School district policy mandated that we buy from a specific list of vendors, and that list does not include small, independent bookstores. In other words, a form of systemic racism is at work. (Again, I am not blaming or shaming any one in our organization. We don't know what we don't know.) I had already been pushing the envelope for several years; i.e., not ordering magazines from our periodical vendor because I could not find culturally relevant titles such as *Hype Hair*. The business manager at my school and the district library coordinator worked with the central office purchasing department, discussed the importance of this book order, and were able to secure prepayment of the order. It was a first in my tenure. I sent both people who work in that department a thank-you note and a gift card to let them know how much their flexibility meant to the students at North View. I felt like we had taken a small step forward in breaking down systemic racism.

USING READING ZONE TO BUILD A CULTURE OF READING

Being a priority school meant that we needed to raise test scores—and do it quickly—if we wanted to "get off the list." One of the ways that we attempted to engage more students in reading was to incorporate Reading Zone, a 15-minute sustained silent reading time, into one of our advisory periods. In graduate school, we had discussed the decline in pleasure reading for junior high school students, and our literacy coach and I had discussed this problem as well. My theory was not that junior high students did not like or did not want to read for pleasure—it was that they were not given time to read, or if they were, they were not given time to go to the library on a weekly basis to check out books as they had in elementary school. I proposed that we implement a schedule where each subject-area teacher brought their students to the library so that each week, all students had the opportunity to check out books. It was an easy sell to the principal, but not as easy to the teachers.

When I presented the idea to my secondary teachers, I received many wide-eyed stares. The idea that certain subject areas (math, for example) had anything to do with reading and they would need to use their class time to come to the library was difficult for them to wrap their heads around. I was surprised at the number of questions that they asked during the presentation. It was a wonderful opportunity to tell them about the library and how it worked. It was also very heartwarming to me that they were concerned about doing it right when they got there. I assured them I would be there to help kids find books, and the teachers would not be left alone. I made sure to model in front of the teachers how I would casually ask kids questions about themselves in order to get to know them, and in turn know what they might like to read.

The first year of Reading Zone—with department visits to the library—was somewhat of a struggle, but students were starting to read more, and our collection statistics grew. The second and third years of implementation were our transformative years. Teachers were consistently bringing their classes to the library to check out books, and students were checking them out and reading them. Our circulation numbers really took off! District staff who did not even work in the school noticed that our kids were always walking around with a book in their hands. Students were coming in the library in the morning, between classes, at lunch, and after school to return and check out books. We had started to build a culture of reading at North View.

Every week, I gave booktalks to our kids in the Success program, which is our "school within a school" alternative program. At first, I would do typical booktalks with the groups, trying to find books that would hook them into reading. After the diversity trainings and focusing on my Whiteness and the Whiteness of libraries, I changed my strategy for booktalks. I started with a group of students with whom I had developed relationships and selected a variety of books with different covers for our sessions. Some covers were stereotypical, and some were not. I asked the group if they would read the synopsis of the books and offer me their insights on the content and covers. I added in more culturally relevant books that were empowering, rather than stereotypical. Along with guidance from their teachers, we were able to help the students understand how and why certain covers were stereotypical. "Do you mean how some people think all Black people sell drugs?" noted one student.

Learning the skills needed to have real conversations about race and racism with our students is exceedingly important. We are not only connecting students to books that they want to read, but content that will empower them. I spent more time searching through the collection to find different examples. I did not do a display of African American historical figures for Black History Month; instead, I displayed as many culturally relevant books as I could throughout the year.

THE JOURNEY CONTINUES

I continue to examine my White privilege and how it affects my personal and professional daily practices. My principal sent me to Coaching for Racial Equity training this year. The facilitator taught us how to be champions of racial equity work. He challenged us to keep the humanity of our students at the forefront of our work. I try to keep this idea prominent in my practice, when I'm offering my opinion at our instructional team meetings, when bringing the subject of race into the room, or having a difficult conversation with a teacher about a classroom book choice. It should be about our students and their humanity. Always.

Make It Happen in Your Library

- Examine your own racial consciousness, reflect on the impact of race in your own life, be prepared to engage in courageous conversations, and commit to acknowledge what you do not know.
- Deepen your understanding of how systemic racism affects the lives of your students.
- Bring attention to and challenge school or district policies that perpetuate systemic racism.
- Look for professional development opportunities.
- Be creative in looking for funding resources.
- Develop partnerships with Black-owned businesses and within your community.
- Do not be afraid to talk with kids about race.

13

We Finally Have a Point Now

Faith Burns and Julie Stivers

We do not learn from experience. We learn from reflecting on experience.

—Dewey (1933, p. 78)

Connecting Research to Practice

As you read this chapter, look for the following characteristics of effective library services for African American youth:

- **Programming**—Develops agency, asset-based, honors/promotes voice, fosters community, challenging
- **Librarians**—Accommodating of culture-based learning practices, committed, caring
- **Instruction**—Cooperative, communal, and iterative, sets high expectations
- **Resources**—Relevant, authentic, provide counterstories

As new librarians who studied theories and perspectives for meeting the needs of youth of color in our library courses at the School of Information and Library Science (SILS) at the University of North Carolina at Chapel Hill (UNC-CH), we have found that it is not enough to study topics such as bias, discrimination, and equity, nor is it enough to simply implement culturally relevant strategies in our practice. In order to be truly effective in working with youth of color (in our case, African American teens), we must constantly reflect upon our practice and then use those reflections to improve our work. We must consider questions such as: How am I incorporating the various tenets of culturally relevant pedagogy into my work? How are the teens responding? What can I do better? Sometimes the best questions that we ask are the most uncomfortable ones, such as: What biases am I bringing into my work, and how can I remove them? Am I aware of and checking my White privilege? Am I willing to address issues of race with students?

Best practices and approaches for teaching African American students include (1) using physical proximity to engage students and connect with their experiences, (2) setting high expectations, (3) creating collaborative learning environments that cultivate voice, and (4) legitimizing the students' culture and lived experiences by providing diverse literature. In this chapter, we share examples of how we have attempted to implement these four approaches, as well as the insights that we have gained by examining our practice in critical and reflective ways.

SOMETIMES, YOU JUST NEED TO SIT THERE (FAITH)

Just like all librarians, when I am at work, I am busy. At any given time, I am balancing a number of tasks and projects. As the coordinator of a teen program at a local public library, one of my responsibilities was to recruit and train teens, called Youth Partners, to deliver storytime programs to students in afterschool care programs at local elementary schools. Typically, the program had 8–10 teen participants, most of whom were African American. I had been working with the Youth Partners for over a year before I understood the importance of using physical proximity as a way to cultivate trust and establish mentoring relationships with the teens.

As part of the Youth Partners program, my colleagues and I picked the teens up at their high schools, transported them to the elementary schools where they would conduct the storytimes, and then took them home at the end of the day. Because of the different dismissal schedules in the school system, there was typically a 10-minute waiting period between the time that the Youth Partners arrived at the elementary schools and the beginning of the storytimes. Before I learned about the importance of using physical space to engage youth, the 10 or 15 minutes that we had before the storytimes began were welcome opportunities to answer just one more e-mail or to check one more box on my to-do list. What I did not know was that those few minutes were also precious opportunities to build relationships with the Youth Partners.

In our diversity class at SILS one day, we were discussing two important aspects of culturally relevant teaching—establishing a community of learners and legitimizing the lived experiences of youth of color. We talked about the importance of body language and proximity, as integral to breaking down racial barriers and establishing meaningful mentoring relationships with youth of color (Moule, 2012). This point was reiterated by a group of African American and Latino high school students from the Blue Ribbon Mentor Advocate (BRMA) program, who joined our class one day to talk about the "students' six"—six strategies for culturally relevant teaching that a group of high school students from the BRMA program had identified as critical to their success in school. One of the key strategies was proximity—"using physical space to engage students and reduce perceived threat" (Meyer & Davis, n.d., p. 2). As they talked, I realized that if I wanted to build a sense of community and trust with the Youth Partners, then I needed to put down my cell phone and just sit there.

The next time I met with the Youth Partners, I put my phone down and sat quietly on the steps to the stage where the teens would be hosting the program. I sat away from everyone else, creating an open space around me for anyone to come and sit down. One or two minutes later, one of the Youth Partners sat down beside me and began to talk with me and ask for my advice on different issues that she was facing. Since that conversation, she now comes and talks to me frequently about different happenings in her life—from who she's dating to college aspirations to anxiety over tests and quizzes in school. After that instance, I began using that 10-minute window as a time to sit and make myself available for conversation with the Youth Partners, and after a short while, they all began coming and talking with me—asking for advice, talking about books, or simply making conversation.

These conversations with the teens would not have taken place if I had continued to use those minutes to check e-mail or do other tasks.

> I will never be able to hear their voices if I do not first quiet my own. I will never be able to show them their lives matter if I do not stop to be a part of them.

Now, as I have transitioned into the role of teen librarian at the same library branch, I constantly reflect on how I can convey to the teens that my office door is always open to them. I have purchased a comfortable, teen-friendly chair for my office (think a college dorm–style chair) and I am decorating my office in a way that is bright and cheerful. The comfortable chair is right beside my desk, making for easy conversation. If I am in my office, my door is always wide open. I also make a point of being visible in the teen section. I introduce myself to teens who are in the area, and I am making a point to memorize their names. I ask them simple questions such as: How was your day? Tell me about your favorite book or video game.

These simple gestures establish proximity and build relationships based on trust, respect, and understanding.

Each day, I remind myself that I will not make a difference in a teen's life if I spend all my time focused on accomplishing the long list of administrative and programmatic tasks that I have. In working with teens, I must make myself available and establish mentoring relationships with them to create a community of learners, where we can openly discuss the challenges that they face and celebrate the joy in their lives. I have to make myself available in close proximity to them, so they will feel comfortable approaching me with whatever topic that they want to discuss. I will never be able to hear their voices if I do not first quiet my own. I will never be able to show them their lives matter if I do not stop to be a part of them. I have learned that sometimes the best way to make a difference or accomplish a goal is to just sit there.

Set High Expectations

The Youth Partners program was established to be a teen-led program. Prior to learning about culturally relevant teaching practices and approaches, I ran it as an adult-directed program. I saw myself as the director and leader, and the teens as just my helpers. In my mind, the program's focus was not the teenagers—it was on providing a quality program for the children in after-school care.

The program operated on a semester basis, with the teens meeting in January, June, and September to plan and prepare the storytime programs. I held the planning meetings, but I never handed control over to the teens. Consequently, the teens were not enthusiastic about the program—I could not get them to engage in the storytimes, or even be committed to showing up for them. I could not figure out why they were so uninterested and disengaged, which frustrated me. And, sadly, I gradually took more and more of their involvement away—ironically, even as I was still asserting that the program was supposed to be teen-led.

In our SILS class one day, we learned that low teacher expectations are one of the primary causes of the low achievement of many youth of color (Edwards et al., 2008). In other words, youth live up to our expectations—if we expect little from them, they will give us little. Conversely, when we set high expectations for youth of color, we challenge the dominant ideology, show them that we trust them, that we respect them, that we value them, and that we believe they are capable (Solórzano & Yosso, 2002).

I suddenly had an "aha" moment. The Youth Partners were not engaged in the storytimes because I had set low expectations for them. I was making all the important decisions, which meant that they had no ownership over the program—no reason to be invested in it. I realized that if I wanted the program to be teen-led, then I needed to set high expectations for the teens, and, perhaps more important, I needed to work with them to create those expectations *together.* Working together to establish the goals for the program would give the teens greater ownership and hopefully lead them to feel like the work that they were doing was meaningful.

At the beginning of January 2015, I changed the planning process. I opened the first brainstorming meeting by intentionally and openly telling the Youth Partners that my vision for the program had changed—that I wanted them to be the decision makers and to lead the activities at the schools. As we talked, I was surprised to learn that they wanted the same thing! In openly discussing both my expectations, and more important, letting them voice their expectations, I found that we were on the same page.

By the end of the session, the teens had decided on the topics that they wanted to cover in their spring 2015 storytimes. Over the course of the month, they worked in small groups and developed specific objectives and activities for each program, and they also selected the books that each program would highlight. They created four programs: Celebrating Dr. Seuss/Oh the Places You'll Go; Be a Buddy, Not a Bully; music and dance; and folklore. During the process, I acted only as discussion facilitator and moderator. As I lessened my control and increased my expectations, the teens gladly assumed more leadership over the program.

My ultimate goal was that eventually I would not talk at all during the programs at the elementary schools. At first, I still introduced the storytime to the elementary children and explained the craft. But then I noticed that the Youth Partners were working together better as a team, and that their enthusiasm for both the program and working with the children was growing. For the first time, some teens were taking leadership roles—something I had never seen before. The transition was working! Eventually, the teens told me that they did not need my help during the program, and that I should "sit down and be quiet, and work the stereo" for the music portion of the program. I have never been so happy to be asked to sit down and be quiet in my life!

To keep those expectations high throughout the semester, I checked in with the teens several times to assess their views of how the program was changing. In one meeting, I asked the teens several different questions during a write-around—one of the culturally relevant teaching techniques that I had learned in my SILS class. One of the questions asked students to write one thing they liked about the program since I had started focusing on the principles of culturally relevant teaching. One student wrote that the program finally "started to have a meaning, a point we're getting at." Because of the high expectations and teen ownership, this teen finally felt like she, and the program, had a purpose and a point.

REMEMBERING COLLABORATION AND VOICE: *RASPUTIN'S BEARD* (JULIE)

Me: *Do you think Rasputin was a confident person?*
Seventh Grade Student: *He had to be. He either believed he really was a healer or was really good at fooling people. But, seriously, if I had a beard that looked like that, I'd be cocky too!*

The mantra "Rasputin's Beard" may seem like a strange way to remember to always include the concept of voice when working with students, but my experiences with a dynamic group of seventh graders have cemented those words in my work with all youth—but particularly African American youth.

In collaboration with a seventh grade social studies team, I had developed a three-day research unit on the Russian Revolution, culminating in a creative writing product where students wrote a diary entry from the point of view of a Russian citizen of their choice. I constructed the final day to allow ample time for writing. I quickly found, however, that many of the African American students were using this time in another way. They were *talking*. And, I welcomed it, as these conversations centered on their research! They were talking about living under house arrest with multiple siblings, the injustice of being murdered for the actions of your parents, surviving Russian winters, and yes, even, the finer points of Rasputin's facial hair.

I taught this lesson with 15 different classes, and there was a commonality about our "writing" days. Many of the African American students used the time to speak about their researched facts and their thoughts on their diary subjects with each other and with me. These conversations not only strengthened their writing assignments and generated dialogue on issues we had not covered in class, but also provided a valuable assessment. *What were my students learning? What interested them? What should I have spent more time on?* After the first day of witnessing this phenomenon, I changed my lead-in on the writing day to include an explicit invitation to speak with me and their classmates, using comments from previous classes to jump-start discussions. In every way, this input from my African American students made my lessons better. It also allowed those students to use their voices—on paper and via the spoken word. What if I had shut those conversations down? What if I had said this common school refrain—*I shouldn't be hearing any talking!*—when I started them on their writing path? Think of all that I would have missed. We need to use great caution when uttering those words and perpetuating that sort of stifling atmosphere. We are doing all of our students a disservice, but we are particularly silencing our African American students. We are taking away their voice.

I realized that when I provided my students with space and acceptance of their actual voices—letting them talk out loud by working together, sharing, and bouncing ideas off each other—I was providing space for their personal and self-empowered voices, their *Voices*. These Voices are crucial for our African American teens to know that they matter, in a society that does not always send that message. To know that we are truly listening to them, and that the world should and will listen. I have discovered that when I am able to hear my African American students' voices raised in discussion or engagement in class, their Voices become louder.

We know from the literature that many African American students thrive in collaborative environments. My experience with the Russian Revolution diary entries taught me that even individual assignments can be collaborative, and that I must support this atmosphere through intentional lesson design, my own willingness to both welcome and support discussion, and by modeling this sort of behavior throughout the school.

Honoring the voices of African American youth can be accomplished no matter the space or time constraints. In my literacy work with youth at a juvenile detention facility, I have found that my most successful "lessons" are those where I essentially *get out of the way*, serving to simply scaffold literacy instruction and giving the teens space to showcase their individual voices. For example, to give teens practice with two writing elements—topic choice and revision—we created Top Ten Lists. After viewing examples of lists ranging from the simple (Top Ten Best Pizza Toppings) to the more complex (Top Ten Ways That Adults Underestimate Teens), my teens worked to create their own lists. It was interesting watching them choose topics and then rank, erase, and reorder their lists, but the most rewarding part was the final products. After their lists were complete—and with their permission—I published the lists at www.thetoptens.com. One of my teens got visibly emotional when viewing her list online for the first time, with her name attached. This simple exercise demonstrated that their Voices mattered. That *they* matter. That not only did I think their thoughts and writing were interesting, but that they were worthy of online publication for other people to see—that their Voices were worth listening to. It was such a simple way to honor their unique Voices.

The Necessity of Diverse Literature: "Because That Is My Life."

Can you help me find a fantasy book series with romance? "Absolutely," I confidently replied to the bright-eyed sixth grader at my elbow. After all, I knew youth literature and I was ready to start translating that knowledge into practice at a new school. I pulled a popular series from the shelves, but found myself becoming increasingly uncomfortable. Every fantasy book that I pulled had a White character on the cover, and it felt like a fraud to only be able to offer these books to an African American student. She finally left with a new series that she squealed with happiness over, but I felt like a cheat. I knew about the importance of diverse literature and could rattle off many "important" titles, but when faced with a specific genre request, I was woefully unprepared. I learned that day that I had to be intentional in my research—and in my own learning about diverse books.

As a librarian who works with African American youth, being familiar with literature written by and about African Americans never feels like an extra part of what I do. It is a core part of my practice. My social media feeds, my professional reading, and my learning networks are diverse. But, just as important, I now work to ensure that my own reading of middle grade and young adult books is inclusive and covers a wide range of reflected experiences—*and genres!* Beyond that, I want my collection, and my own reading, to be particularly reflective of my community—the African American students and teens which I serve. We know that all our students need to see themselves in the literature in our libraries, that in fact including diverse literature in our collections improves engagement, motivation, and comprehension among students. In addition, youth need to be exposed to counterstories where the stories of underrepresented groups are told, serving to challenge dominant—and stereotypical—narratives. I have learned to look beyond only collecting diverse award-winning titles, historical fiction, social issue books, and biographies and searching out more titles with "casual diversity." Malinda Lo (2015) explains this beautifully: "Even though we need books that talk about race and racism, we also need books where characters of color can simply have the same kind of plot-driven adventures that white characters have all the time."

Can we read every book on our shelves? Of course not. We are forced to rely on reviews. I am more comfortable when I do not rely solely on mainstream reviewers, but instead search out reviewers—and publishers—who focus on diverse texts (see the box entitled "Blogs, Reviewers, and Publishers That Include African American Authors and Characters"). My favorite review sources? Actual teen readers. I had read Coe Booth's *Tyrell* (Booth, 2007) in a young adult literature class that focused on diversity. This helped me know enough to recommend it to African American male youth in a literacy group at a youth detention facility. It was their feedback, however, that helped me realize its amazing potential in reaching teens—even for an "older" title—and this has helped inspire creative writing and drawing exercises built around the novel. The covers of both *Tyrell* and its sequel, *Bronxwood* (Booth, 2011), feature the protagonist pictured from the back. I challenged my teens to describe or draw what they thought Tyrell looked like from the front. The *Youth Voices* section for this chapter contains some of this artwork that inspired so much discussion of the novels during their creation. *Bronxwood* is so intensely beloved with some of my teens that I always have a copy when I visit. In speaking of the characters and situations in *Bronxwood*, a teen said, simply: *"They live where we live."*

Of course, it is important to note that not all our African American male teens would automatically relate to the experiences in *Bronxwood*. This is why it is important to have many Black voices represented on our shelves. For example, many of my students relate more to the experiences in *The Crossover* (Alexander, 2014), which focuses on African American brothers growing up in a happy, middle-class, two-parent home, or *The Great Greene Heist* (Johnson, 2014), which chronicles a diverse group of students as they try to stop a bully from winning a middle school student council election.

In addition to diversifying our collections across genres, we must not forget reviewing our formats. If audiobooks are featured in our collection, are diverse voices and authors represented? What about our graphic novel collections? Are a variety of stories being represented? I have had great success with promoting titles with a superhero of color, such as the *Legend of the Mantamaji* series (Seaton, 2014) and the *Ultimate Comics Spider-Man* series (Bendis, 2012) featuring African American Miles Morales as the new Spider-Man. I will never forget when an eighth grader handed me back the first volume of this new *Spider-Man* series, saying: "This is the *first* book I've ever finished reading."

> Diverse literature also holds great potential—and power—for opening up dialogues with teens on issues related to equity, social justice, race, and racism.

When we have diverse collections on our shelves, we can then incorporate them in meaningful and authentic ways into our practice: individual readers' advisory, book clubs, summer reading lists, classroom booktalks, and library programming. In schools, when we collaborate with teachers to incorporate diverse texts across the curriculum, we are taking a first step toward implementing culturally relevant pedagogy.

Diverse literature also holds great potential—and power—for opening up dialogues with teens on issues related to equity, social justice, race, and racism. Entering these conversations via the safe avenue of a literary character makes these discussions more accessible for youth—and us! Our youth need us to address race in our libraries. *Open Mic: Riffs on Life Between Cultures in Ten Voices* (Perkins, 2013) contains excellent short stories written by writers from many different races and ethnicities that can springboard meaningful discussions. After reading the graphic short story *Why I Won't Be Watching* The Last Airbender *Movie* (Yang, 2013) together, a group of eighth graders discussed the topic of whitewashing in movies. After their initial surprise that I wanted to talk about race—*during school!*—the students began to share other examples of whitewashing, such as in video games. The conversation eventually morphed into body image portrayed on screen. If I had started out our discussion by asking what they thought about racism and Hollywood casting, I would have gotten a fair share of blank looks. Using literature can provide a concrete entry point for conversations that can be uncomfortable, but are so critical. After our discussion, I wanted to unpack the method and topic with my students, and I specifically asked them if an issue of race had ever come up in any of their classes. *NOs* from every side of our table. "Well, we've talked about slavery." These were eighth graders! It's unforgivable—and detrimental—for us as educators to not include these issues in our schools. I asked if they wanted these conversations to happen more. Every student said yes, one succinctly voicing: "Yes, because that is my life."

Youth Voices

Teen Drawing: A different perspective of the *Tyrell* cover (Booth, 2007).

Teen Drawing: A different perspective of the *Bronxwood* cover (Booth, 2011).

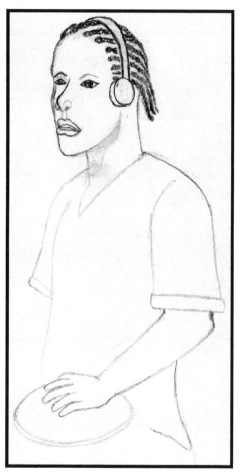

CONCLUDING THOUGHTS

We continue to reflect upon our practice as librarians and how our actions and words—or lack thereof—can affect the teens that we serve. It is a cliché, but still true: sometimes, the smallest actions make the biggest difference. Sit right down next to your African American teen patrons and students. Ask them to suggest a book to be purchased for the library. Get their opinion on your next program idea.

Most of all, we encourage you to not be afraid: do not be afraid to challenge your own actions, beliefs, and biases. Do not be afraid to admit that you made a mistake. (We've made plenty!) Do not be afraid to try something differently. Do not be afraid to challenge societal stereotypes and systemic prejudices, even when—*especially when*—they are occurring in your own library system or school. And, most important, we encourage you to engage your African American teens, to provide spaces and outlets for their voices and talents, and to advocate for and celebrate their Voices.

Make It Happen in Your Library

- Continually reflect on ways to improve your library practice. What is not working? What can I do better? Are my African American patrons and students engaged and using my library services? Why . . . or why not?
- Use physical proximity to more authentically engage youth. Sit at the same table. Stand *next* to your teens when engaging in conversation. Move throughout the teaching space to sit or kneel next to your teens.
- Set high expectations to coincide with building personal relationships based on trust and mutual respect.
- Provide ownership of assigned projects and tasks.
- Create collaborative learning environments. Even individual projects can include time for small-group and classwide discussions.
- Use great caution when using phrases such as *"I shouldn't be hearing any talking."* Instead, develop an environment that gives youth space and time to talk—to engage with you, each other, and the material.
- Provide, promote, and use diverse literature to legitimize students' culture and lived experiences. Stay current with diverse literature and topics by including people of color—authors, bloggers, publishers, and educators—in your professional learning network.

Blogs, Reviewers, and Publishers That Include African American Authors and Characters

Most of these resources have multiple social media feeds. I've found it most efficient to choose one—for me, Twitter—making it easy to stay up to date with all the current information from these advocates for African American literature— and students.

- The Brown Bookshelf at thebrownbookshelf.com
- Diversity in YA at www.diversityinya.com
- Just Us Books at www.justusbooksonlinestore.com
- Lee & Low Books at www.leeandlow.com
- Rich in Color at richincolor.com
- We Need Diverse Books at weneeddiversebooks.org

14

Implementing I-LEARN with K–2 Students: The Story of a Successful Research Partnership

Delia Neuman, Allen Grant, Vera Lee, and Mary Jean Tecce DeCarlo

Connecting Research to Practice

As you read this chapter, look for the following characteristics of effective library services for African American youth:

- **Instruction**—Cooperative and iterative, sets high expectations, fosters agency, authentic and relevant
- **Resources**—Relevant, authentic

In 2012–2013, an interdisciplinary team of researchers from Drexel University in Philadelphia worked with teachers to plan and implement a project in a K–8 school in a nearby neighborhood. The goal for the researchers was to study and validate an inquiry-learning model that is based on research and theory, while the goal for the school was to implement such a model with guidance and support from the university. This chapter describes the steps involved in the project—both those related to research and those related to instruction. Overall, it demonstrates how a partnership between a school and a university can help translate theory into practice, how school-based personnel can help to advance the integration of theory and practice, and how a partnership like this one can have an impact on student learning.

BACKGROUND: THE MODEL AND THE SCHOOL

The I-LEARN Model

The project was centered on the I-LEARN model (Neuman, 2011a, 2011b), which is depicted in Figure 14.1. I-LEARN—Identify, Locate, Evaluate, Apply, Reflect, kNow—is a *learning* model that expands traditional information-seeking models in important ways. It assumes that learning (not just finding information) is the goal of inquiry in schools and that information in its various formats and representations is the basic building block for lifelong learning in the 21st century. The model is grounded in research and theory from both information science and instructional systems design and draws upon the author's own research and writing over more than a decade. Ultimately, it is an inquiry-for-learning model that builds on the traditional information literacy paradigm—accessing, evaluating, and using information—and expands it to provide a conceptual and pedagogical tool linked directly to information-age learning.

The Fairmount School

Located in a neighborhood near downtown Philadelphia that President Barack Obama designated as one of the country's first five "Promise Zones" in 2014, the Fairmount School (a pseudonym) is a K–8 university-assisted public school affiliated with Drexel University. At the time that the I-LEARN project was planned and implemented, 90 percent of the students were African American; 95 percent were classified as "economically disadvantaged"; and only 3 percent of the children in grades 3–8 scored at the proficient level on Pennsylvania's statewide assessments in reading and math (School District of Philadelphia, 2012). Threatened with closure and faced with a number of other difficulties while the project was under way, Fairmount provided an especially grim picture of a city school in trouble. While the situation has improved—thanks in large part to the variety of programs and services now in place through Fairmount's affiliation with Drexel—reviewing how the I-LEARN project was implemented offers a glimpse of both the problems and potential solutions related to urban schools in disadvantaged areas.

GETTING STARTED

Fairmount's status as one of Drexel's university-assisted schools (Community-School of Education, n.d.) led to its selection as a research site, and a small seed grant from the university's School of Education underwrote the project. Three faculty members from that school and one from the College

FIGURE 14.1   The I-LEARN Model

I: Identify	Choose a problem, topic, or question that can be addressed through information. • Activate a sense of curiosity about the world. • Scan the environment for a suitable topic within that world to investigate. • Formulate a problem or question about that topic that can be addressed with information.
L: Locate	Access information, either recorded or in the environment, related to the problem/topic/question through a variety of people and media. • Focus on what is to be learned. • Find the information potentially useful for that learning. • Extract the most relevant and salient information for that learning.
E: Evaluate	Judge the quality and relevance of the information found by ascertaining whether it has • Authority, as evidenced by the credibility of the source and/or author, internal logic, accuracy, etc. • Relevance to the topic at hand, suitability in its level of depth for the question, and appropriateness to the topic. • Timeliness, as evidenced by its currency or historicity (as appropriate to the topic) and its appropriateness in terms of its match with the learner's developmental level.
A: Apply	Use the information to generate a new understanding—that is, to learn • Generate a new understanding that has personal meaning. • Organize that learning in an appropriate cognitive structure (e.g., chronological, hierarchical, etc.). • Create an appropriate product to convey that structure.
R: Reflect	Examine the adequacy of the process and product of learning and revise as appropriate. • Analyze the quality of the process and of the product's form and content. • Revise the product as necessary and determine how to improve the process for the next instance. • Refine the product, polishing it as appropriate.
N: kNow	Instantiate the knowledge gained so it can be used in the future. • Integrate the new learning into existing knowledge. • Personalize the new knowledge by recognizing it as a personal, individual construct. • Activate the new knowledge by drawing upon it as necessary and/or appropriate to generate and answer new questions.

of Computing and Informatics, which hosts Drexel's School Library/Media Program, formed a research team focused on studying and validating the I-LEARN model with the youngest students in the school. While other efforts to study and validate the model have since been undertaken in both K–12 and postsecondary environments, the Fairmount project marked the model's debut as an instructional tool. Several publications have described the context, theory, methods, and results of that effort (e.g., Neuman, Grant, Lee, & Tecce DeCarlo, 2015; Tecce De Carlo, Grant, Lee, & Neuman, 2014), while this chapter focuses on its implementation, specifically on the practical considerations involved in orchestrating the many facets of the I-LEARN project with K–2 students.

Obtaining Permissions

Before the team could begin to work at Fairmount, the researchers had to complete the usual steps required for a university to conduct research in a public school: first gaining the principal's permission to host this particular study and then completing the procedures required by the School District of Philadelphia and Drexel University. Securing approval for a study in any school district is time consuming because it involves several levels of bureaucracy, and the conditions in Philadelphia at the time introduced additional complexities. Concurrent with the team's efforts to win District approval were efforts to secure approval from the University's Institutional Review Board, as required by federal law. The team developed the proposal—including writing a description of the project and creating a consent form to be completed by parents, an assent form to be completed by students, and interview guides and other materials to be used in the study—and made sure all appropriate state and federal clearances for team members were current. Ultimately, completing these efforts and gaining approval from both the School District of Philadelphia and the University took approximately nine months.

Enlisting Participants

Originally, the team had envisioned Fairmount's school library as the focal point for the work: the I-LEARN model operationalizes inquiry learning, and the team members have expertise in areas that are traditionally supported by school libraries (i.e., information literacy, digital literacy, early literacy, K–12 literacy, and early-childhood education and technology integration). However, the library had been closed for years, and the school's plan to reopen and staff it was scuttled because of the dire financial situation in the School District that peaked in the winter and spring of 2013. Although the library offered a large, well-lighted, and well-furnished space, and its collection had been weeded through and organized by Drexel volunteers, the District did not have the funds to staff it.

Fortunately, when the research team proposed the project to Fairmount's six primary-level teachers, four expressed interest in participating: two kindergarten teachers, one first-grade teacher, and one second-grade teacher. The kindergarten teacher, who was finishing a master's degree with a focus on school librarianship, had hoped to be the school's new librarian and was especially interested in the project because of its focus on information and digital literacies. All four teachers were eager to participate because they saw the project as a unique opportunity to help students boost their 21st-century knowledge and skills.

Professional Development Sessions

The first step in implementing I-LEARN in the classroom was to introduce the model formally to the teachers. Three professional-development sessions were designed: one held at Fairmount and two at Drexel. Holding these sessions at both the school and the University stemmed from a conscious attempt to reinforce the principle that the project was a partnership between the two organizations rather than a situation in which university researchers simply brought an innovation to a school, implemented it, and then left. This attention to partnership undergirded the entire project, and it is also inherent in the idea of a university-assisted school (Borthwick et al., 2003; Vissa & Streim, 2006). The Drexel-Fairmount partnership closely aligns with Slater and Ravid's (2010) description of an "interagency partnership" and brings together a number of School District, community, and University entities with the common goal of creating "institutional change" (p. 10) at Fairmount.

The first professional-development session, held at Fairmount, allowed the research team to explain the project, the I-LEARN model, and the generic I-LEARN rubric designed to specify related learning outcomes (Figure 14.2). The original rubric was designed both as a teaching tool and as a guide to assessing students' achievement related to each stage of the model. To make it more useful for this project, the teachers agreed to simplify its language and the complexity of its ideas to make it more suitable for young students. Figure 14.3 shows the version of the model that the teachers created, which proved useful for guiding their instruction and determining how well their students mastered its individual stages and the overall sequence.

The second professional-development session involved introducing the Technological Pedagogical and Conceptual Knowledge (TPACK) survey (Koehler, 2011), a tool for collecting data about teachers' levels of knowledge and skill related to integrating technology into instruction. At this session, all four teachers were asked to complete the survey in the next week or so through a link provided to them. Also at this session, the researchers—based on their expertise in and familiarity with technology for young learners—suggested digital portfolios as the medium for the students' final projects because these tools provide a clear structure for students' work, a technology that is easy for them to master, and an attractive way for them to display and share the results of their efforts. The teachers agreed that this format was promising, and the researchers proposed two free digital-portfolio platforms that they had identified as appropriate for the students to use for creating and storing their final projects.

The third session involved the researchers' demonstrations of the two portfolios and the teachers' experimentation with and selection of the ones that

FIGURE 14.2 The I-LEARN Rubric

Outcome	4	3	2	1
Identifies a meaningful question or problem	Formulates an original, information-based question or problem based on personal curiosity and a review of information related to the topic	Formulates an original, information-based question or problem, but without reviewing related information	Formulates an original question or problem that cannot be addressed through information	Fails to formulate an original question that can be addressed with information
Locates information appropriate to the question or problem	Searches for and selects a variety of information focused on a particular aspect of the question or problem	Searches for and selects limited information focused on a particular aspect of the question or problem	Searches for and selects information that is generally related to, but not focused on, the question or problem	Fails to find any appropriate information
Evaluates the information critically	Systematically evaluates information for authenticity/credibility, topical and other relevance, and timeliness as these relate to the question or problem at hand	Evaluates candidate information unsystematically, or based on only one or two criteria	Evaluates candidate information unsystematically, or based on inappropriate criteria	Fails to evaluate information on any basis
Applies relevant information to the question or problem	Generates an original response to the question or problem and organizes it in a representation that communicates it effectively	Generates an original response, but either organizes it illogically or communicates it ineffectively	Generates an original response, but organizes it illogically and communicates it ineffectively	Fails to generate an original response
Reflects on the information process and product	Thoroughly analyzes the process and product of the first four steps, revises either or both as necessary, and creates a polished final version	Analyzes the process and product and revises either or both to a limited degree, and/or, creates an unpolished final version	Analyzes only the process or product, revises either or both inappropriately, and/or creates a deficient final version	Fails to analyze or revise the process and product

FIGURE 14.3   The Fairmount I-LEARN Rubric

Outcome	3	2	1	0
Identifies a meaningful problem	Chooses between given topics and writes a question that makes sense	Chooses a topic and writes a question that doesn't make sense or writes a statement [rather than a question]	Chooses a topic	Does not choose a topic
Locates information related to the problem	Finds 3 sources (ideally a mix of electronic, books, oral, and pictorial)	Finds 2 sources	Finds 1 source	Finds 0 sources
Evaluates the information critically	Selects a preferred resource and explains why this is good information, using the I-LEARN criteria	[Selects a preferred resource and] Explains why it's good using emotional criteria (e.g., I like it)	Selects a preferred resource but does not explain why	Does not select a preferred resource
Applies relevant information to the question	Answers question with information from identified source, using product criteria	Answers question with emotional or other irrelevant data	Partially answers question	Does not answer question
Reflects on the information process and product	Creates an accurate statement of what went well and what did not	Creates a statement . . . but [it] is inaccurate or just makes something up	Gives a broad or blanket statement with no detail	Does not create a statement

they would use. The two kindergarten teachers chose Little Bird Tales (https://littlebirdtales.com), which is largely student centered and provides tools that allow young students to create their own digital tales. The second-grade teacher selected Weebly (http://education.weebly.com), which is more teacher centered and allows a teacher to create a template for a website that individual students can then complete. At this point, the first-grade teacher—who was greatly affected by the tumult at the school and District levels, and who also was concerned about possible reassignment to another school at the end of the school year—decided not to participate in the classroom component of the project. She did, however, participate in all the professional-development sessions and in the exit interview.

Topic Selection

The three teachers still involved with the effort identified the overall topic for the students' projects: "What Makes Philadelphia Special?" This topic is related to the District's Social Studies objectives for K–2 students, and several of the teachers had used it previously and believed it would work well for the I-LEARN project. "What Makes Philadelphia Special?" allowed the teachers to apply the unfamiliar I-LEARN model to familiar territory, so they could focus more directly on implementing the model rather than on designing and implementing a totally new instructional unit.

Acquiring Technology

As planning moved forward, it became clear that Fairmount did not have the technology resources necessary for the project. The school had only one computer lab, which was designated for older students, and no computers for its elementary classrooms. Through contacts at the University, the research team identified and acquired the necessary equipment. Discarded central-processing units came from one academic unit; another unit's information technology (IT) specialists found used keyboards and screens and spent several weeks refurbishing the equipment and uploading the software needed to make the computers functional. A member of the research team, along with technical support staff from the University, delivered the machines and related equipment and power cords and set up stations in the participating teachers' classrooms. As a result, each of the four teachers received three or four classroom computer setups.

IMPLEMENTING I-LEARN

Prior to the classroom implementation of the project, the research team provided informal consultation and guidance as the teachers planned their instructional approaches. The planning was organic, as the teachers worked primarily individually to develop approaches, strategies, and materials as they determined how to approach the unit. The creation of digital projects—the key outcome for all three teachers—provided a common focal point, but each teacher developed her own unit. The following discussion focuses only on the implementation experiences of two teachers (identified here as Ms. A and Ms. B) because the study yielded insufficient data about the experience of the third teacher.

Throughout the actual implementation—in April and part of May 2013—two members of the research team provided extensive, almost daily support, to help both participating teachers and their students as they moved through the stages of the I-LEARN model and created their portfolios. This support was crucial, since inquiry learning was familiar to only one of the teachers—Ms. A, who had a background in school libraries—and both teachers were challenged by having to create instructional materials related to I-LEARN that were targeted to their students. Furthermore, it became clear that only Ms. A was technologically sophisticated enough to proceed with the actual creation of the portfolios on her own. The researchers also played an active role in helping the students in a variety of ways. Inquiry learning was new to them as well, and they needed guidance in locating and evaluating information on the Internet and in preparing the drafts for their portfolios. Because they lacked experience with computers, the students also required extensive, side-by-side support in the mechanics of using the equipment.

The Teachers' Differing Approaches

Undoubtedly, the most interesting facet of the implementation involves how each teacher's pedagogical philosophy, experience, and style influenced her students' learning. Ms. B, a senior teacher who had extensive classroom experience but only limited experience with technology, used a teacher-directed approach; Ms. A, a new teacher with far less classroom experience but whose academic background in newer pedagogical approaches as well as in school libraries familiarized her with problem-based inquiry learning and technology, carefully structured the students' work to maximize their independence at every stage of the I-LEARN model. Both teachers guided their students to create attractive portfolios that reflect an understanding and application of the model, suggesting that I-LEARN is flexible enough to support very different teaching styles. Ms. A's students, however, developed more sophisticated skills in both inquiry and digital literacies because her approach focused specifically on that development.

Ms. B's Approach

Early in the project, Ms. B determined that her second graders' limited knowledge and experience with the City of Philadelphia beyond their own neighborhood required her to adapt the model to meet their needs. She led them in some opening discussions, but in the end, as she stated in the exit interview, "I fed them different things" rather than promoting their own inquiry skills. She limited their choices of projects to four famous sites—the Philadelphia Zoo, the Liberty Bell, Fairmount Park, and Memorial Hall—rather than letting them "Identify" their own topics, as suggested in the first stage of the model. Next, she printed out information on the topics (from a source that she never identified) and distributed it as a handout rather than allowing students to "Locate" information themselves (the second stage). Students' comments to one of the researchers about how they "Evaluated" their sources—e.g., "It is good because my teacher gave it to me"—suggest that Ms. B also overlooked the opportunity to help students develop their knowledge and skills related to the third stage of the model. In addition, because she believed that many of her students' poor computer skills would lead them to take too long to create their portfolios, she asked the researcher to work with those who needed help in the "Apply" stage by uploading their notes and inserting stock photos of the sites they had chosen into the Weebly classroom site. The researcher also asked the students to respond to the "Reflect" questions included in the I-LEARN template for their portfolios and typed their answers into the program for them.

Ultimately, 23 of Ms. B's second graders (10 boys and 13 girls) completed their Weebly portfolios; 2 students did not complete portfolios. Figure 14.4 shows the I-LEARN "Reflection" page from "Eddie's" portfolio. ("Eddie" is a pseudonym, used here to protect the student's privacy.) Completion of Ms. B's students' projects spilled into the month of May, and students had to come into her classroom during lunch and gym periods to finish their work. It is unclear whether the students had an opportunity to share their completed projects with the class.

Ms. A's Approach

Ms. A took a very different approach than Ms. B—one reflecting a deep understanding of culturally responsive instruction (Howard, 2003; Ladson-Billings, 1995) that no doubt influenced the sophisticated outcomes her students achieved. Although she, too, realized that "a lot of kids don't even realize necessarily that they live in Philadelphia," she addressed this learning need by helping them understand where they live. She had them talk about their neighborhood community and about places in the City they had visited with their families; she read aloud books about places and activities there. For the "Identify" stage of the model, she had the students brainstorm possible topics before allowing them to select their own. To support them in the "Locate" stage, she brought in guest speakers (including a Philadelphia firefighter) and explained that families, as well as computers and books, are good sources of information.

While she and the researcher served as final judges of the quality of the information, she encouraged the students to discuss the "Evaluation" criteria at their own level: one student proclaimed that "going to the park" is a good source because "you can see and look around." To support them through the "Apply" stage, Ms. A created and explained a model portfolio based on her own family's experience in Philadelphia and provided a specific structure for students to use in building their portfolios. Following this structure, each student created a kind of storyboard, with clip art and brief statements about the chosen illustrations; discussed this phase of the work with Ms. A; and—with her guidance—uploaded the visual information into Little Bird Tales and recorded a brief narrative with the platform's recording tool. To guide them in the "Reflect" stage, Ms. A asked each student a series of questions: "What was your favorite part of the project? What part do you think you did the best? The worst? What is your favorite source that you used? Why is [that source] a good way to learn about Philadelphia?" Finally, she scored the students' projects according to the revised version of the generic I-LEARN rubric to assess what students came to "kNow" (the final stage) through their work.

Ultimately, 24 of Ms. A's kindergarteners (11 boys and 13 girls) completed their Little Bird Tales portfolios. The portfolio created by "Jane" (a pseudonym) was entitled "I Like My City" and contained a mural she had drawn showing

FIGURE 14.4   The I-LEARN "Reflection" Page in "Eddie's" Weebly Portfolio

I-LEARN Reflection
I—Identify a topic or question
What question do you want to answer? What do you want to know?
What would people do there [at Fairmont Park]?

L—Locate information
Where did you find your information? How many sources did you find?
My teacher gave it to me, used only one source.

E—Evaluate the information
Is the information good? How do you know?
I trust her because she's nice.

A—Apply—use the information to answer the question
What's the answer to your question? What information did you use to answer it?
No, I don't have an answer.

R—Reflect
What worked to help you answer the question? What didn't work?
I could talk to an adult.

kNow
What did you learn? What new questions do you have?
I learned that it is located west of the Schuylkill River and the corner of East Memorial Hall Drive.

row houses, a familiar sight to Philadelphia residents. Figure 14.5 shows the final page of the portfolio, which lists the sources Jane used in her research. Jane—like all Ms. A's students—completed her work within the month of April and had an opportunity to share her "tale" with the rest of the class.

ANALYZING THE DATA

Both Ms. A and Ms. B provided copies of their students' portfolios for analysis, and all four teachers participated in a focus-group exit interview that was recorded and then transcribed by a transcription service. The corpus for analysis also included copies of the Fairmount rubric that Ms. A. had used to help students assess their work, and of the worksheets that she had used in the follow-up interviews to help them reflect on their experience (Figures 14.6 and 14.7). Ms. B did not provide any evidence to suggest that she had done any formal assessment of her students' work.

FIGURE 14.5. List of Sources Identified in Jane's Little Bird Tales Portfolio

My Sources:

Bing Clip Art

My sister [name]

Stories we read in class

Visiting places

Analysis of Teacher Data

Exit-interview questions focused primarily on the teachers' past experience with research, how they organized this project, what worked well (and didn't), how they addressed instructional challenges related to I-LEARN, their evaluation of the project's success according to their own criteria, their understanding of the I-LEARN model itself, and their beliefs about the importance of digital and information literacy and how best to help students master these areas. Detailed responses related to all these areas provided a rich data set that the research team recognized as the primary data source for the project.

To analyze these data, the team designed and implemented an innovative, recursive approach to coding the transcripts and identifying the key findings that it yielded. First, the team jointly developed a coding scheme based on the study's research questions; then, each team member used this scheme independently to code the transcripts. Next, the team worked as a group to review all four team members' coded transcripts, both to establish intercoder reliability and to expand the initial scheme to encompass codes that had emerged through the independent coding. Lastly, the researchers worked as a group to apply this revised and expanded scheme to performing a final analysis of the transcripts. Done on a copy of the transcripts projected on a whiteboard in a conference room, this analysis yielded a document that became the basis for identifying the study's major findings. This group-individual-group approach drew on each team member's disciplinary expertise and resulted in a comprehensive picture of the teachers' experience with the I-LEARN project.

Analysis of Student Data

Analysis of the student data—the portfolios created by the students in both classes and Ms. A's students' self-assessments and her records of her interviews with them—began when Ms. A anonymized the data by assigning pseudonyms to the students and organized their work to make it more usable by the

FIGURE 14.6   Sample of Ms. A's Completed Rubric

Outcome	3	2	1	0
Identifies a meaningful problem	Chooses between given topics and writes a question that makes sense	Chooses a topic and writes a question that doesn't make sense or writes a statement [rather than a question]	Chooses a topic	Does not choose a topic
Locates information related to the problem	Finds 3 sources (ideally a mix of electronic, books, oral, pictorial)	Finds 2 sources	Finds 1 source	Finds 0 sources
Evaluates the information critically	Selects a preferred resource and explains why this is good info, using the I-LEARN criteria	Explains why it's good using emotional criteria (e.g., I like it)	Selects a preferred resource but does not explain why	Does not select a preferred resource
Applies relevant information to the question	Answers question with info from identified source, using product criteria	Answers question with emotional or other irrelevant data	Partially answers question	Does not answer question
Reflects on the information process and product	Creates an accurate statement of what went well and what did not	Creates a statement . . . but [it] is inaccurate or just makes something up	Gives a broad or blanket statement with no detail	Does not create a statement

Score: 12

research team (a task for which she received a small stipend through the seed grant that had funded the project). Anonymizing data is one of the federal government's requirements to protect the privacy of participants in research, and the approval for this study suggested that this process should be done within the school so that the researchers could analyze the data without being influenced by knowledge of any particular individual.

After Ms. A had completed her task, the research team members organized all the nonelectronic data into Microsoft Word tables and Microsoft Excel spreadsheets and also examined the students' completed portfolios in detail to

FIGURE 14.7   Jane's "Reflection" Interview with Ms. A

I-Learn Project Self-Assessment
Name: Jane

1. *What was your favorite part of the Philadelphia Project?*
   Making the Tale on the computer.

2. *What part do you think you did the best? The worst?*
   The best was telling what I saw for the mural.

3. *What is your favorite source you used? Why is it good to learn about Philadelphia?*
   The computer is good because I got to see lots of murals.

determine how successfully each student had used the I-LEARN model to determine what makes Philadelphia special to him or her. The team analyzed the data both individually and collectively, organizing and synthesizing it to see what trends in the data emerged. Although this analysis involved less formal coding and recursion than the analysis of the teacher data, some patterns emerged that helped the team understand some of the details of the students' experience. For example, the analysis of the sources that students identified in their portfolios revealed that Ms. A's students used nine sources for their information, while Ms. B's students used only four.

FINDINGS OF THE STUDY

Data from the exit interview show that all four teachers concluded that the I-LEARN model had successfully supported their students in problem-based, inquiry learning. Both the teachers who had participated fully in the project and those whose participation had been limited praised the model for turning the abstract concept of research into a concrete, step-by-step process that even young students can understand and use. All four teachers expressed interest in integrating the model and the use of digital portfolios into their curriculum and instruction in the future.

Data related to students' products show that the great majority of students for whom data were submitted completed their portfolios successfully, as judged by the teachers and the researchers. These data are qualitative rather than quantitative—befitting both the relatively small number of teachers and students involved and the fact that the intent of the project was to validate the I-LEARN model, rather than to measure its impact. Despite its many challenges, then, the project provided evidence of the model's potential for promoting problem-based, inquiry learning and digital and information literacy, even with very young students. It showed that even very young children can master the key concepts involved in 21st-century learning when they are guided by knowledgeable teachers to use a clear, focused, step-by-step model like I-LEARN.

CONCLUDING THOUGHTS

Implementing the I-LEARN project at Fairmount—both as a curriculum initiative and as a research study—was challenging and rewarding. The challenges stemmed mostly from the turmoil within the School District and uncertain conditions within the school itself. At the time of the project, the District's growing budget and staffing crisis were making daily headline news in all the local media (Strauss, 2013). The stress of potential of transfers (and even layoffs) among Fairmont's faculty and administration cannot be overstated. In addition, Fairmount itself had a long-standing reputation as a troubled school in an impoverished community; its affiliation with Drexel was only the latest in a series of attempts to improve it.

Overall, the turmoil within the District and the school created an environment that was a clear distraction to participants in the study. Indeed, the researchers faced serious losses in both teacher and student data: only two teachers actually completed the TPACK questionnaire, rendering the analysis of the project's quantitative data inappropriate. The project lost much of its qualitative data as well: one of the original four teachers was unable to focus on implementing the project at all, and another erased her students' data at the end of the school year. Ultimately, then, the only student work that was analyzed were the portfolios produced by the students in Ms. A's and Ms. B's classrooms.

The situation in the school also created advantages for both the instructional intervention and the research study. Fairmount's new affiliation with Drexel and its designation by the School District as a "Promise Academy" provided new opportunities that seemed to energize both teachers and students. The affiliation with the University brought cadres of University faculty and students into the school to initiate and support various projects. The designation as a Promise Academy brought extra financial resources from the District, a longer school day for teachers and students, and greater autonomy for the principal. All the teachers involved with the project were excited about the prospects of more resources, more attention for their students, and a new school-wide focus on curriculum innovation. They were deeply committed to their students and eager to use the I-LEARN project to help them start to catch up on information and digital skills that they had not had a chance to learn.

The near-daily presence of the research team was a key element in helping both teachers and students achieve successful outcomes with the project. While Ms. A could easily have orchestrated the project on her own, the other teachers (including those whose participation was limited) needed coaching both in problem-based, inquiry learning and in integrating technology into their instruction. In their technology-impoverished school, they had not had the opportunity to become familiar with much, if any, of the growing repertoire of approaches to digital pedagogy. Their eagerness to learn about these approaches suggests that hands-on, on-site coaching for other teachers in similar schools would be a welcome and successful strategy for helping them succeed as 21st-century teachers.

It is important to note that the fact that the I-LEARN project occurred with no involvement by Fairmount's school library has serious implications for the school-library field. In many schools that serve disadvantaged children, school libraries have been shuttered or turned into reading rooms or storytelling venues that rely on uncertified volunteers. This trend suggests that the children of poverty who rely on urban public schools are facing even more disadvantage as they lag behind in developing the information and digital skills that they will need throughout their adult lives.

It is also important to note that the theory of culturally relevant pedagogy (Howard, 2003; Ladson-Billings, 1995) offers an additional conceptual and analytic lens for examining the data from Fairmount and from future studies. While the research team did not initially use this lens, it is clear in retrospect that the teachers exhibited characteristics that are consistent with this approach to help their students be successful. For instance, both Ms. A and Ms. B gave all their students an equal opportunity to participate in the project and never spoke about them in deficit terms—a stance that is consistent with Ladson-Billings's (1995) notion that culturally relevant teachers believe that "all students are capable of academic success" (p. 478) and Howard's (2001) idea that maintaining such a positive approach is particularly important for African American students, who have often experienced negative perceptions and labeling in schools.

> Ms. A commented that her students "really enjoyed seeing each other's Little Bird Tales, and kept asking to see them over and over again," while Ms. B stated that her students "were able to get in groups and actually critique each other [i.e., their projects] with positive words."

In addition, both teachers also encouraged collaborative learning, in keeping with Ladson-Billings's (1995) assertion that culturally relevant teachers "encourage students to learn collaboratively and be responsible for one another" (p. 480). Ms. A commented that her students "really enjoyed seeing each other's Little Bird Tales, and kept asking to see them over and over again," while Ms. B stated that her students "were able to get in groups and actually critique each other [i.e., their projects] with positive words." A third way in which the teachers exhibited culturally relevant pedagogy was by "scaffold[ing], or build[ing] bridges, to facilitate learning" (Ladson-Billings, 1995, p. 481), so that all students could achieve according to their own abilities and needs. While it can be argued that Ms. A was much more successful in scaffolding the different phases of the I-LEARN project than Ms. B, it is clear that both teachers believed that it was important to build "bridges" of knowledge so their students could be successful with the project.

The research team believes that the data from the study revealed a number of things that are important for both researchers and practitioners. First, the findings confirm that the I-LEARN model works with young students, even those who face serious disadvantages. Second, they suggest that research partnerships like this one can be beneficial to both universities and schools. Third, they point to the need for the school-library field to develop new models and approaches to providing essential 21st-century skills in light of the sobering realities that face today's urban schools.

Finally, they suggest the importance of studying I-LEARN's implementation through the lens of culturally relevant pedagogy. In future research—particularly studies with the urban students who are the focus of the team's current efforts—we plan to incorporate this theory into our conceptual framework in specific and detailed ways. We hope to learn much more about how teachers' beliefs about their students, their pedagogical practices, and their racial/cultural backgrounds (Howard, 2001, 2003) influence the ways in which they teach I-LEARN to students of color.

References

Adichie, C. N. (2009). *The danger of a single story.* Retrieved from http://www.ted
 .com/talks/chimamanda_adichie_the_danger_of_a_single_story?language=en

Adoff, J. (2005). *Jimi & me.* New York: Jump at the Sun.

Alemán, E. (2007). Situating Texas school finance policy in a CRT framework: How
 "substantially equal" yields racial inequity. *Educational Administration Quarterly,* 43(5): 525–558.

Alexander, K. (2014). *The crossover.* Boston: Houghton Mifflin Harcourt.

Allington, R., & Cunningham, P. (2007). *Schools that work: Where all children read
 and write.* 3rd ed. New York: Pearson.

Angelou, M. (1969). *I know why the caged bird sings.* New York: Random House.

Astolfi, M. (2012). *Are our students seeing reflections of themselves in the texts that
 are being read by their teachers? A case study of read aloud texts from a North
 Carolina elementary school.* Unpublished master's thesis. Univ. of North Carolina at Chapel Hill, Chapel Hill, NC.

Bailey, C. T., & Boykin, A. W. (2001). The role of task variability and home contextual
 factors in the academic performance and task motivation of African American
 elementary school children. *Journal of Negro Education,* 70 (1/2): 84–95.

Banks, J. A. (1993a). Multicultural education: Development, dimensions, and challenges. *Phi Delta Kappan,* 75(1): 22–28.

Banks, J. A. (1993b). Multicultural education: Historical development, dimensions,
 and practice. *Review of Research in Education,* 19: 2–49.

Banks, J. A. (1994). Transforming the mainstream curriculum. *Educational Leadership,* 51(8): 4–8.

Banks, J. A. (1995). Multicultural education and curriculum transformation. *Multicultural Education,* 1(2): 8–11.

Banks, J. A. (1999). *An introduction to multicultural education.* 2nd ed. Boston: Allyn
 and Bacon.

Banks, J. A. (2009). *Teaching strategies for ethnic studies.* 8th ed. New York:
 Pearson.

Banks, J. A. (2015). *Cultural diversity and education: Foundations, curriculum, and teaching.* 6th ed. New York: Routledge.

Barnes, D. (2010). *We could be brothers.* New York: Scholastic.

Bathina, J. (2015, July 4). Student voices. *Literate Voices* blog. Retrieved from http://literatevoices.org/2015/07/04/student-voice

Belgrave, F., & Brevard, J. K. (2015). *African American boys: Identity, culture, and development.* New York: Springer.

Bell, D. (1992). *Faces at the bottom of the well: The permanence of racism.* New York: Basic Books.

Bell, Y. R., & Clark, T. R. (1998). Culturally relevant reading material as related to comprehension and recall in African American children. *Journal of Black Psychology,* 24(4): 455–475.

Bendis, B. M. (2012). *Ultimate comics Spiderman, Vol. 1.* New York: Marvel.

Bernier, A. (2010). Spacing out with young adults: Translating YA space concepts back into practice. In D. E. Agosto & S. Hughes-Hassell (Eds.), *Urban teens in the library: Research and practice* (pp. 113–126). Chicago: ALA Editions.

Binns, B. A. (2010). *Pull.* Lodi, NJ: WestSide Books.

Black Males Speak (2011). Building a Bridge to Literacy for African American Youth website. Retrieved from http://bridgetolit.web.unc.edu/?page_id=748

Board of Governors of the Federal Reserve System (2014). *Changes in U.S. family finances from 2010 to 2013: Evidence from the survey of consumer finances.* Washington, DC: Federal Reserve. Retrieved from http://www.federalreserve.gov/pubs/bulletin/2014/pdf/scf14.pdf

Book Harvest (2016). *Book babies.* Durham, NC: Book Harvest. Retrieved from http://bookharvestnc.org/programs/book-babies

Booth, C. (2007). *Tyrell.* New York: Push Books.

Booth, C. (2011). *Bronxwood.* New York: Push Books.

Borthwick, A. C., Stirling, T., Nauman, A. D., & Cook, D. L. (2003). Achieving successful school-university collaboration. *Urban Education,* 38(3): 330–371.

Boykin, A. W. (1982). Task variability and the performance of Black and White schoolchildren: Vervistic explorations. *Journal of Black Studies,* 12(4): 469–485.

Boykin, A. W. (1983). The academic performance of Afro-American children. In J. T. Spence (Ed.), *Achievement and achievement motives psychological and sociological approaches* (pp. 324–371). New York: W. H. Freeman.

Boykin, A. W. (1986). The triple quandary and the schooling of Afro-American children. In U. Neisser (Ed.), *The school achievement of minority children: New perspectives* (pp. 57–92). Hillsdale, NJ: Erlbaum.

Boykin, A. W. (1994a). Afrocultural expression and its implications for schooling. In. E.R. Hollins (Ed.), *Teaching diverse populations: Formulating a knowledge base.* New York: State University.

Boykin, A. W. (1994b). Harvesting talent and culture: African-American children and education reform. In R. J. Rossi (Ed.), *Schools and students at risk: Context and framework for positive change* (pp. 116–138). New York: Teachers College Press.

Boykin, A. W. (2013). On enhancing academic outcomes for African American children and youth. In *Being black is not a risk factor: A strengths-based look at the state of the Black child.* Washington, DC: National Black Child Development Institute.

Boykin, A. W., & Cunningham, R. T. (2001). The effects of movement expressiveness in story content and learning context on the analogical reasoning performance of African American children. *Journal of Negro Education,* 70(1/2): 72–83.

Boykin, A. W., Lilja, A. J., & Tyler, K. M. (2004). The influence of communal vs. individual learning context on the academic performance in social studies of grade 4–5 African-Americans. *Learning Environments Research,* 7(3): 227–244.

Boykin, A. W., & Noguera, P. (2011). *Creating the opportunity to learn: Moving from research to practice to close the achievement gap.* Alexandria, VA: ASCD.

Boykin, A. W., Tyler, K. M., Watkins-Lewis, K., & Kizzie, K. (2006). Culture in the sanctioned classroom practices of elementary school teachers serving low-income African American students. *Journal of Education for Students Placed at Risk,* 11(2): 161–173.

Branch, A. J. (2012). Ethnic and racial identity: Educational implications. In J. Banks (Ed.), *Encyclopedia of diversity in education,* Vol. 2 (pp. 825–828). Thousand Oaks, CA: Sage Publications.

Braun, L. W., Hartman, M. L., Hughes-Hassell, S., & Kumasi, K. (2014). *The future of library service for and with teens: A call to action.* Chicago: YALSA. Retrieved from http://www.ala.org/yaforum/sites/ala.org.yaforum/files/content/YALSA_nationalforum_final.pdf

Britt-Harris, A., Valrie, C. R., Kurtz-Costes, B., & Rowley, S. J. (2007). Perceived racial discrimination and self-esteem in African-American youth: Racial socialization as a protective factor. *Journal of Research on Adolescence,* 17(4): 669–682.

Brooks, W., & Savage, L. (2009). Critiques and controversies of street literature: A formidable literary genre. *The ALAN Review,* 36(2): 48–55.

Bruce, A. (2015). On being white: A raw, honest conversation. *Children and Libraries,* 13(3): 3–6.

Buehler, J. (2010). "Their lives are beautiful, too": How Matt de la Peña illuminates the lives of urban teens. *The Alan Review,* 37(2): 36–43.

Bunner, T. (2014, July 21). The magic of author visits. *Nerdy Book Club* blog. Retrieved from https://nerdybookclub.wordpress.com/2014/07/21/the-magic-of-author-visits-by-teresa-bunner/

Bureau of Justice Statistics (2014). *Prisoners in 2013.* Washington, DC: Department of Justice. Retrieved from http://www.bjs.gov/content/pub/pdf/p13.pdf

Burt, J. M., & Halpin, G (1998). *African American identity development: A review of the literature.* Presentation at the Mid-South Educational Research Association, New Orleans, November 4–6, 1998.

Butts, M. G. (2011, August 13). Book club growing readers through a social experience. *The Herald Sun.*

Cabrera, N. J. (2013). Minority children and their families: A positive look. In *Being Black is not a risk factor: A strengths-based look at the state of the Black child.* Washington, DC: National Black Child Development Institute. Retrieved from http://www.nbcdi.org/sites/default/files/resource-files/Being%20Black%20Is%20Not%20a%20Risk%20Factor_0.pdf

Camangian, P. R. (2015). Teach like lives depend on it: Agitate, arouse, and inspire. *Urban Education,* 50(4): 424–453.

Canada, G. (1995). *Fist, stick, knife, gun.* Boston: Beacon Press.

Carter, D. J. (2008). Achievement as resistance: The development of a critical race achievement ideology among Black achievers. *Harvard Educational Review,* 78(3): 466–497.

Center for an Urban Future (2013). *Branches of opportunity.* New York. Retrieved from http://nycfuture.org/pdf/Branches_of_Opportunity.pdf

Christensen, L. (2009). *Teaching of joy and justice: Reimaging the language arts classroom.* Milwaukee, WI: Rethinking Schools. Retrieved from http://www.rethinkingschools.org/publication/tfjj/tfjj_intro.shtml

Christensen, L. (2012). The danger of a single story: Writing essays about our lives. *Rethinking Schools, 26*(4): 19–25.

Christensen, L. (2013–2014). Trayvon Martin and my students: Writing toward justice. *Rethinking Schools, 28*(2): 22–27.

Clark, J. A. (2006). Social justice, education and schooling: Some philosophical issues. *British Journal of Educational Studies, 54*(3): 272–287.

Coates, T. (2015). *Between the world and me.* New York: Spiegel & Grau.

Cole, J. M., & Boykin, A. W. (2008). Examining culturally structured learning environments with different types of music-linked movement opportunity. *Journal of Black Psychology, 34*(3): 331–355.

Colesante, R. J., & Biggs, D. A. (2015). *Discovering gifted youth in inner-city schools.* Research Gate. Retrieved from https://www.researchgate.net/publication/252799923_DISCOVERING_GIFTED_YOUTH_IN_INNER_CITY_SCHOOLS

Community—School of Education (n.d.). Retrieved from http://drexel.edu/soe/outreach-support/community

Cook-Sather, A. (2006). Sound, presence, and power: "Student voice" in educational research and reform. *Curriculum Inquiry, 36*(4): 359–390.

Cooperative Center for Children's Books (2015). *Multicultural literature 2014: Statistics gathered by the Cooperative Children's Book Center School of Education, University of Wisconsin-Madison.* Retrieved from https://ccbc.education.wisc.edu/books/2014statistics.asp

Craft, J. (n.d.). *It will take a village to raise diversity in the children's book industry.* CBC Diversity Blog. Retrieved from http://www.cbcdiversity.com/post/130274147033/it-will-take-a-village-to-raise-diversity-in-the

Crime in Philadelphia (2016). Retrieved from http://data.inquirer.com/crime/neighborhood/north-philadelphia_west/?start_date=2015-01-01&end_date=2015-12-31

Cross, W. E., Jr. (1991). *Shades of Black: Diversity in African-American identity.* Philadelphia: Temple University Press, 1991.

Cross, W. E., Jr. (1995). The psychology of nigrescence: Revising the Cross model. In J. G. Ponterotto, J. M. Casa, L. S. Suzuki, & C. M. Alexander (Eds.), *Handbook of multicultural counseling* (pp. 93–122). Thousand Oaks, CA: Sage Publications.

Daniels, H., & Daniels, E. (2013). *The best kept teaching secret: How written conversations engage kids, activate learning, grow fluent writers . . . K–12.* Thousand Oaks, CA: Corwin Literacy.

Darling-Hammond, L., French, J. C., & Garcia-Lopez, S. P. (2002). *Learning to teach for social justice.* New York: Teachers College Press.

Davis, S., Jenkins, G., & Hunt, R. (2005). *We beat the street: How a friendship pact led to success.* New York: Dutton Children's Books.

DeCuir, J. T., & Dixson, A. D. (2004). "So when it comes out, they aren't that surprised that it is there": Using critical race theory as a tool of analysis of race and racism in education. *Educational Researcher, 33*(5): 26–31.

DeCuir-Gunby, J. T. (2009). A review of the racial identity development of African American adolescents: The role of education. *Review of Educational Research 79*(1): 103–124.

de la Peña, M. (2005). *Ball don't lie.* New York: Delacorte Press.

de la Peña, M. (2010). *Mexican WhiteBoy.* New York: Delacorte Press.

de la Peña, M. (2013). *The living.* New York: Delacorte Press.

DeLeón, L. (2002). Multicultural literature: Reading to develop self-worth. *Multicultural Education,* 10(2): 49–51.

Delgado, R. (1989). Storytelling for oppositionists and others: A plea for narrative. *Michigan Law Review Association,* 87(8): 2437.

Delgado, R., & Stefanic, J. (2001). *Critical race theory: An introduction.* New York: New York University Press.

Delpit, L. (1988). The silenced dialogue: Power and pedagogy in educating other people's children. *Harvard Educational Review,* 58(3), 280–298.

Delpit, L. (2002). *The skin we speak: Thoughts on language and culture in the classroom.* New York: New Press.

Delpit, L. (2006). *Other people's children: Cultural conflict in the classroom.* New York: W. W. Norton & Company.

Delpit, L. (2012). *Multiplication is for white people: Raising expectations for other people's children.* New York: New Press.

Derman-Sparks, L. (1993). Empowering children to create a caring culture in a world of differences. *Childhood Education,* 70(2): 66–71.

Dill, E. M., & Boykin, A.W. (2000). The comparative influence of individual, peer tutoring, and communal learning contexts on the text recall of African American children. *Journal of Black Psychology,* 26(1): 65–78.

Dixson, A. D. (2006). The fire this time: Jazz, research, and critical race theory, In A. D. Dixson & C. K. Rousseau (Eds.), *Critical race theory in education* (pp. 213–230). New York: Routledge.

Douglas, F. (1885/1997). *Narrative of the life of Frederick Douglass, an American slave.* New York: Signet Classics.

Draper, S. (2015). *Stella by starlight.* New York: Atheneum Books.

Early, J. S., & Flores, T. (2015). *Cuentos del corazón/*Stories from the heart: An after-school writing project for bilingual students and their families. *Rethinking Schools* 30(1): 13–19.

Eccles, J. S., Wong, C. S., & Peck, S. C. (2006). Ethnicity as a social context for the development of African-American adolescents. *Journal of School Psychology,* 44(5): 407–426.

Edwards, P. A., McMillon, G. T., & Turner, J. D. (2010). *Change is gonna come: Transforming literacy education for African American students.* Newark, DE: International Reading Association.

Erikson, E. H. (1950). *Childhood and society.* New York: Norton.

Erikson, E. H. (Ed.) (1963). *Youth: Change and challenge.* New York: Basic Books.

Erikson, E. H. (1968). *Identity: Youth and crisis.* New York: W. W. Norton and Company.

Fearon, J. D. (1999). *What is identity (as we now use the word)?* Stanford University. Retrieved from https://web.stanford.edu/group/fearon-research/cgi-bin/wordpress/wp-content/uploads/2013/10/What-is-Identity-as-we-now-use-the-word-.pdf

Fisher, M. (2008). *Black literate lives: Historical and contemporary perspectives.* New York: Routledge.

Flake, S. G. (2007a). *Bang.* New York: Jump at the Sun.

Flake, S. G. (2007b). Who says black boys won't read? *Journal of Children's Literature,* 34(1): 13–14.

Flake, S. G. (2009). *You don't even know me: Stories and poems about boys.* New York: Jump at the Sun.

Flake, S. G. (2012). *Pinned.* New York: Scholastic.

Flake, S. G. (2014). *Unstoppable Octobia May.* New York: Scholastic.

Fordham, S., & Ogbu, J. U. (1986). Black students' school success: Coping with the "burden of 'acting white.'" *Urban Review,* 18(3): 176–193.

Freedom Writers with E. Grunwell (1999). *The freedom writers diary: How a teacher and 150 teens used writing to change themselves and the world around them.* New York: Broadway Books.

Furner, J. (2007). Dewey deracialized: A critical race-theoretic perspective. *Knowledge Organization,* 34(3): 144–168.

Gangi, J. M. (2008). The unbearable whiteness of literacy instruction: Realizing the implications of the proficient reader research. *Multicultural Review,* 17(1): 30–35.

Gaspaire, Brent (n.d). Redlining (1937–). In *The Black past remembered and reclaimed: The online reference guide to African American history.* Retrieved from http://www.blackpast.org/aah/redlining-1937

Gay, G. (2000). *Culturally responsive teaching.* New York: Teachers College Press.

Geilig, N. (2015, February 18). How Oregon's second-largest city vanished in a day. *Smithsonian Magazine.* Retrieved from http://www.smithsonianmag.com /history/vanport-oregon-how-countrys-largest-housing-project-vanished -day-180954040/?no-ist

Giroux, H. A. (2010, October 17). Lessons from Paulo Freire. *Chronicle of Higher Education.* Retrieved from http://chronicle.com/article/Lessons-From-Paulo -Freire/124910

Glazier, J., & Seo, J. (2005). Multicultural literature and discussion as mirror or window? *Journal of Adolescent & Adult Literacy,* 48(8): 686–700.

Gorski, P. C. (2013). *Teaching and reaching students in poverty: Strategies for erasing the opportunity gap.* New York: Teachers College Press.

Gorski, P. C. (2014). Imagining equity literacy. Retrieved from Teaching Tolerance website: http://www.tolerance.org/blog/imagining-equity-literacy?elq=c1866 89bf1984d34a8e3f8fa951e870b&elqCampaignId=248

Gorski, P. C., & Swalwell, K. (2015). Equity literacy for all. *Educational Leadership,* 72(6): 34–40.

Graham, K. A. (2015). School cuts have decimated librarians. Retrieved from http:// articles.philly.com/2015-02-02/news/58679838_1_school-library-librarian -philadelphia-school-district

Grimes, N. (1998). *Bronx masquerade.* New York: Dial Books.

Hale, J. E. (2001). *Learning while Black: Creating educational excellence for African American children.* Baltimore: Johns Hopkins University Press.

Hale-Benson, J. (1989). The school learning environment and academic success. In G. L. Berry & J. K. Keiko (Eds.), *Black students: Psychosocial issues and academic achievement* (pp. 83–98). Newbury Park, CA: SAGE Publications.

Hanley, M. S., & Noblit, G. W. (2009). *Cultural responsiveness, racial identity, and academic success: A review of the literature.* Retrieved from http://www.heinz .org/UserFiles/Library/Culture-Report_FINAL.pdf

Hannah-Jones, N. (2011, May 6). In Portland's heart, 2010 census shows diversity dwindling. *The Oregonian.* Retrieved from http://www.oregonlive.com/pacific -northwest-news/index.ssf/2011/04/in_portlands_heart_diversity_dwindles .html

Hansen-Krening, N. (1992). Authors of color: A multicultural perspective. *Journal of Reading,* 36(2): 124–129.

Harper, B. E. (2007). The relationship between Black racial identity and academic achievement in urban settings. *Theory into Practice,* 46(3): 230–238.

Harris-Britt, A., Valrie, C. R., Kurtz-Costes, B., & Rowley, S. J. (2007). Perceived racial discrimination and self-esteem in African American youth: Racial socialization as a protective factor. *Journal of Research on Adolescence*, 17(4): 669–682.

Harvard Project Zero (n.d). *Circle of viewpoints thinking routine.* Cambridge, MA: Harvard Graduate School of Education. Retrieved from http://www .visiblethinkingpz.org/VisibleThinking_html_files/03_ThinkingRoutines/03e _FairnessRoutines/Fairness_pdfs/VT_CircleofViewpoints.pdf

Hasson, E. A. (1991). Reading with infants and toddlers. *Day Care and Early Education,* 19(1): 35–37.

Hawley, W. (n.d.). *Strategies for reducing racial and ethnic prejudice: Essential principles for program design.* Retrieved from http://www.tolerance.org /supplement/strategies-reducing-racial-and-ethnic-prejudice-essential-pr

Heflin, B. R., & Barksdale-Ladd, M. A. (2001). African American children's literature that helps students find themselves: Selection guidelines for grades K-3. *Reading Teacher,* 54(8): 810–819.

Helms, J. E. (1993). An overview of black racial identity theory. In J. E. Helms (Ed.), *Black and White racial identity: Theory, research, and practice* (pp. 9–32). Westport, CT: Praegar Publishers.

Helms, J. E. (1995). An update of Helms's white and people of color racial identity models. In J. G. Ponterotto, J. M. Casa, L. S. Suzuki, & C. M. Alexander (Eds.), *Handbook of multicultural counseling* (pp. 181–198). Thousand Oaks, CA: Sage Publications.

Hernandez, D. J. (2010). *Double jeopardy: How third-grade reading skills and poverty influence high school graduation.* Albany, NY: Annie E. Casey Foundation. Retrieved from http://www.aecf.org/~/media/Pubs/Topics/Education /Other/DoubleJeopardyHowThirdGradeReadingSkillsandPovery/DoubleJeo pardyReport040511FINAL.pdf

Hinton-Johnson, K. (2009). Sharon M. Draper: Reaching reluctant readers. *The ALAN Review,* 36(2): 89–93.

Horning, K. T., Febry, C., Lindgren, M. V., & Schliesman, M. (2014). *Thoughts on publishing in 2013.* Madison, WI: Cooperative Children's Book Center. Retrieved from http://ccbc.education.wisc.edu/books/choiceintro14.asp

Hottman, S. (2013, January 14). Black pioneers came to Oregon with the railroad, stayed through determination. *The Oregonian.* Retrieved from http://www .oregonlive.com/portland/index.ssf/2013/01/black_pioneers_came_to_ore gon.html

Howard, G. R. (2006). *We can't teach what we don't know: White teachers, multiracial schools.* 2nd ed. New York: Teachers College Press.

Howard, T. C. (2001). Powerful pedagogy for African American students: A case of four teachers. *Urban Education,* 36(2): 179–202.

Howard, T. C. (2003). Culturally relevant pedagogy: Ingredients for critical teacher reflection. *Theory into Practice,* 42(3): 195–202.

Howard, T. C. (2010). *Why race and culture matter in schools: Closing the achievement gap in America's classroom.* New York: Teachers College Press.

Hughes-Hassell, S. (2013). Multicultural young adult literature as a form of counter-storytelling. *Library Quarterly: Information, Community, Policy,* 83(3): 212–228.

Hughes-Hassell, S., Barkley, H. A., & Koehler, E. (2009). Promoting equity in children's literacy instruction: Using a critical race theory framework to examine transitional books. *SLMR:* 12. Retrieved from http://www.ala.org/ala/mgrps

/divs/aasl/aaslpubsandjournals/slmrb/slmrcontents/volume12/hughes
_hassell.cfm

Hughes-Hassell, S., Hassell, L., & Agosto, D. E. (2010). Moving beyond the stereo-
types: Seeing urban teenagers as individuals. In D. E. Agosto & S. Hughes-
Hassell (Eds.), *Urban teens in the library: Research and practice* (pp. 9–19).
Chicago: American Library Association.

Hughes-Hassell, S., Kumasi, K., Rawson, C. H., & Hitson, A. (2010). *Building a
bridge to literacy for African American male youth: A call to action for the
library community.* Unpublished manuscript. School of Information and
Library Science, University of North Carolina at Chapel Hill, Chapel Hill,
NC. Retrieved from http://sils.unc.edu/sites/default/files/news/Building-a
-Bridge-to-Literacy.pdf

Hurley, E. A., Boykin, A. W., & Allen, B. A. (2005). Communal versus individual
learning of a math-estimation task: African American children and the culture of learning contexts. *Journal of Psychology*, 139(6): 513–527.

Irizarry, J. G. (2011). *The Latinization of U.S. schools: Successful teaching and learning in shifting cultural contexts.* Boulder, CO: Paradigm Publishers.

Irvine, J. J. (2003). *Educating teachers for diversity: Seeing with a cultural eye.* New
York: Teachers College Press.

Ito, M., Gutiérrez, K., Livingstone, S., Penuel, B., Rhodes, J., Salen, K., Schor, J.,
Sefton-Green, J., & Watkins, S. C. (2013). *Connected learning: An agenda for
research and design.* Irvine, CA: Digital Media and Learning Research Hub.

Jalongo, M. R. (1998). *Young children and picture books: Literature from infancy to
six.* Washington, DC: National Association for the Education of Young Children.

Johnson, V. (2014). *The great Greene heist.* New York: Arthur Levine Books.

Johnston, P. H., & Nicholls, J. G. (1995). Voices we want to hear and voices we
don't. *Theory Into Practice*, 34(2): 94–100.

Jones, C., Sohl, K., & Woodward, M. F. (2011). *Preparing African American children
for kindergarten: A library planning grant.* Portland, OR: MLC. Retrieved from
http://www.oregon.gov/OSL/LD/LSTA/2010/10-04-3pconsultrpt.pdf

Jones, J. M. (2013). U.S. Blacks, Hispanics have no preferences on group labels.
Retrieved from http://www.gallup.com/poll/163706/blacks-hispanics-no
-preferences-group-labels.aspx

Katz, P. A. (1993). *Development of racial attitudes in children.* Presentation given to
the University of Delaware.

Kirk, B. J. (2012). 55 percent of Philadelphia households lack access to internet.
Technical.ly Philly. Retrieved from http://technical.ly/philly/2012/04/04/55
-percent-of-philadelphia-households-lack-access-to-internet-new-early-data
-shows-rate-higher-than-previously-thought/

Kirkland, D. (2012). Teaching Englishes. *The Engaged Scholar Magazine*, 7(1–2).
Retrieved from http://engagedscholar.msu.edu/magazine/volume7/kirkland
.aspx

Kirkland, D. (2013). *A search past silence: The literacy of young Black men.* New
York: Teachers College Press.

Knaus, C. B. (2009). Shut up and listen: Applied critical race theory in the classroom. *Race Ethnicity and Education*, 12(2): 133–154.

Koehler, M. (2011, May 13). *What is TPACK?* Retrieved from http://www.tpack.org

Koester, A. (2015, February 8). Selection is a privilege. *The Show Me Librarian* blog.
Retrieved from http://showmelibrarian.blogspot.com/2015/02/selection-is
-privilege.html

Kozol, J. (2012, August 1). The other America: Giving our poorest children the same
opportunities as our richest. *School Library Journal* blog. Retrieved from

http://www.slj.com/2012/08/literacy/the-other-america-giving-our-poorest-children-the-same-opportunities-as-our-richest/

Kumasi, K. (2012). Roses in the concrete: A critical race perspective on urban youth and school libraries. *Knowledge Quest,* 40(4): 12–17.

Kurz, R. F. (2012) Missing faces, beautiful places: The lack of diversity in South Carolina picture book award nominees. *New Review of Children's Literature and Librarianship,* 18(2): 128–145.

Ladson-Billings, G. (1995). Toward a theory of culturally relevant pedagogy. *American Educational Research Journal,* 32(3): 465–491.

Ladson-Billings, G. (1998). Just what is critical race theory and what's it doing in a nice field like education. *International Journal of Qualitative Studies in Education,* 11(1): 7–24.

Ladson-Billings, G. (2006). From the achievement gap to the education debt: Understanding achievement in U.S. schools. *Educational Researcher* 35(7): 3–12.

Ladson-Billings, G. (2009). *The dreamkeepers: Successful teaching of African American children.* 2nd ed. San Francisco: Jossey Bass.

Ladson-Billings, G., & Tate, W. F. (1995). Toward a critical race theory of education. *Teachers College Record,* 97(1): 47–68.

Lankes, R. D. (2011). *The atlas of new librarianship.* Cambridge, MA: MIT Press.

Larson, L. [Lars] (2012, May 31). Does anybody think this is a good idea, paid for with your tax dollars: Youth librarian Kirby McCurtis leads the new Black storytime program at Midland Library [Facebook status update]. Retrieved from https://www.facebook.com/TheLarsLarsonShow/posts/451823918179429

Lazar, A., Edwards, P. A., & McMillon, G. T. (2012). *The essential guide to social equity teaching.* New York: Teachers College Press.

Lenhart, A., Ling, R., Campbell, S., & Purcell, K. (2010). *Teens & mobile phones.* Pew Internet & American Life Project. Retrieved from http://pewinternet.org.

Levin, B. (2000). Putting students at the centre of education reform. *Journal of Educational Change,* 1(2): 155–172.

Lewis, S., Simon, C. Uzzell, R., Horwitz, A., & Casserly, M. (2010). *A call for change: The social and educational factors contributing to the outcomes of Black males in urban schools.* Washington, DC: The Council of the Great City Schools. Retrieved from http://www.edweek.org/media/black_male_study.pdf

Lewis, S., Casserly, M., Simon, C., Uzzell, R., & Palacios, M. (2013). *A call for change: Providing solutions for Black male achievement.* Washington, DC: The Council of the Great City Schools. Retrieved from http://www.cgcs.org/cms/lib/DC00001581/Centricity/Domain/88/A%20Call%20For%20Change_Finale Book.pdf

Lo, M. (2015, February 19). *Perceptions of diversity in book reviews.* Retrieved from www.malindalo.com/2015/02/perceptions-of-diversity-in-book-reviews.

Lundy, Garvey F. (2003). The myths of oppositional culture. *Journal of Black Studies,* 33(4): 450–467.

Lyons, K. S. (2007). *One million men and me.* New York: Just Us Books.

Lyons, K.S. (2012). *Tea cakes for Tosh.* New York: Putnam.

Magoon, K. (2010). *The rock and the river.* New York: Aladdin.

Majors, R., & Billson, J. M. (1992). *Cool pose: The dilemmas of Black manhood in America.* New York: Lexington Books.

Maker Ed. (2015). *Youth Makerspace playbook.* San Francisco: Maker Education Initiative. Retrieved from http://makered.org/wp-content/uploads/2015/09/Youth-Makerspace-Playbook_FINAL.pdf

Marcia, J. (1966). Development and validation of ego-identity status. *Journal of Personality and Social Psychology,* 3(5): 551–558.

Marcia, J. (1980). Identity in adolescence. In J. Adelson (Ed.), *Handbook of adolescent psychology* (pp. 159–187). New York: John Wiley & Sons.

Martin, B. L. (1991). From Negro to Black to African American: The power of names and naming. *Political Science Quarterly,* 106(1): 83–107.

Mattoon, M. (2015). *What are protocols? Why use them?* Bloomington, IN: National School Reform Faculty, Harmony Education Center. Retrieved from http://www.nsrfharmony.org/system/files/protocols/WhatAreProtocols%2BWhyUse_0.pdf

McCullough, R. G. (2008). Untapped cultural support: The influence of culturally bound prior knowledge on comprehension performance. *Reading Horizons,* 49(1): 1–30.

McDonald, J. P., Mahr, N., Dicter, A., & McDonald, E. C. (2013). *The power of protocols: An educator's guide to better practice.* 3rd ed. New York: Teacher's College Press.

McDougald Terrace Library. (2003). Unpublished manuscript. School of Information and Library Science, University of North Carolina at Chapel Hill, Chapel Hill, NC.

McGregor, M. (2003). The Vanport flood and racial change in Portland. *Oregon History Project.* Retrieved from http://www.oregonhistoryproject.org/articles/essays/the-vanport-flood/#.V3fN4DUbyqw

McLagan, E. (n.d.). The Black laws of Oregon, 1844–1857. *The Black Past remembered and reclaimed: The online reference guide to African American history.* Retrieved from http://www.blackpast.org/perspectives/black-laws-oregon-1844-1857#sthash.ntytqoXc.dpuf

McManus, M. (2016, October 12). Why do rich kids do better than poor kids in school? It's not the "word gap." *New Republic Online.* Retrieved from http://www.newrepublic.com/article/123093/why-do-rich-kids-do-better-poor-kids-school

McNair, J. C. (2008a). The representation of authors and illustrators of color in school-based book clubs. *Language Arts,* 65(3): 193–201.

McNair, J. C. (2008b). Innocent though they may seem . . . A critical race theory analysis of Firefly and Seesaw Scholastic book club order forms. *Multicultural Review,* 17(1): 24–29.

Mead, S. (2010, June 13). Reading for life. *The American Prospect.* Retrieved from http://prospect.org/article/reading-life-0

Mestre, L. S. (2010). Culturally responsive instruction for teacher-librarians. *Teacher Librarian,* 36(3): 8–12.

Meyer, G., & Davis, B. (n.d.). *Students' six: Teaching strategies that work for students of color.* Chapel Hill, NC: Chapel Hill-Carrboro City Schools. Retrieved from http://www.theequitycollaborative.com/wp-content/uploads/2015/06/Students-Six-Cover.pdf

Michigan Education Association (n.d.). *What is cultural competence?* Retrieved from http://www.mea.org/diversity/index.html

Miller, D. B., & Macintosh, R. (1999). Promoting resilience in Urban African American adolescents: Racial socialization and identity as protective factors. *Social Work Research,* 23(3): 159–169.

Mitra, D. L. (2004). The significance of students: Can increasing "student voice" in schools lead to gains in youth development? *Teachers College Record,* 106(4): 651–688.

Mitra, D. L., & Serrier, S. C. (2012). Student voice in elementary school reform: Examining youth development in fifth graders. *American Educational Research Journal,* 49(4): 743–774.

Morrell, E. (2002). Toward a critical pedagogy of popular culture: Literacy development among urban youth. *Journal of Adolescent & Adult Literacy,* 46(1): 72–77.

Morrell, E. (2004a). *Becoming critical researchers: Literacy and empowerment for urban youth.* New York: Peter Lang.

Morrell, E. (2004b). *Linking literacy and popular culture: Finding connections for lifelong learning.* Norwood, MA: Christopher Gordon.

Morrell, E. (2006). Youth-initiated research as a tool for advocacy and change in urban schools. In S. Ginwright, P. Noguera, & J. Cammarota (Eds.), *Beyond resistance! Youth activism and community change: New democratic possibilities for practice and policy for America's youth* (pp. 111–128). New York: Routledge.

Morrell, E., & Duncan-Andrade, J. (2002). Promoting academic literacy with urban youth through hip-hop culture. *English Journal,* 91(6): 88–92.

Morris, V. J. I. (2010). Street lit: Before you can recommend it, you have to understand it. In D. E. Agosto & S. Hughes-Hassell (Eds.), *Urban teens in the library: Research and practice* (pp. 53–66). Chicago: ALA.

Moule, Jean. (2012). *Cultural competence: A primer for educators.* Belmont, CA: Wadsworth.

Mowry, J. (2007). *Skeleton key.* Port Orchard, WA: Orchard House Press.

Myers, W. D. (2006). *Autobiography of my dead brother.* New York: Harper Collins.

Myers, W. D. (2009). *Sunrise over Fallujah.* New York: Scholastic.

Myers, W. D. (2010a). *The cruisers.* New York: Scholastic.

Myers, W. D. (2010b). *Lockdown.* New York: Harper Collins.

Myers, W. D. (2011). *Checkmate.* New York: Scholastic.

Myers, W. D. (2012). *A star is born.* New York: Scholastic.

Myers, W. D. (2013). *Oh, snap!* New York: Scholastic.

Nasir, N. S. (2012). *Racialized identities: Race and achievement among African American youth.* Stanford, CA: Stanford University Press.

National Association for Educational Progress (2014). *The nation's report card: Reading 2013.* Retrieved from http://nces.ed.gov/nationsreportcard/naepdata

National Center for Education Statistics (2009). *The nation's report card: Reading 2009* (NCES 2010–458). Washington, DC: Institute of Education Sciences, U.S. Department of Education. Retrieved from http://nces.ed.gov/nationsreportcard/pdf/main2009/2010458.pdf

National Center for Health Statistics (2009). *Health, United States 2012: Homicide chart.* Retrieved from http://www.cdc.gov/nchs/data/hus/2012/034.pdf

National Council of Teachers of English (2013). *The NCTE definition of 21st-century literacies.* Retrieved from http://www.ncte.org/positions/statements/21stcentdefinition

Neri, G. (2010). *Yummy: The last days of a Southside shorty.* New York: Lee & Low.

Neuman, D. (2011a). Constructing knowledge in the 21st Century: I-LEARN and using information as a tool for learning. *School Library Media Research,* 14. Retrieved from http://www.ala.org/aasl/sites/ala.org.aasl/files/content/aaslpubsandjournals/slr/vol14/SLR_ConstructingKnowledge_V14.pdf

Neuman, D. (2011b). *Learning in information-rich environments: I-LEARN and the construction of knowledge in the 21st century.* New York: Springer.

Neuman, D., Grant, A., Lee, V., & Tecce DeCarlo, M. J. (2015). Information literacy in a high-poverty urban school: An I-LEARN project. *School Libraries Worldwide,* 21(1): 38–53.

Neuman, S. B., & Celano, D. (2001). Access to print in low-income and middle-income communities: An ecological study of four neighborhoods. *Reading Research Quarterly,* 36(1): 8–26.

Noguera, P. A. (2008). *The trouble with Black boys: And other reflections on race, equity, and the future of public education.* San Francisco: Jossey-Bass.

Office for Civil Rights (2015). *Frequently asked questions about racial harassment.* Washington DC: Department of Education. Retrieved from http://www2.ed.gov/about/offices/list/ocr/qa-raceharass.html

Ogbu, J. U. (2004). Collective identity and the burden of "acting White" in Black history, community, and education. *The Urban Review,* 36(1): 1–35.

Okun, T. (2010). *The emperor has no clothes: Teaching about race and racism to people who don't want to know.* Charlotte, NC: Information Age Publishing.

Older, D. J. (2015). *Shadowshaper.* New York: Arthur Levine.

Oldfather, P. (1995). Songs "come back most to them": Students' experiences as researchers. *Theory into Practice,* 34(2): 131.

olsson, j. (1997). *Detour spotting for white anti-racists: A tool for change.* Questa, NM: Cultural Books. Retrieved from http://www.racialequitytools.org/resourcefiles/olson.pdf

Overall, P. M. (2009). Cultural competence: A conceptual framework for library information science professionals. *The Library Quarterly,* 79(2): 175–204.

Parham, T. A. (1989). Cycles of psychological nigrescence. *The Counseling Psychologist,* 17(2): 187–226.

Parker, L., & Stovall, D. O. (2004). Actions following words: Critical race theory connects to critical pedagogy. *Educational Philosophy,* 36(2): 167–182.

Parsons, E. C. (2008). Learning contexts, Black cultural ethos, and the science achievement of African American students in an urban middle school. *Journal of Research in Science Training,* 45(6): 665–683.

Pateman, J. V. (2010). *Public libraries and social justice.* Farnham, UK: Ashgate Publishing.

Perkins, M. (Ed.) (2013). *Open mic: Riffs on life between cultures in ten voices.* Somerville, MA: Candlewick Press.

Pettaway, A. (2015). Book smarts. *Teaching Tolerance,* 51. Retrieved from http://www.tolerance.org/magazine/number-51-fall-2015/feature/book-smarts

Phinney, J. S. (1989). Stages of ethnic identity development in minority group adolescents. *Journal of Early Adolescence,* 9(1–2): 34–49.

Phinney, J. S. (1990). Ethnic identity in adolescents and adults: Review of research. *Psychological Bulletin,* 108(3): 499–514.

Phinney, J. S. (1993). A three-stage model of ethnic identity development in adolescence. In M. E. Bernal & G. P. Knight (Eds.), *Ethnic identity: Formation and transmission among Hispanics and other minorities* (pp. 61–79). Albany: State University of New York Press.

Phinney, J. S. (1995). Ethnic identity and self-esteem: A review and integration. In A. M. Padilla (Ed.), *Hispanic psychology: Critical issues in theory and research* (pp. 57–70). Thousand Oaks, CA: Sage Publications.

Phinney, J. S., & Rotherman M. J. (Eds.) (1987). *Children's Ethnic Socialization: Pluralism and Development.* Newbury Park, CA: Sage Press.

Pinkney, A. D. (2010). *Sit-in: How four friends stood up by sitting down.* New York: Little Brown Books.

Powell, R. (2009). Introduction. In L. S. Spears-Bunton & R. Powell (Eds.), *Toward a literacy of promise: Joining the African Americans in the struggle* (pp. 1–16). New York: Routledge.

Purves, A., & Beach, R. (1972). *Literature and the reader.* Urbana, IL: National Council of Teachers of English.

Quiroz, P. A. (2001). The silencing of Latino student "voice": Puerto Rican and Mexican narratives in eighth grade and high school. *Anthropology and Education Quarterly,* 32(3): 326–349.

Racial Equity Tools (2013). Glossary. Retrieved from http://www.racialequitytools
.org/images/uploads/RET_Glossary913L.pdf

Rawls, J. (1972). *A theory of justice.* Oxford, UK: Clarendon Press.

Rawls, J. (2001). *Justice as fairness: A restatement.* Cambridge, MA: Belknap Press.

Rawson, C. (2014). Are all lists created equal? In H. Booth & K. Jensen (Eds.), *The whole library handbook: Teen services* (pp. 97–104). Chicago: ALA Editions.

Renee, B. (2015). I'm not African-American, I'm Black: Why racial labels matter. *Elite Daily.* Retrieved from http://elitedaily.com/life/culture/im-not-african -american-im-black-racial-labels-matter/1008819/

Rhuday-Perkovich, O. (2013). Confessions of a Black geek. In M. Perkins (Ed.), *Open mic: Riffs on life between cultures in ten voices* (pp. 69–78). Somerville, MA: Candlewick Press.

Roberts, D. D., & Taylor, R. D. (2012). Racial identity as a buffer to *discriminación* among low-income African American adolescents: An examination of academic performance. In J. M. Sullivan & A. M. Esmail (Eds.), *African American identity: Racial and cultural dimensions of the Black experience* (pp. 317–343). Plymouth, UK: Lexington Books.

Roc, M. (2014). *Connected learning: Harnessing the information age to make learning more powerful.* Washington, DC: Alliance for Excellent Education. Retrieved from http://all4ed.org/wp-content/uploads/2014/03/ConnectedLearning.pdf

Rodriguez, L. F., & Brown, T. M. (2009). From voice to agency: Guiding principles for participatory action research with youth. *New Directions for Youth Development,* 123: 19–34.

Roth, V. (2011). *Divergent.* New York: Harper Collins.

Rudd, T. (2014). *Racial disproportionality in school discipline: Implicit bias is heavily implicated.* Columbus, OH: Kirwan Institute for the Study of Race and Ethnicity, The Ohio State University. Retrieved from http://kirwaninstitute.osu .edu/wp-content/uploads/2014/02/racial-disproportionality-schools-02 .pdf

Rudduck, J., & Flutter, J. (2000). Pupil participation and perspective: "Carving a new order of experience." *Cambridge Journal of Education,* 30(1): 75–89.

Sánchez, L. (2014). Fostering wide-awakeness: Third-grade community activists. In P. Gorski and J. Landsman (Eds.), *The poverty and education reader* (pp. 183–194). Sterling, VA: Stylus.

Scharf, A. (2015). *Critical practices for anti-bias education.* Atlanta: Southern Poverty Law Center. Retrieved from http://www.tolerance.org/sites/default/files /general/PDA%20Critical%20Practices.pdf

School District of Philadelphia (2012). *School progress report.* Retrieved from http:// webgui.phila.k12.pa.us/offices/s/strategic-analytics/annual-reports /school-progress- reports

Schwartz, M. (2013). Engaging the elusive non-user. *Library Journal* blog. Retrieved from http://lj.libraryjournal.com

Search Institute (2016). Developmental assets. Minneapolis: Search Institute. Retrieved from http://www.search-institute.org/research/developmental -assets

Seaton, E. D. (2014). *Legend of the Mantamaji.* Los Angeles: And . . . Action! Entertainment.

Sebring, P. B., Brown, E. R., Julian, K. M., Ehrlich, S. B., Sporte, S. E., Bradley, E., & Meyer, L. (2013). *Teens, digital media, and the Chicago public library.* Chicago: University of Chicago Consortium on Chicago School Research.

Segal, S. (2013, September 13). Closing school libraries? This means war. *Philadelphia Weekly.* Retrieved from http://philadelphiaweekly.com/2013/sep/13 /Closing-school-libraries-This-means-war-223651501/

Serpell, Z. N., Boykin, A. W., Serge, M., & Nasim A. (2006). The significance of contextual factors in African American students' transfer of learning. *Journal of Black Psychology, 32* (4): 418–441.

Shakur, T. (1999). *The rose that grew from concrete.* New York: MTV Books.

Slater, J. J., & Ravid, R. (2010). *Collaboration in education.* New York: Routledge.

Sleeter, C. E. (2012). Confronting the marginalization of culturally responsive pedagogy. *Urban Education, 47*: 562–584.

Small, C., White, R., Chavou, T., & Sellers, R. (2007). Racial ideological beliefs and racial discrimination experiences as predictors of academic engagement among African American adolescents. *Journal of Black Psychology, 33*(3): 299–330.

Smith, C. R., Jr. (2008). *Chameleon.* Cambridge, MA: Candlewick Press.

Solórzano, D. G. (1997). Images and words that wound: Critical race theory, racial stereotyping, and teacher education. *Teacher Education Quarterly, 24*(3): 5–19.

Solórzano, D. G., & Delgado Bernal, D. (2001). Critical race theory and transformational resistance: Chicana/o students in an urban context. *Urban Education, 36*(3): 308–342.

Solórzano, D. G., & Yosso, T. J. (2002). Critical race methodology: Counter-story telling as an analytical framework for education. *Qualitative Inquiry, 8*(1): 26.

Solórzano, D. G., Villalpando, O., & Oseguera, L. (2005). Education inequities and Latina/o undergraduate students in the United States: A critical race analysis of their educational progress. *Journal of Hispanic Higher Education, 4*(3): 274–292.

Steele, C. M. (1997). A threat in the air: How stereotypes shape intellectual identity and performance. *American Psychologist, 52*(6): 613–629.

Steele, C. (2003). Stereotype threat and African American student achievement. In T. Perry, C. Steele, and A. Hilliard (Eds.), *Young, gifted, and black: Promoting high achievement among African American students* (pp. 109–130). Boston: Beacon Press.

Stivers, J., & Hughes-Hassell, S. (2015). #act4teens: The inclusive library: More than a diverse collection: Part 1. *YALSA* blog. Retrieved from http://yalsa.ala.org/blog/2015/03/07/act4teens-the-inclusive-library-more-than-a-diverse-collection-part-1

Strauss, V. (2013, June 8). Philadelphia school district laying off 3,783 employees. *Washington Post.* Retrieved from http://www.washingtonpost.com/blogs/answersheet/wp/2013/06/08/philadelphia-school-district-laying-off-3783-employees

Sue, D. W., Capodilupo, C., Torino, G, Bucceri, J., Holder, A., Nadal, K., & Equin, M. (2007). Racial microaggressions in everyday life: Implications for clinical practice. *The American Psychologist, 62*(4): 271–286.

Tate, W. F. (1997). Critical race theory and education: History, theory, and implications. *Review of Research in Education, 95*(1): 195–246.

Tatum, A. W. (2009). *Reading for their life: (Re)building the textual lineages of African American adolescent males.* Portsmouth, NH: Heinemann Educational Books.

Tatum, A. W. (2013). *Fearless voices: Engaging a new generation of African American adolescent male writers.* New York: Scholastic.

Tatum, B. D. (1997). *"Why are all the Black kids sitting together in the cafeteria?" and other conversations about race.* New York: Basic Books.

Teaching Tolerance (2014). *Perspectives for a Diverse America* [Curriculum]. Atlanta: Teaching Tolerance. Retrieved from http://perspectives.tolerance.org

Tecce DeCarlo, M. J., Grant, A., Lee, V. J., & Neuman, D. (2014). Information literacy in the kindergarten classroom: An I-LEARN case study. In S.

Kurbanoglu, S. Spiranec, F. Grassian, D. Mizrachi, & R. Catts (Eds.), *Information literacy: Lifelong learning and digital literacy in the 21st century* (pp. 243–252). New York: Springer.

Theoharis, J. (2014). *The rebellious life of Mrs. Rosa Parks.* Boston, Beacon Press.

Thomas, W. (2015). How to foster teen activism. *School Library Journal.* Retrieved from http://www.slj.com/2015/11/teens-ya/how-to-foster-teen-activism

Tyler, K. M., Boykin, A. W., Boelter, C. M., & Dillihunt, M. L. (2005). Examining mainstream and afro-cultural value socialization in African American households. *Journal of Black Psychology,* 31(3): 291–310.

Tyler, K. M., Boykin, A. W., Miller, O., & Hurley, E. (2007). Cultural values in the home and school experiences of low-income African-American students. *Social Psychology of Education,* 9(4): 363–380.

Tyler, K. M., Boykin, A. W., & Walton, T. R. (2006). Cultural considerations in teacher's perceptions of student classroom behavior and achievement. *Teaching and Teacher Education,* 22(8): 998–1005.

U.S. Bureau of Labor (2014). *The employment situation: April 2014.* Retrieved from http://www.bls.gov/news.release/pdf/empsit.pdf

U.S. Census Bureau (2013). *About race.* Retrieved from http://www.census.gov /topics/population/race/about.html

U.S. Department of Education (2016). National—Regulatory adjusted cohort graduation rate, Black. Retrieved from http://eddataexpress.ed.gov/data-element -explorer.cfm/tab/trend/deid/5324/state/US/

U.S. Department of Education, Office for Civil Rights (2012). *Revealing new truths about our nation's school.* Washington, DC: U.S. Department of Education. Retrieved from http://www2.ed.gov/about/offices/list/ocr/docs/crdc-2012 -data-summary.pdf

Van Ausdale, D., & Feagin, J. R. (2001). *The first R: How children learn race and racism.* New York: Rowman & Littlefield Publishers.

Van den Berghe, P. L. (1967). *Race and racism.* New York: Wiley.

Villarosa, L. (Ed.). (2012). Mobilizing community power to address structural racism. *PRE Critical Issue* 4. Washington, DC. Philanthropic Initiatives for Racial Equity. Retrieved from http://racialequity.org/docs/CIF4FullWeb.pdf

Vissa, J., & Streim, N. (2006). Perspectives on boundary spanning: University faculty as managers of public schools. In N. L. Zimpher & K. R. Howley (Eds.), *Boundary spanners: Key to success in P–16 university-school partnerships* (pp. 168–188). New York: American Association of State College and Universities and National Association of State Universities and Land-Grant Colleges.

Watkins, M. (1979, September 23). James Baldwin writing and talking. *New York Times Book Review,* pp. 3, 36–37.

Wellman, David. (1977). *Portraits of white racism.* Cambridge, UK: Cambridge University Press.

Wiggins, G. (2007). What is an essential question? *Big Ideas: An Authentic Education e-Journal.* Retrieved from http://www.authenticeducation.org/ae _bigideas/article.lasso?artid=53

Wildhagen, T. (2012). How teachers and schools contribute to racial differences in the realization of academic potential. *Teachers College Record,* 114(7): 1–27.

Winters, S., & Gregg, E. (2009). Before it's reading, it's writing: Urban teens as authors in the public library. In D. E. Agosto & S. Hughes-Hassell (Eds.), *Urban teens in the library: Research and practice* (pp. 153–169). Chicago: ALA.

Wong, C. A., Eccles, J. S., & Sameroff, A.(2003). The influence of ethnic discrimination and ethnic identification on African American adolescents' school and socioemotional adjustment. *Journal of Personality,* 71(6): 1197–1232.

Wright, B. L. (2009). Racial-ethnic identity, academic achievement, and African American males: A review of literature. *Journal of Negro Education,* 78(2): 123–134.

Yang, G. L. (2013). Why I won't be watching the Last Airbender movie. In M. Perkins (Ed.), *Open mic: Riffs on life between cultures in ten voices.* Somerville, MA: Candlewick Press.

Young Adult Library Services Association (2012). *National teen space guidelines.* Retrieved from http://www.ala.org

About the Editors and Contributors

SARAH ALVERSON is the Children's Librarian at Stanford L. Warren Library, a historically African American Library in Durham County, North Carolina. Receiving her MLS from North Carolina Central University in 2011, she now works closely with the community surrounding the college. At Stanford L. Warren Library, Ms. Alverson has worked with both children and teens, providing a diverse range of services and programs. She successfully established "Sensory Storytime: A Storytime for Adults with Special Needs," a program that was then replicated for local youth with special needs, gaining nationwide recognition following an article published by the Urban Libraries Council. She serves on the Book Babies Task Force, a Book Harvest program that provides books for Medicaid eligible families, and is active on a number of committees for Durham County Library, including Summer Reading, Youth Services, and Hispanic Services.

PAULETTA BROWN BRACY is professor in the School of Library and Information Sciences at North Carolina Central University, where she also serves as director of the Office of University Accreditation. She began her library career in the Pittsburgh, Pennsylvania, public schools as a middle school librarian. Her areas of teaching and research are school library media librarianship and children's and young adult literature and services, with foci on ethnic perspectives in literature and meeting the needs of African American children and adolescents in school and public libraries. She is the current chair of the Coretta Scott King Book Award Committee. She has also taught at the University of Iowa, the University of North Carolina at Chapel Hill (UNC-CH), and the University of North Carolina at Greensboro. She holds a BA in English from Fisk University, an MLS from the University of Pittsburgh and a PhD in library science from the University of Michigan.

TERESA BUNNER currently works in Wake County Schools, North Carolina, as the Coordinating Literacy Teacher for High Schools. She works with literacy efforts across the district. Previously, she served as the academic support specialist for the Blue Ribbon Mentor-Advocate (BRMA) program in the Chapel Hill–Carrboro City Schools, working with the 130 students in the program by coordinating academic support and enrichment. She also cofacilitated (with 20 high school students) the Student Six project, a professional development series on creating culturally responsive classrooms. In her past life, Bunner was a classroom teacher and reading specialist at the elementary, middle, and high school levels. When she is not working, she serves as the CEO for her wonderful family, which includes her husband and four boys.

FAITH BURNS is a teen librarian at Durham County Library's Main Library in Durham, North Carolina, where she loves working with her phenomenal group of young people. They keep her laughing! She graduated from the School of Information and Library Science at the University of North Carolina at Chapel Hill (UNC-CH) in 2015 and from Duke University in 2010. When she is not at the library, she spends her time with her husband, Adam, and their dog, Humphrey.

HEATHER CUNNINGHAM earned her master's degree in library and information science at the University of North Carolina at Chapel Hill (UNC-CH), with a focus on school and public librarianship. While working on her degree, she accepted a position at the Durham County Public Library and began to work her way up through the ranks. In 2013, she received *Library Journal*'s Outstanding Mention for Paralibrarian of the Year, in recognition of her work establishing a successful teen program at the Stanford L. Warren Branch Library. From then on, she split her time working in teen and children's services until 2014, when she officially became the library's first teen librarian. She is currently working within an international school setting in Switzerland, as well as serving as a contributor for NoveList.

ALLEN GRANT is an assistant clinical professor and the department head for policy, organization, and leadership in the School of Education at Drexel. An education change agent with a wide variety of experiences, he has taught kindergarten, served as a language instructor, consulted for the International Baccalaureate program, and worked for state agencies. He was the program director for a state virtual school (Louisiana) and a policy expert and grants coordinator for the Louisiana Board of Elementary and Secondary Education. His expertise in curriculum design and development underlies his service as a master reviewer for Quality Matters and as an online learning council fellow at Drexel. Other parts of his experience include his work at Louisiana State University, University of Maryland University College, and Southern University. Dr. Grant earned a PhD at LSU, an M.Ed. at George Mason University, and a BA in history from the College of William and Mary. His research centers on emerging technologies, urban school reform, and K–12 virtual schooling.

SANDRA HUGHES-HASSELL, PhD, is a professor and coordinator of the School Library Media Program in the School of Information and Library Science at the University of North Carolina at Chapel Hill (UNC-CH). She is President-elect of the Young Adult Library Services Association (YALSA). In her current research, she focuses on social justice issues in youth library services, diverse youth literature, and the role of school library media specialists in education reform. She has written and presented extensively on culturally relevant pedagogy, Critical Race Theory (CRT), and the role of libraries in serving diverse youth. With funding from a 2011 grant awarded by the Institute of Museum and Library Services (IMLS), the School of Information and Library Science at UNC-CH and the School of Library and Information Science at North Carolina Central University, she hosted the summit "Building a Bridge to Literacy for African American Male Youth: A Call to Action for the Library Community" in June 2012. The outcome of this summit was the development and dissemination of a report and website that focused on how the library community can actively address the literacy needs of African American male youth.

VERA LEE is an assistant clinical professor of literacy studies in Drexel University's School of Education, where she teaches literacy courses for the pre-K–4 certification program and the ESL Specialist program. She is also affiliated with the university's Lindy Center for Civic Engagement, where she serves as the faculty advisor for the center's America Reads, America Counts program and facilitates workshops for undergraduates who tutor K–4 students in a local elementary school. Dr. Lee taught middle school language arts and high school English for seven years, completed the Reading Specialist program at the University of Pennsylvania, and holds Instructional II certification in several states in secondary English. Her degrees include an MS.Ed. and an Ed.D. in reading, writing, and literacy from the University of Pennsylvania. Her current research focuses on preservice/in-service teacher development in the English as a Second Language (ESL) specialist program, information/digital literacy development of K–12 urban teachers and students, and fostering the home/school early literacy and language practices of immigrant families.

KIRBY MCCURTIS is a youth librarian for Multnomah County Library. She has worked as a youth librarian at Multnomah County Library's Midland branch since January 2012, focusing on youth ages 0–18 and service to the African and African American communities. She was a 2013 *Library Journal* Mover & Shaker for her efforts in community building. Prior to coming to Multnomah County Library, McCurtis worked at San Diego Public Library, where she launched the "Cuddle up & Read" program—storytimes for pregnant and parenting teens. She is active professionally, serving on committees for both Multnomah County Library and the American Library Association (ALA). In addition to being on the Black Caucus of the American Library Association (BCALA) executive board, McCurtis is currently the president of the New Members Round Table (NMRT). She earned her MLIS from the University of California, Los Angeles (UCLA) in 2008, and her areas of interest are early literacy, equity and empowerment, and community engagement.

DELIA NEUMAN is a professor in the College of Computing and Informatics at Drexel University, where she is also the director of the School Library Media (SLiM) Program. An instructional designer before becoming a university faculty member, she developed curriculum materials for elementary and high school students who are hearing impaired and for middle school students who are learning disabled. She has published over 150 publications and presentations and was the writer for the American Association of School Librarians/Association for Educational Communications and Technology's 1998 standards, *Information Power: Building Partnerships for Learning.* Her book *Learning in Information-Rich Environments: I-LEARN and the Construction of Knowledge in the 21st Century* (Springer, 2011) brings together the research and theory from information science and instructional design that led to the development of the I-LEARN model. Dr. Neuman holds an A.B in English from Chestnut Hill College, an A.M. in English from the University of Michigan, and a PhD in education from The Ohio State University.

THERESA RAMOS began her career at the Free Library of Philadelphia as a LEAP Afterschool Leader. She subsequently managed the library's nationally recognized Books Aloud! program, which focused on early literacy; an $18 million library renovation project; and several IMLS Laura Bush 21st-Century Librarian grants, focused on diversity and children's service. Over the past 20 years, she has developed and managed dozens of the Free Library's grant-funded initiatives serving children, teens, and families, including most recently the library's Hot Spot program funded by the Knight Foundation and the IMLS-funded Maker Jawn initiative. As program development coordinator, she seeks to further the scope of the library's programs and community outreach partnerships, especially those designed to provide resources to and amplify the voices of nondominant youth.

CASEY H. RAWSON, PhD, is currently a postdoctoral research associate in the School of Information and Library Science at the University of North Carolina at Chapel Hill (UNC-CH), where she earned an MSLS in 2011 with a concentration in school library media. She also holds an MAT in middle grades education from the University of Louisville and is a former sixth- and seventh-grade science teacher. Her research interests include teacher-librarian collaboration in science, technology, engineering, and mathematics (STEM) content areas and diversity and equity in library materials and services for youth. Her articles include "Are All Lists Created Equal? Diversity in Award-Winning and Best-selling Young Adult Fiction," which received the 2012 YALSA Writing Award; and "Rethinking the Texts We Use in Literacy Instruction with Adolescent African American Males," written with Sandra Hughes-Hassell, which received a 2013 Virginia Hamilton Essay Award Honor Citation.

SONYA L. SCOTT is a senior youth information services specialist at Pearl Bailey Library in Newport News, Virginia. In her 10 years there, she has worked closely with youth and community members to develop programs and services that have made Pearl Bailey one of the busiest branches in the city.

JULIE STIVERS has worked with teens in different settings, including schools in Durham and Wake counties and with incarcerated youth at the Durham Youth Home. She is currently the librarian at Mount Vernon School, an alternative public middle school in Raleigh, North Carolina, where she loves finding engaging, reflective literature to put in her students' hands. Stivers has presented on diverse youth literature at a number of conferences, including the Young Adult Library Services Association (YALSA) Young Adult Literature Symposium and the National Conference of African American Librarians and Librarianship. Her research and writing have appeared in *School Libraries Worldwide* and on websites such as YALSA, *School Library Journal*, and American Indians in Children's Literature (AICL). She earned her MSLS in 2015 from the University of North Carolina at Chapel Hill (UNC-CH).

MARY JEAN TECCE DECARLO is an assistant clinical professor of literacy studies in the School of Education at Drexel University, where she designs and teaches courses in the Teacher Education program and the Special Education program. During her 20 years in education, Dr. DeCarlo has been a classroom teacher, a curriculum leader, and a college professor in suburban and urban communities in the Philadelphia area. She earned her B.S.Ed. from West Chester University and her M.S.Ed. and Ed.D. in reading, writing, and literacy from the University of Pennsylvania. She is a certified Reading Specialist and currently focuses on issues and challenges regarding effective reading and writing instruction for delayed readers and writers and the development of information and digital literacy skills for children K–8. She chooses to situate much of her research in urban schools in order to highlight the strengths and needs of teachers and students in these underresourced environments.

ANNA TEEPLE started working as a residential counselor at the Bar None treatment center after graduating from Hamline University in St. Paul, Minnesota. While there, she received an M.Ed from Bethel University and starting teaching special education for Osseo Area Schools. After seven years as a special education teacher, she earned her Library Media Specialist (LMS) licensure from St. Cloud State University. She has started her 10th year as an LMS and works at North View Middle IB World School in Brooklyn Park. Outside of work, Teeple enjoys training her dog, Sadie, to be a therapy dog, teaching yoga, and gardening.

DEMETRIA TUCKER is senior family and youth services librarian for the Pearl Bailey Library in Newport News, Virginia. She was the recipient of the 2013 Coretta Scott King–Virginia Hamilton Award for Lifetime Achievement. The award is sponsored by the American Library Association (ALA). She earned her MSLS in 1978 from the University of North Carolina at Chapel Hill (UNC-CH).

Index

CPSIA information can be obtained
at www.ICGtesting.com
Printed in the USA
LVHW061555120319
610370LV00008B/222/P